Lyra Germanica

First and Second Books

Translated from the German by Catherine Winkworth
This Edition Edited by Anthony Uyl

Woodstock, Ontario, Canada 2018

Lyra Germanica: First and Second Books
Translated from the German by Catherine Winkworth
This Edition Edited by Anthony Uyl

The text of Lyra Germanica: First and Second Books is all in the Public Domain. The layout and Devoted Publishing logo are Copyright ©2018 Devoted Publishing. This edition is published by Devoted Publishing a division of 2165467 Ontario Inc.

**What kind of philosophies do you have?
Let us know!**

Visit our website: www.devotedpublishing.com
Contact us at: devotedpub@hotmail.com
Visit us on Facebook: @DevotedPublishing

Published in Woodstock, Ontario, Canada 2018.

For bulk educational rates, please contact us at the above email address.

ISBN: 978-1-77356-242-1

Table of Contents

Book I: Lyra Germanica: Hymns for the Sundays & Chief Festivals of The Christian Year 7

Dedication 8

Preface... 9

    First Sunday in Advent 14

    Second Sunday in Advent.................... 16

    Third Sunday in Advent........................ 18

    Fourth Sunday in Advent..................... 20

    Christmas Eve 22

    Xmas Day.. 24

    St. Stephen's Day 26

    Saint John the Evangelist.................... 27

    Innocents Day 29

    Emmanuel: Sunday after Christmas-day 31

    The Circumcision of Christ: A Hymn for New Year's Day 33

    The Adoration of the Magi 36

    First Sunday After Epiphany 38

    Second Sunday after Epiphany............ 39

    Third Sunday after Epiphany............... 42

    Fourth Sunday After Epiphany............ 43

    Fifth Sunday After Epiphany............... 45

    Sixth Sunday after Epiphany 47

    Septuagesima Sunday 49

    Sexagesima Sunday 51

    Quinquagesima Sunday 53

    Quinquagesima Sunday 55

    Ash Wednesday 57

    First Sunday in Lent............................. 58

    Second Sunday in Lent 60

    Third Sunday in Lent 61

    Fourth Sunday in Lent 62

    Fifth Sunday in Lent 64

    Palm Sunday 66

    Monday in Passion Week 68

    Tuesday in Passion Week 70

    Wednesday in Passion Week 72

    Thursday in Passion Week................... 74

    Good Friday. Morning 76

    Good Friday. Evening 78

    Easter Even 80

    Easter Day. Morning............................. 82

    Easter Day. Evening.............................. 84

    Monday in Easter Week....................... 85

    Tuesday in Easter Week 87

    First Sunday after Easter...................... 89

    Second Sunday after Easter 91

    Third Sunday After Easter 92

    Fourth Sunday After Easter 95

    Fifth Sunday after Easter 97

    Ascension Day 98

    Sunday After Ascension Day............... 99

    Whit Sunday....................................... 101

    Monday in Whitsun-Week 103

    Tuesday in Whitsun-Week................. 106

    Trinity Sunday.................................... 107

    First Sunday after Trinity................... 109

    Second Sunday after Trinity 112

    Third Sunday after Trinity 114

    Fourth Sunday after Trinity 116

    Fifth Sunday after Trinity 117

    Sixth Sunday after Trinity.................. 120

    Seventh Sunday after Trinity 121

    Eighth Sunday after Trinity 124

    Ninth Sunday after Trinity................. 126

    Tenth Sunday after Trinity................. 128

    Eleventh Sunday after Trinity............ 130

    Twelfth Sunday after Trinity 132

    Thirteenth Sunday after Trinity 134

    Fourteenth Sunday after Trinity........ 136

    Fifteenth Sunday after Trinity............ 138

    Sixteenth Sunday after Trinity........... 141

    Seventeenth Sunday after Trinity 142

    Eighteenth Sunday after Trinity......... 145

    Nineteenth Sunday after Trinity 146

Twentieth Sunday after Trinity 148

Twenty-first Sunday after Trinity 150

Twenty-second Sunday after Trinity. 152

Twenty-third Sunday after Trinity 155

Twenty-fourth Sunday after Trinity .. 157

Twenty-fifth Sunday after Trinity 159

St. Andrew's Day 160

St. Thomas the Apostle 162

Presentation in the Temple 163

St. Matthias' Day 165

The Annunciation 167

St. Barnabas' Day 169

St. Michael and all Angels 172

All Saint's Day 174

Morning Hymns[1] 176

Evening Hymns[2] 183

For the Sick & Dying[3] 188

For the Burial of the Dead[4] 196

Appendix I: Alternate Versions 200

Appendix II: Manuscript Addenda 202

Biography 203

In Memory of CATHERINE
WINKWORTH 205

Footnotes: 206

Book II: Lyra Germanica: Second Series:
The Christian Life 207

PREFACE 208

PART I. AIDS OF THE CHURCH 211

HOLY SEASONS 211

ADVENT 211

I. The Dayspring from on High 211

II. The Deliverer 213

III. The Heart longing for the inner advent 215

IV. The New Year 217

CHRISTMAS 220

I. A Song of Joy at Dawn 220

II. We love Him for He first loved Us 223

III. God with Us 225

EPIPHANY 227

I. The King of Men 227

II. The Light of the World 228

III. Forsaking all for the True Light ... 229

IV. Christ our Example 230

PASSION WEEK 231

I. In the Garden 231

II. At the Foot of the Cross 233

III. Our Heritage 236

IV. Our Requital 237

V. At the Sepulchre 239

VI. Our Rest 240

EASTER 241

I. The Song of Triumph 241

II. Christ our Champion 243

III. The Whole World restored in Christ
.... 244

IV. The Resurrection from the Death of Sin 245

V. The Walk to Emmaus 247

ASCENSION 249

I. The Way opened 249

II. Christ's Ascension the Ground of Ours 250

III. The Kingdom of Christ 251

IV. The Throne of Grace 253

WHITSUNTIDE 255

I. The Work of the Holy Spirit 255

II. The Spirit of Wisdom, Love, and Joy
.... 257

III. The unity of the Spirit 259

IV. The Strength of the Church 260

V. The Diffusion of the Gospel 261

TRINITY 262

I. A Morning Hymn 262

II. Our Father, Redeemer, Guide 263

III. An Evening Hymn 264

Services 265

MORNING PRAYER 265

I. For The Sabbath Morning 265

II. Before Public Worship 267

III. In Time of War and Persecution .. 268

IV. In Time of Distress 269

V. The Christian's Morning Sacrifice 270

VI. A Morning Song of Gladness 271

VII. A Morning Prayer 272

EVENING PRAYER 274

I. Trust in God 274

II. An Evening Thanksgiving 275

III. In Sickness 277

IV. For a Wakeful Night 279

V. At the Close of the Sabbath 280

BAPTISM 281

I. The Command 281

II. The Name 283

III. The Blessing 284

IV. For a Christian Child 285

V. Renewal of the Vow 286

THE HOLY COMMUNION 288

I. The Preparation 288

II. The Thanksgiving 289

III. The exceeding great Love of our Master and only Saviour Jesus Christ 291

IV. The Christian Sacrifice 293

V. The Christian Fellowship 294

VI. The Remembrance 296

VII. After Participation 298

FOR TRAVELLERS 301

I. At the Outset of any Journey 301

II. On a Long and Perilous Journey ... 302

III. Prayers at Sea 305

IV. On the Sea-Shore 306

V. The Parting 307

VI. On the Voyage 309

AT THE BURIAL OF THE DEAD .. 310

I. The Sure and Certain Hope 310

II. The Departure of a Christian 312

III. The Lord doth all Things Well 313

IV. The Light in Darkness 314

V. The Death of a little Child 315

VI. On the Death of His Son 316

PART II. THE INNER LIFE 319

PENITENCE 319

I. The Only Helper 319

II. Submission 321

III. In great inward Distress 323

IV. The Weakness and Restlessness of Sin 325

V. A Christian's Daily Prayer 327

VI. The Deliverer from Bondage 329

VII. The Safe Refuge 331

PRAISE AND THANKSGIVING 333

I. The Chorus of God's Thankful Children 333

II. The Goodness of God 334

III. The Glory of God in Creation 336

IV. The Faithfulness of God 337

V. The Holiness of God brought near to Man in Christ 340

VI. To the Saviour 341

VII. For Public Peace 342

THE LIFE OF FAITH 344

I. Faith 344

II. Faith that worketh by Love 346

III. The Christian's Trust 347

IV. The Anchor of the Soul 348

V. The Resolve 349

VI. The Christian Race 350

VII. The Christian's Joy 351

VIII. Under Clouds 353

IX. Aspiration 354

X. Song of the Christian Pilgrim 356

XI. Longing for Home 358

SONGS OF THE CROSS 360

I. Queen Maria of Hungary's Song 360

II. In Outward and Inward Distress ... 362

III. The only Refuge in Time of Trouble 363

IV. Under a Heavy Private Cross or Bereavement 364

V. The one True Friend 366

VI. Under the Pressure of Care or Poverty 368

VII. The Resting-Place amid Changes 370

VIII. Rest in the Lord 371

IX. The Christian's Confidence 372

X. Childlike Submission 373

XI. The quiet hoping Heart 375

XII. The Courage of perfect Trust 377

XIII. The Sufficiency of God 379

THE FINAL CONFLICT AND HEAVEN 381

I. The Uncertainty of Life 381

II. Preparation for Death 382

III. A Weary Pilgrim's Song 384

IV. In Time of dangerous Duty 386

V. In the near prospect of Death 388

VI. In Weakness and Distress of Mind 389

VII. Resignation 391

VIII. The Faithful Servant Longing for Peace 392

IX. The Christian Soldier rejoicing that he has overcome 394

X. Jerusalem 396

XI. The new Heavens and new Earth 398

XII. The Final 400

XIII. The End 401

Footnotes: 402

Book I: Lyra Germanica: Hymns for the Sundays & Chief Festivals of The Christian Year

Translated from the German by Catherine Winkworth
Originally Published by: London: Longman, Green, Longman, and Roberts. 1861.

Dedication

To His Excellency the Chevalier Bunsen, these Hymns are by His Kind Permission Respectfully and Gratefully Dedicated by the Translator.

Preface

The following hymns are selected from the Chevalier Bunsen's "Versuch eines allgemeinen Gesang und Gebetbuchs," published in 1833. From the large number there given, about nine hundred, little more than one hundred have been chosen. This selection contains many of those best known and loved in Germany; but in a work of this size it is impossible to include all that have become classical in that home of Christian poetry. In reading them it must be remembered that they are hymns, not sacred poems, though from their length and the intricacy of their metres, many of them may seem to English readers adapted rather to purposes of private than of public devotion. But the singing of hymns forms a much larger and more important part of public worship in the German Reformed Churches than in our own services. It is the mode by which the whole congregation is enabled to bear its part in the worship of God, answering in this respect to the chanting of our own liturgy.

Ever since the Reformation, the German Church has been remarkable for the number and excellence of its hymns and hymn-tunes. Before that time it was not so. There was no place for congregational singing in public worship, and therefore the spiritual songs of the latter part of the middle ages assumed for the most part an artificial and unpopular form. Yet there were not wanting germs of a national Church poetry in the verses rather than hymns which were sung in German on pilgrimages and at some of the high festivals, many of which verses were again derived from more ancient Latin hymns. Several of Luther's hymns are amplifications of verses of this class, such as the Pentecostal hymn here given, "Come, Holy Spirit, God and Lord," which is founded on a German version of the "Veni Sancte Spiritus, Reple." By adopting these verses, and retaining their well-known melodies, Luther enabled his hymns to spread rapidly among the common people. He also composed metrical versions of several of the Psalms, the Te Deum, the Ten Commandments, the Lord's Prayer, the Nunc Dimittis, the Da nobis Pacem, &c., thus enriching the people, to whom he had already given the Holy Scriptures in their own language, with a treasure of that sacred poetry which is the precious inheritance of every Christian church.

The hymn, "In the midst of life," is one of those founded on a more ancient hymn, the "Media in vita" of Notker, a learned Benedictine of St. Gall, who died in 912. He is said to have composed it while watching some workmen, who were building the bridge of Martinsbruck at the peril of their lives. It was soon set to music, and became universally known; indeed it was used as a battle song, until the custom was forbidden on account of its being supposed to exercise magical influences. In a German version it formed part of the service for the burial of the dead, as early as the thirteenth century, and is still preserved in an unmetrical form in the Burial Service of our own Church.

The carol, "From Heaven above to earth I come," is called by Luther himself, "A Christmas child's song concerning the child Jesus." He wrote it for his little boy Hans, when the latter was five years old, and it is still sung from the dome of the Kreuzkirche in Dresden before day-break on the morning of Christmas Day. It refers to the custom, then and long afterwards prevalent in Germany, of making at Christmas-time representations of the manger with the infant Jesus. But the most famous of his hymns is the noble version of the 46th Psalm, "A sure stronghold our God is He," which may be called the national hymn of his Protestant countrymen. Luther's hymns are wanting in harmony and correctness of metre to a degree which often makes them jarring to our modern ears, but they are always full of fire and strength, of clear Christian faith, and brave joyful trust in God.

From his time there has been a constant succession of hymn writers in the German Church. Paul Eber, an intimate friend of Melancthon, wrote for his children the hymn, "Lord Jesus Christ, true Man and God," which soon became a favorite hymn for the dying. Hugo Grotius asked that it might be repeated to him in his last moments, and expired ere its conclusion. Another hymn of the same class is, "Now hush your cries, and shed no tear," the "Jam moesta quiesce querela" of Prudentius II. translated by Nicholas Hermann, the pious precentor of Joachimsthal, a hymn long sung at every festival.

The terrible times of the Thirty years' War were rich in sacred poetry. Rist, a clergyman in North Germany, who suffered much in his youth from mental conflicts, and in after years from plunder, pestilence, and all the horrors of war, used to say, "the dear cross hath pressed many songs out of me," and this seems to have been equally true of many of his contemporaries. It certainly was true of Johann Hermann, the author of some of the most touching hymns for Passion Week, who wrote his sweet songs under great physical sufferings from ill health, and amidst the perils of war, during which he more than once esaped murder as by a miracle. So too the hymns of Simon Dach, professor of poetry in the University of Koningsberg, speak of the sufferings of the Christian, and his longing to escape from the strife of earth to the peace of heaven.

But the Christians of those days had often not only to suffer, but to fight for their faith, and in the hymns of Altenburg and von Löwenstern we have two that may be called battle songs of the Church. The former published his hymn, "Fear not, O little flock, the foe," in 1631, with this title: "A heart-cheering song of comfort on the watch word of the Evangelical Army in the battle of Leipsic, September 5th, 1631, God with us." It was called Gustavus Adolphus's battle song, because the pious hero often sang it with his army; and he sang it for the last time immediately before the battle of Lützen. The latter, von Löwenstern, was the son of a saddler, but was ennobled by the Emporer, Ferdinand III. for his public services: he was at once a statesman, poet, and musician. His hymn, "Christ, Thou the champion of the band," was a favorite of Niebuhr.

Another favorite hymn of Niebuhr was the hymn to Eternity, the greater part of which is of very ancient but uncertain date. It received its present form about the middle of the 17th century.

Many of the hymns of Paul Gerhardt belong to this period, though he lived until 1676, long after the conclusion of peace. He is without doubt the greatest of the German hymn writers, possessing loftier poetical genius, and a richer variety of thought and feeling than any other. His beautiful hymn, "Commit thou all thy [griefs and] ways," is already well known to us through Wesley's translation, and many others of his are not inferior to it. He was a zealous preacher for several years at the Nicolai-Kirch in Berlin; whence he retired because he had not sufficient freedom in preaching the truth, and became Archdeacon of Lübben. With him culminated the elder school of German sacred poetry, a school distinguished by its depth and simplicity. Most of its hymns are either written for the high festivals and services of the Church, or are expressive of a simple Christian faith, ready to dare or suffer all things for God's sake. To this school we must refer, from their spirit, two hymns written a little later; the first is "Jesus my Redeemer Lives," one of the most favorite Easter hymns, written by the pious Electress of Brandenburgh, who founded the Orphan House at Oranienburg. The other, "Leave God to order all thy ways," was written by George Neumarck, Secretary to the Archives at Weimar. It spread rapidly among the common people, at first without the author's name. A baker's boy in New Brandenburgh used to sing it over his work, and soon the whole town and neighbourhood flocked to him to learn this beautiful new song.

In the latter half of the seventeenth century a new school was founded by Johann Franck, and Johann Scheffler, commonly called Angelus. The former was burgomaster of Guben in Lusatia; the latter physician to Ferdinand III., but in 1663 he became a Roman Catholic, and afterwards a priest. The pervading idea of this school is the longing of the soul for that intimate union with the Redeemer of the world, which begins with the birth of Christ in the heart, and is perfected after death. This longing breathes through the hymns of Franck given in this collection; one of them, "Redeemer of the nations, come," is a translation of the "Veni, Redemptor gentium" of St. Ambrose. Angelus dwells rather on the means of attaining this union by the sacrifice of the Self to God through the great High-priest of mankind, an idea expressed in his hymns with peculiar tenderness and sweetness. We find much of his spirit and sweetness lingering in modern times about the few hymns of the gifted Novalis.

The greatest poet of this school is however Gerhard Tersteegen, who lived during the early part of the eighteenth century as a ribbon manufacturer at Mühlheim. His hymns have great beauty, and bespeak a tranquil and childlike soul filled and blessed with the contemplation of God. The well-known hymn of Wesley's, "Lo God is here! let us adore," belongs to him, and in its original shape is one of the most beautiful he ever wrote, but is frequently met with only in a disfigured and mutilated form. To this school belong a large number of the hymns in this collection, among which those of Deszler, an excellent philologist of Nuremburgh, and of Anton Ulrich, the pious and learned Duke of Brunswick, are particularly good. Those of Schmolck, the pastor of Schweidnitz, who exercised great influence over the hymn-writing of his day, have more simplicity than most of the rest, but are characterized by a curious mixture of real poetry and deep feeling with occasional vulgarities of expression. The defects of this school, which showed themselves strongly in the course of the eighteenth century, were a tendency that the feeling should degenerate into sentimentality, and the devout dwelling of the heart on Christ's great sacrifice into compassion and gratitude for His physical sufferings,-- defects which greatly disfigure many of the Moravian hymns. In some of the hymns here translated the expression "Christi Wundenhöhle" occurs, which has been rendered by the blood or cross of Christ, as being phrases at once more scriptural and more consonant to our feelings. There were not wanting, however, even at this period, many hymns fit for good soldiers of Jesus Christ, such as "Who seeks in weakness an excuse," and others of the same kind.

Germany is rich in Morning and Evening Hymns, and Hymns for the Dying, of which a few are given in these translations. Among these is the morning hymn of Baron von Canitz: I was not aware until after translating it that it had been already published at the close of one volume of Dr. Arnold's sermons.

The hymn "How blest to all Thy followers, Lord, the road," was the favourite hymn of Schelling.

In translating these hymns the original form has been retained, with the exception, that single rhymes are generally substituted for the double rhymes which the structure of the language renders so common in German poetry, but which become cloying to an English ear when constantly repeated; and that English double common or short metre is used instead of what may be called the German common metre, the same that we call Gay's stanza, to which it approximates closely in the number of syllables, while its associations in our minds are somewhat more solemn. In a few instances slight alterations have been made in the metre, when, as is the case with some excellent hymns in our own language, it is hardly grave and dignified enough for the poetry. These alterations are but slight, and seemed justifiable, since these hymns have been translated, not so much as specimens of German hymn-writing, as in the hope that these utterances of German piety which have comforted and strengthened the hearts of many true Christians in their native country, may speak to the hearts of some among us, to help and cheer those who must strive and suffer, and to make us feel afresh what a deep and true Communion of Saints exists among all the children of God in different Churches and lands.

Alderley Edge,
July 16th,
1855

In the second edition a few corrections have been made and additional verses given in some of the hymns: a few among them are however still given in an abbreviated form, where the omitted verses appeared to be decidedly inferior in merit, or to contain no new thought. I have also exchanged the former version of "Ein feste Burg" for one, as it seems to me, much superior, which I owe to the kindness of the Rev. William Gaskell.
Nov. 30, 1855.

First Sunday in Advent
The night is far spent, the day is at hand; let us therefore cast off the works of darkness, and let us put on the armour of light
     From the Epistle. [Rom. 13:12]
Richter. 1704.
trans. by Catherine Winkworth, 1855

O Watchman, will the night of sin
Be never past?
O watchman, doth the tarrying day begin
To dawn upon thy straining sight at last?
Will it dispel
Ere long the mists of sin wherein I dwell?

Now all the earth is bright and glad
With the fresh morn;
But all my heart is cold and dark and sad;
Sun of the soul, let me behold Thy dawn!
Come, Jesus, Lord!
Oh quickly come, according to Thy word!

Do we not live in those blest days
So long foretold,
When Thou shouldst come to bring us light and grace?
And yet I sit in darkness as of old,
Pining to see
Thy glory; but Thou still art far from me.

Long since Thou camest for the light
Of all men here;
And still in me is nought but blackest night,
Yet I am thine, Oh hasten to appear,
Shine forth and bless
My soul with vision of Thy righteousness!

If thus in darkness ever left,
Can I fulfil
The works of light, while yet of light bereft?
Or how discern in love and meekness still
To follow Thee,
And all the sinful works of darkness flee?

The light of reason cannot give
Light to my soul;
Jesus alone can make me truly live,

Catherine Winkworth

One glance of His can make my spirit whole,
Arise and shine,
O Jesus, on this longing heart of mine!

Single and clear, not weak or blind,
The eye must be,
To which Thy glory shall and entrance find;
For if Thy chosen ones would gaze on Thee,
No earthly screen
Between their souls and Thee must intervene.

Jesus, do Thou mine eyes unseal,
And let them grow
Quick to discern whate'er thou dost reveal,
So shall I be deliver'd from that woe,
Blindly to stray
Through hopeless night, while all around is day.

Second Sunday in Advent

Behold the fig-tree and all the trees; when they now shoot forth, ye see and know of your own selves that summer is now nigh at hand. So likewise ye, when ye see these things come to pass, know ye that the kingdom of God is nigh at hand.

    From the Gospel. [Mk 13:28-29]
Rist. 1651.
trans. by Catherine Winkworth, 1855

Awake, thou careless world, awake!
The final day shall surely come;
What Heaven hath fixed Time cannot shake,
It cannot sweep away thy doom.
Know, what the Lord Himself hath spoken
Shall come at last and not delay;
Though heaven and earth shall pass away,
His steadfast word can ne'er be broken.

Awake! He comes to judgment, wake!
Sinners, behold His countanance
In beauty terrible, and quake
Condemned beneath His piercing glance.
Lo! He to whom all power is given,
Who sits at God's right hand on high,
In fire and thunder draweth nigh,
To judge all nations under heaven.

Awake, thou careless world, awake!
Who knows how soon our God shall please
That suddenly that day should break?
We fathom not such depths as these.
Oh guard thee well from lust and greed;
For as the bird is in the snare,
Or ever of its foe aware,
So comes that day with silent speed.

The Lord in love delayeth long
The final day, and grants us space
To turn away from sin and wrong,
And mourning seek His help and grace.
He holdeth back that best of days,
Until the righteous shall approve
Their faith and hope, their constant love;
So gentle us-ward are His ways!
But ye, O faithful souls, shall see

Catherine Winkworth

That morning rise in love and joy;
Your Saviour comes to set you free,
Your Judge shall all your bonds destroy:
He, the true Joshua, then shall bring
His people with a mighty hand
Into their promised father-land,
Where songs of victory they shall sing.

Rejoice! The fig-tree shows her green,
The springing year is in its prime,
The little flowers afresh are seen,
We gather strength in this great time;
The glorious summer draweth near,
When all this body's earthly load,
In light that morning sheds abroad,
Shall wax as sunshine pure and clear.

Arise, and let us day and night
Pray in the Spirit ceaselessly,
That we may heed our Lord aright,
And ever in His presence be;
Arise, and let us haste to meet
The Bridegroom standing at the door,
That with the angels evermore
We too may worship at His feet.

Third Sunday in Advent

And it shall be said in that day, Lo, this is our God; we have waited for Him, and He will save us: this is the Lord; we have waited for Him, we will be glad and rejoice in His salvation.
    From the Lesson. [Is. 25:9]
Paul Gerhardt. 1653.
trans. by Catherine Winkworth, 1855

How shall I meet Thee? How my heart
Receive her Lord aright?
Desire of all the earth Thou art!
My hope, my sole delight!
Kindle the Lamp, Thou Lord, alone,
Half-dying in my breast,
And make thy gracious pleasure known
How I may greet Thee best.

Her budding boughs and fairest palms
Thy Zion strews around;
And songs of praise and sweetest psalms
From my glad heart shall sound.
My desert soul breaks forth in flowers,
Rejoicing in Thy fame;
And puts forth all her sleeping powers,
To honour Jesus' name.

In heavy bonds I languished long,
Thou com'st to set me free;
The scorn of every mocking tongue--
Thou com'st to honour me.
A heavenly crown wilt Thou bestow,
And gifts of priceless worth,
That vanish not as here below,
The fading wealth of earth.

Nought, nought, dear Lord, had power to move
Thee from Thy rightful place,
Save that most strange and blessed Love
Wherewith Thou dost embrace
This weary world and all her woe,
Her load of grief and ill
And sorrow, more than man can know;--
Thy love is deeper still.

Catherine Winkworth

Oh write this promise in your hearts,
Ye sorrowful, on whom
Fall thickening cares, while joy departs
And darker grows your gloom.
Despair not, for your help is near,
He standeth at the door
Who best can comfort you and cheer,
He comes, nor stayeth more.

Nor vex your souls with care, nor grieve
And labour longer thus,
As though your arm could ought achieve,
And bring Him down to us.
He comes, He comes with ready will,
By pity moved alone,
To soothe our every grief and ill,
For all to Him is known.

Nor ye, O sinners, shrink aside,
Afraid to see His face,
Your darkest sins our Lord will hide
Beneath His pitying grace.
He comes, He comes to save from sin,
And all its pangs assuage,
And for the sons of God to win
Their proper heritage.

Why heed ye then the craft and noise,
The fury of His foes?
Lo, in a breath the Lord destroys
All who His rule oppose.
He comes, He comes, as King to reign!
All earthly powers may band
Against Him, yet they strive in vain,
His might may none withstand.

He comes to judge the earth, and ye
Who mocked Him, feel His wrath;
But they who loved and sought Him see
His light o'er all their path.
O Sun of Righteousness! arise,
And guide us on our way
To yon fair mansion in the skies
Of joyous cloudless day.

Fourth Sunday in Advent

Rejoice in the Lord alway, and again I say, Rejoice. The Lord is at hand.
    From the epistle. [Philip. 4:4]
Weiszel. 1635.
trans. by Catherine Winkworth, 1855

Lift up your heads, ye mighty gates,
Behold the King of glory waits,
The King of kings is drawing near,
The Saviour of the world is here;
Life and salvation doth He bring,
Wherefore rejoice, and gladly sing
Praise, O my God, to Thee!
Creator, wise is Thy decree!

The Lord is just, a helper tried,
Mercy is ever at His side,
His kingly crown is holiness,
His sceptre, pity in distress,
The end of all our woe He brings;
Wherefore the earth is glad and sings
Praise, O my God, to Thee!
O Saviour, great Thy deeds shall be!

Oh, blest the land, the city blest,
Where Christ the ruler is confessed!
Oh, happy hearts and happy homes
To whom this King in triumph comes!
The cloudless Sun of joy He is,
Who bringeth pure delight and bliss;
Praise, O my God, to Thee!
Comforter, for Thy comfort free!

Fling wide the portals of your heart,
Make it a temple set apart
From earthly use for Heaven's employ,
Adorned with prayer, and love, and joy;
So shall your Sovereign enter in,
And new and nobler life begin.
Praise, O my God, be Thine,
For word, and deed, and grace divine.

Catherine Winkworth

Redeemer, come! I open wide
My heart to Thee, here, Lord, abide!
Let me Thy inner presence feel,
Thy grace and love in me reveal,
Thy Holy Spirit guide us on
Until our glorious goal is won!
Eternal praise and fame,
Be offered, Saviour, to Thy Name!

Christmas Eve

Behold, I bring you good tidings of great joy, which shall be to all people.
    Luke 2:10.
Written for his little son Hans. 1540
trans. by Catherine Winkworth, 1855

From Heaven above to earth I come
To bear good news to every home;
Glad tidings of great joy I bring
Whereof I now will say and sing:

To you this night is born a child
Of Mary, chosen mother mild;
This little child, of lowly birth,
Shall be the joy of all your earth.

'Tis Christ our God who far on high
Hath heard your sad and bitter cry;
Himself will your Salvation be,
Himself from sin will make you free.

He brings those blessings, long ago
Prepared by God for all below;
Henceforth His kingdom open stands
To you, as to the angel bands.

These are the tokens ye shall mark,
The swaddling clothes and manger dark;
There shall ye find the young child laid,
By whom the heavens and earth were made.

Now let us all with gladsome cheer
Follow the shepherds, and draw near
To see this wondrous gift of God
Who hath His only Son bestowed.

Give heed, my heart, lift up thine eyes!
Who is it in yon manger lies?
Who is this child so young and fair?
The blessed Christ-child lieth there.

Welcome to earth, Thou noble guest,
Through whom e'en wicked men are blest!
Thou com'st to share our misery,
What can we render, Lord, to Thee!

Catherine Winkworth

Ah, Lord, who hast created all,
How hast Thou made Thee weak and small,
That Thou must choose Thy infant bed
Where ass and ox but lately fed!

Were earth a thousand times as fair,
Beset with gold and jewels rare,
She yet were far too poor to be
A narrow cradle, Lord, for Thee.

For velvets soft and silken stuff
Thou hast but hay and straw so rough,
Whereon Thou King, so rich and great,
As 'twere Thy heaven, art throned in state.

Thus hath it pleased Thee to make plain
The truth to us poor fools and vain,
That this world's honour, wealth and might
Are nought and worthless in Thy sight.

Ah! dearest Jesus, Holy Child,
Make Thee a bed, soft, undefiled,
Within my heart, that it may be
A quiet chamber kept for Thee.

My heart for very joy doth leap,
My lips no more can silence keep;
I too must sing with joyful tongue
That sweetest ancient cradle-song-

Glory to God in highest Heaven,
Who unto man His Son hath given!
While angels sing with pious mirth
A glad New Year to all the earth.

Xmas Day

And the word was made flesh, and dwelt among us.
      From the Gospel. [Jn. 1:14]
Laurenti. 1700.
trans. by Catherine Winkworth, 1855

O Thou essential Word,
Who from eternity
Didst dwell with God, for thou wast God,
Who art ordained to be
The Saviour of our race;
Welcome indeed Thou art,
Blessed Redeemer, Fount of Grace,
To this my longing heart!

Come, self-existant Word,
And speak within my heart,
That from the soul where Thou art heard
Thy peace may ne'er depart.
Thou Light that lightenest all,
Abide through faith in me,
And let me never from Thee fall,
And seek no guide but Thee.

Why didst Thou leave Thy throne,
O Jesus, what could bring
Thee to a world where e'en Thine own
Knew not their rightful King?
Thy love beyond all thought
Stronger than Death or Hell,
And my deep woe, this wonder wrought,
That Thou on earth dost dwell.

Then help me, Lord, to give
My whole heart unto Thee,
That all my life while here I live
One song of praise may be.
Yes, Jesus, form anew
This stony heart of mine,
And let it e'en in death be true
To Thee, for ever Thine.

Let nought be left within
But cometh of Thy hand;
Root quickly out the weeds of sin,

Catherine Winkworth

My cunning foe withstand.
From Thee comes nothing ill,
'Tis he doth sow the tares;
Make plain my path before me still,
And save me from his snares.

Thou art the Life, O Lord!
Sole Light of Life Thou art!
Let not Thy glorious rays be poured
In vain on my dark heart.
Star of the East, arise!
Drive all my clouds away,
Guide me till earth's dim twilight dies
Into the perfect day!

St. Stephen's Day

And Stephen, full of faith and power, did great wonders and miracles among the people. . . . Then they stirred up the people. . . . and caught him, and set up false witnesses against him.
     From the Lesson. [Acts 7:8-11]
Gustavus Adolphus' Battle-song. 1631.
trans. by Catherine Winkworth, 1855

Fear not, O little flock, the foe
Who madly seeks your overthrow,
Dread not his rage and power:
What though your courage sometimes faints,
His seeming triumph o'er God's saints
Lasts but one little hour.

Be of good cheer; your cause belongs
To Him who can avenge your wrongs,
Leave it to Him our Lord.
Though hidden yet from all our eyes,
He sees the Gideon who shall rise
To save us, and His word.

As true as God's own word is true,
Nor earth nor hell with all their crew
Against us shall prevail.
A jest and by-word are they grown;
God is with us, we are His own,
Our victory cannot fail.

Amen, Lord Jesus, grant our prayer!
Great Captain, now Thine arm make bare;
Fight for us once again!
So shall Thy saints and martyrs raise
A mighty chorus to Thy praise,
World without end. Amen.

Saint John the Evangelist
If I will that he tarry till I come, what is that to thee? Follow thou me.
        From the Gospel. [Jn. 21:22]
Sinold. 1710.
trans. by Catherine Winkworth, 1855

If Thou, True Life, wilt in me live,
Consume whate'er is not of Thee;
One look of Thine more joy can give
Than all the world can offer me.
O Jesus, be Thou mine for ever,
Nought from thy love my heart can sever,
As Thou hast promised in Thy Word;
Oh deep the joy whereof I drink,
Whene'er my soul in Thee can sink,
And own her Bridegroom and her Lord!

O Heart, that glowed with love and died,
Kindle my soul with fire divine;
Lord, in the heart Thou'st won, abide,
And all in it that is not Thine
Oh let me conquer and destroy,
Strong in Thy love, Thou Fount of Joy,
Nay, be Thou conqueror, Lord, in me;
So shall I triumph o'er despair,
O'er death itself Thy victory share,
Thus suffer, live, and die in Thee.

And let the fire within me move
My heart to serve Thy members here;
Let me their need and trials prove,
That I may know my love sincere
And like to Thine, Lord, pure and warm;
For when my soul hath won that form
Is likest to Thy holy mind,
Then I shall love both friends and foes,
And learn to grieve o'er others' woes,
Like Thee, my Pattern, true and kind.

The light and strength of Faith, oh grant,
That I may bring forth holy fruit,
A living branch, a blooming plant,
Fast clinging to my vine--my root:
Thou art my Saviour, whom I trust,
My Rock,--I build not on the dust,--

The ground of faith, eternal, sure.
When hours of doubt o'ercloud my mind,
Thy ready help then let me find,
Thy strength my sickening spirit cure!

And grant that Hope may never fail,
But anchored safely on Thy cross,
Through Thee who art mine All, prevail
O'er every anguish, dread, and loss.
The world may build on what decays,
O Christ, my Sun of Hope, my gaze
Cares not o'er lesser lights to range;
To Thee in love I ever cleave,
For well I know Thou ne'er wilt leave
My soul,--Thy love can never change.

Wouldst Thou that I should tarry here,
I live because Thou willest it;
Or Death should suddenly appear,
I shall not fear him, Lord, one whit,
If but Thy life still in me live,
If but Thy death my strength shall give,
When earthly life draws near its end;
To Thee I give away my will,
In life and death remembering still
Thou wilt my good, O truest Friend.

Innocents Day

Except ye be converted, and become as little children, ye shall not enter into the kingdom of Heaven.
     Matt. 18:3
Gerhard Tersteegen. 1731.
trans. by Catherine Winkworth, 1855

Dear Soul, couldst thou become a child
While yet on earth, meek, undefiled,
Then God Himself were ever near,
And Paradise around thee here.

A child cares nought for gold or treasure,
Nor fame nor glory yield him pleasure;
In perfect trust, he asketh not
If rich or poor shall be his lot.

Little he recks of dignity,
Nor prince nor monarch feareth he;
Strange that a child so weak and small
Is oft the boldest of us all!

He hath not skill to utter lies,
His very soul is in his eyes;
Single his aim in all, and true,
And apt to praise what others do.

No questions dark his spirit vex,
No faithless doubts his soul perplex,
Simply from day to day he lives,
Content with that the present gives.

Scarce can he stand alone, far less
Would roam abroad in loneliness;
Fast clinging to his mother still,
She bears and leads him at her will.

He will not stay to pause and choose,
His father's guidance e'er refuse,
Thinks not of danger, fears no harm,
Wrapt in obedience' holy calm.

For strange concerns he careth nought;
What others do, although were wrought
Before his eyes the worst offence,

Stains not his tranquil innocence.

His dearest work, his best delight,
Is, lying in his mother's sight,
To gaze for ever on her face,
And nestle in her fond embrace.

O childhood's innocence! the voice
Of thy deep wisdom is my choice!
Who hath thy lore is truly wise,
And precious in our Father's eyes.

Spirit of childhood! loved of God,
By Jesu's Spirit now bestowed!
How often have I longed for thee;
O Jesus, form Thyself in me!

And help me to become a child
While yet on earth, meek, undefiled,
That I may find God always near,
And Paradise around me here.

Catherine Winkworth

Emmanuel: Sunday after Christmas-day
Behold, a Virgin shall be with child, and shall bring forth a son, and they shall call his name Emmanuel, which being interpreted is, God with us.
    From the Gospel. [Matt. 1:23]
Paul Gerhardt. 1650.
trans. by Catherine Winkworth, 1855

Thee, O Immanuel, we praise,
The Prince of Life, and Fount of Grace,
The Morning Star, the Heavenly Flower,
The Virgin's Son, the Lord of Power.

With all Thy saints, Thee, Lord, we sing,
Praise, honour, thanks to Thee we bring,
That Thou, O long-expected guest,
Hast come at last to make us blest!

Since first the world began to be,
How many a heart hath longed for Thee;
Long years our fathers hoped of old
Their eyes might yet Thy Light behold:

The prophets cried; "Ah, would He came
To break the fetters of our shame;
That help from Zion came to men,
Israel were glad, and prospered then!"

Now art Thou here; we know Thee now,
In lowly manger liest Thou;
A child, yet makest all things great,
Poor, yet is earth Thy robe of state.

From Thee alone all gladness flows,
Who yet shalt bear such bitter woes;
Earth's light and comfort Thou shalt be,
Yet none shall watch to comfort Thee.

All heavens are Thine, yet Thou didst come
To sojourn in a stranger's home;
Thou hangest on Thy mother's breast
Who art the joy of spirits blest.

Now fearless I can look on Thee,

From sin and grief Thou sett'st me free;
Thou bearest wrath, Thou conquerest Death,
Fear turns to joy Thy glance beneath.

Thou art my Head, my Lord Divine,
I am Thy member, wholly Thine,
And in Thy Spirit's strength would still
Serve Thee according to Thy will.

Thus will I sing Thy praises here
With joyful spirit year by year;
And they shall sound before Thy throne,
Where time nor number more are known.

The Circumcision of Christ: A Hymn for New Year's Day

So teach us to number our days, that we may apply our hearts unto wisdom.
    Psalm 90:12.
WÃlffer. 1648.
trans. by Catherine Winkworth, 1855

Eternity! Eternity!
How long art thou, Eternity!
And yet to thee Time hastes away,
Like as the warhorse to the fray,
Or swift as couriers homeward go,
Or ship to port, or shaft from bow.
Ponder, O Man, Eternity!

Eternity! Eternity!
How long art thou, Eternity!
For ever as on a perfect sphere
End nor beginning can appear,
Even so, Eternity, in thee
Entrance nor exit can there be.
Ponder, O Man, Eternity!

Eternity! Eternity!
How long art thou, Eternity!
A circle infinite art thou,
Thy centre an Eternal Now,
Never, we name thy outer bound,
For never end therein is found.
Ponder, O Man, Eternity!

Eternity! Eternity!
How long art thou, Eternity!
A little bird with fretting beak
Might wear to nought the loftiest peak,
Though but each thousand years it came,
Yet thou wert then, as now, the same.
Ponder, O Man, Eternity!

Eternity! Eternity!
How long art thou, Eternity!
As long as God is God, so long
Endure the pains of sin and wrong,
So long the joys of heaven remain;

Oh lasting joy, Oh lasting pain!
Ponder, O Man, Eternity!

Eternity! Eternity!
How long art thou, Eternity!
O man, full oft thy thoughts should dwell
Upon the pains of sin and hell,
And on the glories of the pure,
That both beyond all time endure.
Ponder, O Man, Eternity!

Eternity! Eternity!
How long art thou, Eternity!
How terrible art thou in woe,
How fair where joys for ever glow!
God's goodness sheddeth gladness here,
His justice there wakes bitter fear.
Ponder, O Man, Eternity!

Eternity! Eternity!
How long art thou, Eternity!
They who lived poor and naked rest
With God, for ever rich and blest,
And love and praise the Highest Good,
In perfect bliss and gladsome mood.
Ponder, O Man, Eternity!

Eternity! Eternity!
How long art thou, Eternity!
A moment lasts all joy below,
Whereby man sinks to endless woe,
A moment lasts all earthly pain,
Whereby an endless joy we gain.
Ponder, O Man, Eternity!

Eternity! Eternity!
How long art thou, Eternity!
Who ponders oft on thee, is wise,
All fleshly lusts will he despise,
The world finds place with him no more;
The love of vain delights is o'er.
Ponder, O Man, Eternity!

Eternity! Eternity!
How long art thou, Eternity!
Who marks thee well would say to God,
Here judge, burn, smite me with Thy rod,
Here let me all Thy justice bear,
When time of grace is past, then spare!
Ponder, O Man, Eternity!

Catherine Winkworth

Eternity! Eternity!
How long art thou, Eternity!
Lo, I, Eternity, warn thee,
O Man, that oft thou think on me,
The sinner's punishment and pain,
To them who love their God, rich gain!
Ponder, O Man, Eternity!

The Adoration of the Magi
Epiphany.
Arise, shine, for thy light has come, and the glory of the Lord is risen upon thee!
     From the Lesson. [Is. 60:1]
Rist. 1655.
trans. by Catherine Winkworth, 1855

All ye Gentile lands awake!
Thou, O Salem, rise and shine!
See the day spring o'er you break,
Heralding a morn divine,
Telling, God hath called to mind
Those who long in darkness pined.

Lo! the shadows flee away,
For our Light is come at length,
Brighter than all earthly day,
Source of being, life, and strength!
Whoso on this Light would gaze
Must forsake all evil ways.

Ah how blindly did we stray
Ere shone forth this glorious Sun,
Seeking each his separate way,
Leaving Heaven, unsought, unwon;
All our looks were earthward bent,
All our strength on earth was spent.

Earthly were our thoughts and low,
In the toils of Folly caught,
Tossed of Satan to and fro,
Counting goodness all for nought!
By the world and flesh deceived,
Heaven's true joys we disbelieved.

Then were hidden from our eyes
All the law and grace of God;
Rich and poor, the fools and wise,
Wanting light to find the road
Leading to the heavenly life,
Wandered lost in care and strife.

Catherine Winkworth

But the glory of the Lord
Hath arisen on us today,
We have seen the light outpoured
That must surely drive away
All things that to night belong,
All the sad earth's woe and wrong.

Thy arising, Lord, shall fill
All my thoughts in sorrow's hour;
Thy arising, Lord, shall still
All my dread of Death's dark power:
Through my smiles and through my tears
Still Thy light, O Lord, appears.

Let me, Lord, in peace depart
From this evil world to Thee;
Where Thyself sole Brightness art,
Thou hast kept a place for me:
In the shining city there
Crowns of light Thy saints shall wear.

First Sunday After Epiphany

I beseech you, brethren, by the mercies of God, that ye present your bodies a living sacrifice, holy, acceptable unto God, which is your reasonable service.
   From the Epistle. [Rom. 12:1]
Angelus. 1657.
trans. by Catherine Winkworth, 1855

Great High-priest, who deign'dst to be
Once the sacrifice for me,
Take this living heart of mine,
Lay it on Thy holy shrine.

Love I know accepteth nought,
Save what Thou, O Love, hast wrought;
Offer Thou my sacrifice,
Else to God it cannot rise.

Slay in me the wayward will,
Earthly sense and passions kill,
Tear self-love from out my heart,
Though it cost me bitter smart.

Kindle, Mighty Love, the pyre,
Quick consume me in Thy fire,
Fain were I of self bereft,
Nought but Thee within me left.

So may God, the Righteous, brook
On my sacrifice to look;
In whose sight no gift has worth
Save a Christ-like life on earth.

Second Sunday after Epiphany

Lift up your eyes unto the heavens, and look upon the earth beneath; for the heavens shall vanish away like smoke, and the earth shall wax old like a garment, and the people that dwell therein shall die in like manner; but my salvation shall be for ever, and my righteousness shall not be abolished.
       From the Lesson. [Is. 51:6]
Zihn. 1682.
trans. by Catherine Winkworth, 1855

God liveth ever!
Wherefore, Soul, despair thou never!
Our God is good, in every place
His love is known, His help is found,
His mighty arm, and tender grace
Bring good from ills that hem us round,
Easier than we think can He
Turn to joy our agony;
Soul, remember 'mid thy pains,
God o'er all for ever reigns.

God liveth ever!
Wherefore, Soul, despair thou never!
Say, shall He slumber, shall He sleep,
Who gave the eye its power to see?
Shall He not hear His children weep
Who made the ear so wondrously?
God is God; He sees and hears
All their troubles, all their tears.
Soul, forget not 'mid thy pains,
God o'er all for ever reigns.

God liveth ever!
Wherefore, Soul, despair thou never!
He who can earth and heaven control,
Who spreads the clouds o'er sea and land,
Whose presence fills the mighty Whole,
In each true heart is close at hand;
Love Him, He will surely send
Help and joy that never end.
Soul, remember in thy pains,
God o'er all for ever reigns.

God liveth ever!
Wherefore, Soul, despair thou never!
Scarce canst thou bear thy cross? Then fly

To Him where only rest is sweet;
Thy God is great, His mercy nigh,
His strength upholds the tottering feet;
Trust Him, for His grace is sure,
Ever doth His truth endure;
Soul, forget not in thy pains,
God o'er all for ever reigns.

God liveth ever!
Wherefore, Soul, despair thou never!
When sins and follies long forgot
Upon thy tortured conscience prey,
Oh come to God, and fear Him not,
His love shall sweep them all away;
Pains of hell at look of His,
Change to calm content and bliss.
Soul, remember in thy pains,
God o'er all for ever reigns.

God liveth ever!
Wherefore, Soul, despair thou never!
Those whom the thoughtless world forsakes,
Who stand bewildered with their woe,
God gently to his bosom takes,
And bids them all His fulness know;
In thy sorrows' swelling flood
Own his hand who seeks thy good.
Soul, forget not in thy pains,
God o'er all for ever reigns.

God liveth ever!
Wherefore, Soul, despair thou never!
Let earth and heaven outworn with age,
Sink to the chaos whence they came;
Let angry foes against us rage,
Let hell shoot forth his fiercest flame;
Fear not Death, nor Satan's thrusts,
God defends who in Him trusts;
Soul, remember in thy pains,
God o'er all for ever reigns.

God liveth ever!
Wherefore, Soul, despair thou never!
What though thou tread with bleeding feet
A thorny path of grief and gloom,
Thy God will choose the way most meet
To lead thee heavenwards, lead thee home.

Catherine Winkworth

For this life's long night of sadness
He will give thee peace and gladness;
Soul, remember in thy pains,
God o'er all for ever reigns.

Third Sunday after Epiphany

For as the rain cometh down, and the snow from heaven; and returneth not thither, but watereth the earth, and maketh it bring forth and bud, that it may give seed to the sower, and bread to the eater; so shall my word be that goeth forth out of my mouth: it shall not return unto me void, but it shall accomplish that which I please, and it shall prosper in the thing whereto I sent it.

From the Lesson. [Is. 55:10]
Anon.
trans. by Catherine Winkworth, 1855

Thy Word, O Lord, like gentle dews,
Falls soft on hearts that pine;
Lord, to Thy garden ne'er refuse
This heavenly balm of Thine.
Watered from Thee
Let every tree
Bud forth and blossom to Thy praise,
And bear much fruit in after days.

Thy word is like a flaming sword,
A wedge that cleaveth stone;
Keen as a fire so burns Thy Word,
And pierceth flesh and bone.
Oh send it forth
O'er all the earth,
To shatter all the might of sin,
The darkened heart to cleanse and win.

Thy word a wondrous guiding star,
On pilgrim hearts doth rise,
Leads to their Lord who dwell afar,
And makes the simple wise.
Let not its light
E'er sink in night,
But still in every spirit shine,
That none may miss Thy light divine.

Fourth Sunday After Epiphany

And he said unto them, Why are ye fearful, O ye of little faith? Then He arose and rebuked the winds and the sea, and there was a great calm.
        From the Gospel. [Matt. 8:26]
Drewes. 1797.
trans. by Catherine Winkworth, 1855

My god, lo, here before Thy face
I cast me in the dust;
Where is the hope of happier days,
Where is my wonted trust?
Where are the sunny hours I had
Ere of Thy light bereft?
Vanished is all that made me glad,
My pain alone is left.

I shrink with fear and sore alarm
When threatening ills I see,
As though in time of need Thine arm
No more could shelter me;
As though Thou couldst not see the grief
That makes my courage quail,
As thou Thou wouldst not send relief,
When human helpers fail.

Cannot Thy might avert e'en now
What seems my certain doom,
And still with light and succour bow
To him who weeps in gloom?
Art Thou not evermore the same?
And hast not Thou revealed
That Thou wilt be our strength, Thy Name
Our tower of hope, our shield?

O Father, compass me about
With love, for I am weak;
Forgive, forgive my sinful doubt,
Thy pitying glance I seek;
For torn and anguished is my heart,
Thou seest it, my God,
Oh soothe my conscience' bitter smart,
Lift off my sorrows' load.

I know that I am in Thy hands,
Whose thoughts are peace toward me,
That ever sure thy counsel stands,--
Could I but build on Thee!
I know that Thou wilt give me all
That Thou has promised, Lord,
Here will I cling, nor yield, nor fall,
I live but by Thy Word.

Though mountains crumble into dust,
Thy covenant standeth fast;
Who follows Thee in pious trust
Shall reach the goal at last.
Though strange and winding seem the way
While yet on earth I dwell,
In heaven my heart shall gladly say,
Thou, God, dost all things well!

Take courage then, my soul, nor steep
Thy days and nights in tears,
That soon shalt cease to mourn and weep,
Thou dark are now thy fears.
He comes, He comes, the Strong to save,
He comes nor tarries more,
His light is breaking o'er the wave,
The clouds and storms are o'er!

Fifth Sunday After Epiphany

Oh that Thou wouldst rend the heavens, that Thou wouldst come down, that the mountains might flow down at Thy presence ... To make Thy name known to Thine adversaries, that the nations may tremble at Thy presence.
     From the Lesson. [Is. 64:1-2]
Bogatsky. 1727.
after A. H. Franke (1663-1727).
trans. by Catherine Winkworth, 1855

Awake, Thou Spirit, who of old
Didst fire the watchmen of the Church's youth,
Who faced the foe, unshrinking, bold,
Who witnessed day and night the eternal truth,
Whose voices through the world are ringing still,
And bringing hosts to know and do Thy will!

Oh that thy fire were kindled soon,
That swift from land to land its flame might leap!
Lord, give us but this priceless boon
Of faithful servants, fit for Thee to reap
The harvest of the soul; look down and view
How great the harvest, yet the labourers few.

Lord, let our earnest prayer be heard,
The prayer Thy son Himself hath bid us pray;
For, lo! Thy children's hearts are stirred
In every land in this our darkening day,
To cry for help with fervent soul to Thee;
Oh hear us, Lord, and speak, Thus let it be!

O haste to help ere we are lost!
Send forth evangelist, in spirit strong,
Armed with Thy Word, a dauntless host,
Bold to attack the rule of ancient wrong,
And let them all the earth for Thee reclaim,
To be Thy kingdom, and to know Thy name.

Would there were help within our walls!
Oh let thy promised Spirit come again,
Before whom every barrier falls,
And ere the night once more shine forth as then!
Oh rend the heavens and make Thy presence felt,
The chains tha tbind us at Thy touch would melt!

And let Thy Word have speedy course,
Through every land the truth be glorified,
Till all the heathen know its force,
And gather to Thy churches far and wide;
And waken Israel from her sleep, O Lord!
Thus bless and spread the conquests of Thy Word!

The Church's deserts paths restore,
That stumbling blocks which long in them have lain,
May hinder now Thy Word no more;
Destroy false doctrine, root out notions vain,
Set free from hirelings, let the Church and school
Bloom as a garden 'neath Thy prospering rule!

Catherine Winkworth

Sixth Sunday after Epiphany
Every man that hath this hope in him purifieth himself even as he is pure.
       From the Epistle. [1 Jn. 3:3]
Freylinghausen. 1713.
trans. by Catherine Winkworth, 1855

Pure essence! Spotless Fount of Light,
That fadeth never into dark!
O Thou, whose eyes more clear and bright
Than noonday sun are quick to mark
Our sins; lo, bare before Thy face
Lies all the desert of my heart,
My once fair soul in every part
Now stained with evil foul and base.

Since but the pure in heart are blest
With promised vision of their God,
Sore fear and anguish fill my breast,
Rememb'ring all the ways I trod;
Mourning I see my lost estate,
And yet in faith I dare to cry,
Oh let my evil nature die,
Another heart in me create!

Enough, Lord, that my foe too well
Hath lured me once away from Thee;
Henceforth I know his craft how fell,
And all his deep-laid snares I flee.
Lord, through the Spirit whom Thy Son
Hath bidden us in prayer to ask,
Arm us with might that every task,
Whate'er we do, in Thee be done.

Unworthy am I of Thy grace,
So deep are my transgressions, Lord,
And yet once more I seek Thy face;
My God, have mercy, nor reward
My sins and follies, dark and vain;
Reject, reject me not in wrath,
But let Thy sunshine now beam forth,
And quicken me with hope again.

The Holy Spirit Thou hast given,
The wondrous pledge of love divine,
Who fills our hearts with joys of heaven,

And bids us earthly joys resign;
Oh let His seal be on my heart,
Oh take Him nevermore away,
Until this fleshly house decay,
And Thou shlt bid me hence depart.

But ah! my coward spirit droops,
Sick with the fear that enters in
Whene'er a soul to bondage stoops,
And wears the shameful yoke of sin;
Oh quicken with the strength that flows
From out the Eternal Fount of Life,
My soul half-fainting in the strife,
And make an end of all my woes.

I cling unto Thy grace alone,
Thy steadfast oath my only rest;
To Thee, Heart-searcher, all is known
That lieth hidden in my breast;
Thy joy, O Spirit, on me pour,
Thy fervent will my sloth inspire,
So shall I have my heart's desire,
And serve and praise Thee evermore.

Septuagesima Sunday

I therefore so run, not as uncertainly; so fight I, not as one that beateth the air.
      From the Epistle. [1 Cor. 9:26]
Winkler. 1703.
trans. by Catherine Winkworth, 1855

Strive when thou art called of God,
When He draws thee by his grace,
Strive to cast away the load
That would clog thee in the race!

Fight, though it may cost thy life;
Storm the kingdom, but prevail;
Let not Satan's fiercest strife
Make thee, warrior, faint or quail.

Wrestle, till through every vein
Love and strength are glowing warm,
Love that can the world disdain,
Half-love will not abide the storm.

Wrestle with strong prayers and cries,
Think no time too much to spend,
Though the night be passed in sighs.
Though all day thy voice ascend.

Hast thou won the pearl of price,
Think not thou hast reached the goal,
Conquered every sin and vice
That had power to harm thy soul.

Gaze with mingled joy and fear,
On the refuge thou hast found;
Know, while yet we linger here
Perils ever hem us round.

Art thou faithful? then oppose
Sin and wrong with all thy might;
Care not how the tempest blows,
Only care to win the fight.

Art thou faithful? Wake and watch,
Love with all thy heart Christ's ways,
Seek not transient ease to snatch,
Look not for reward or praise.

Lyra Germanica: Hymns for the Sundays & Chief Festivals of The Christian Year - Book I & II

Art thou faithful? Stand apart
From all all worldly hope and pleasure,
Yonder fix thy hopes and heart,
On the heaven where lies our treasure.

Soldiers of the Cross, be strong,
Watch and war 'mid fear and pain,
Daily conquering woe and wrong,
Till our King o'er earth shall reign!

Sexagesima Sunday

Let them praise the name of the Lord for His name alone is excellent; His glory is above the earth and heaven.
      Psalm 148:13
Angelus. 1657.
trans. by Catherine Winkworth, 1855

Nothing fair on earth I see
But I straightway think on Thee;
Thou art fairest in mine eyes,
Source in whom all beauty lies!

When the golden sun forth goes,
And the east before him glows,
Quickly turns this heart of mine
To Thy heavenly form divine.

On Thy light I think at morn,
With the earliest break of dawn;
Ah, what glories lie in Thee,
Light of all Eternity!

When I watch the moon arise
'Mid Heaven's thousand golden eyes,
Then I think, more glorious far
Is the Maker of yon star.

Or I cry in spring's sweet hours,
When the fields are gay with flowers,
As their varied hues I see,
What must their Creator be!

When along the brook I wander,
Or beside the fountain ponder,
Straight my thoughts take wing and mount
Up to Thee, the purest fount!

Sweetly sings the nightingale,
Sweet the flute's soft plaintive tale,
Sweeter than their richest tone,
Is the name of Mary's Son.

Sweetly all the air is stirred
When the Echo's call is heard;
But no sounds my heart rejoice

Like to my Beloved's voice.

Come then, fairest Lord, appear,
Come, let me behold Thee here,
I would see Thee face to face,
On Thy proper light would gaze.

Take away these veils that blind,
Jesus, all my soul and mind;
Henceforth ever let my heart
See Thee truly as Thou art!

Quinquagesima Sunday

And now abideth faith, hope, charity, these three; but the greatest of these is charity.
     From the Epistle. [1 Cor. 13:13]
Ernst Lange. 1711.
trans. by Catherine Winkworth, 1855

Many a gift did Christ impart,
Noblest of them all is Love,
Love, a balm within the heart
That can all its pains remove;
Love, a star most bright and pure;
Love, a gem of priceless worth,
Richer than man knows on earth;
Love, like beauty, strong to lure;
Love, like joy, makes man her thrall,
Strong to please and conquer all.

Love can give us all things; here
Use and beauty cannot sever;
Love can raise us to that sphere
Whence the soul tends heavenwards ever;
Though one speak with angel tongues
Bravest words of strength and fire,
If no love his heart inspire,
They are but as fleeting songs;
All his eloquence shall pass,
As the noise of sounding brass.

Science with her keen-eyed glance,
All the wisdom of the world,
Mysteries that the soul entrance,
Faith that mighty hills had hurled
From their ancient seats;--all this,
Wherein man takes most his pride,
Valueless is cast aside,
If the spirit there we miss,
That can work from love alone,
Not from pride in what is known.

Though I lavished all I have
On the poor in charity;
Though I shrank not from the grave,
Or unmoved the stake could see;
Though my body here were given

To the all-consuming flame;
If my mind were still the same,
Meeter were I not for heaven,
Till by Love my works were crowned,
Till in Love my strength were found.

Faith must conquer, Hope must bloom,
As our onward path we wend,
Else we came not through the gloom,
But with earth they also end:
Thou, O Love, doth stretch afar
Through the wide eternity,
And the soul arrayed in Thee
Shines for ever as a star.
Faith and hope must pass away,
Thou, O Love, endurest aye.

Come, thou Spirit of pure Love,
Who dost forth from God proceed,
Never from my heart remove,
Let me all Thy impulse heed;
All that seeks self-profit first,
Rather than another's good,
Whether foe or linked in blood,
Let me hold such thought accurst;
And my heart henceforward be
Ruled, inspired, O Love, by thee!

Quinquagesima Sunday

And Jesus said unto him, Receive thy sight; thy faith hath saved thee. And immediately he received his sight, and followed him, glorifying God.
    From the Gospel. [Luke 18:42-43]
trans. by Catherine Winkworth, 1855

I am the light of the world.
    [Jn. 8:12]

God said, let there be light: and there was light.
    [Gen. 1:3]

My Saviour, what Thou didst of old,
When thou wast dwelling here,
Thou doest yet for them, who bold
In faith to Thee draw near.
As thou hadst pity on the blind,
According to Thy Word,
Thou sufferedst me Thy grace to find,
Thy Light hast on me poured.

Mourning I sat beside the way,
In sightless gloom apart,
And sadness heavy on me lay,
And longing gnawed my heart;
I heard the music of the psalms
Thy people sang to Thee,
I felt the waving of their palms,
And yet I could not see.

My pain grew more than I could bear,
Too keen my grief became,
Then I took heart in my despair
To call upon Thy name;
"O Son of David, save and heal,
As Thou so oft hast done!
O dearest Jesus, let me feel
My load of darkness gone."

And ever weeping as I spoke
With bitter prayers and sighs,
My stony heart grew soft and broke,
More earnest yet my cries.
A sudden answer stilled my fear,
For it was said to me,

"O poor blind man, be of good cheer,
Rejoice, He calleth thee."

I felt, Lord, that Thou stoodest still,
Groping Thy feet I sought,
From off me fell my old self-will,
A change came o'er my thought.
Thou saidst, "What is it thou wouldst have?"
"Lord, that I might have sight;
To see Thy countenance I crave:"
"So be it, have thou Light."

And words of Thine can never fail,
My fears are past and o'er;
My soul is glad with light, the veil
Is on my heart no more.
Thou blessest me, and forth I fare
Free from my old discrace,
And follow on with joy where'er
Thy footsteps, Lord, I trace.

Ash Wednesday

Gather the people . . and let the priests, the ministers of the Lord, weep between the porch and the alter, and let them say, Spare Thy people, O Lord.
    From the Passage for the Epistle. [Joel 2:17]
Albinus. 1652.
trans. by Catherine Winkworth, 1855

Not in anger smite us, Lord,
Spare Thy people, spare!
If Thou mete us due reward
We must all despair.
Let the flood
Of Jesus' blood
Quench the flaming of Thy wrath,
That our sin enkindled hath.

Father! Thou hast patience long
With the sick and weak;
Heal us, make us brave and strong,
Words of comfort speak.
Touch my soul,
And make me whole
With Thy healing precious balm;
Ward off all would bring me harm.

Weary am I, Lord, and worn
With my ceaseless pain;
Sad the heart that night and morn
Sighs for help in vain.
Wilt Thou yet
My soul forget,
Waiting anxiously for Thee
In the cave of misery?

Hence, ye foes! God hears my prayer
From His holy place;
Once again with hope I dare
Come before His face.
Satan flee,
Hell touch not me;
God hath given me power o'er all,
Who once mocked and sought my fall.

First Sunday in Lent

Then was Jesus led up of the Spirit into the wilderness to be tempted of the devil. And he fasted forty days and forty nights.
    From the Gospel. [Matt. 4:1-2]
Raisner. 1678.
trans. by Catherine Winkworth, 1855

Am I a stranger here, on earth alone,
When shall my weary days be past and gone?
When shall I find some respite, some relief
From this unsleeping pain, this haunting grief?

The joyful sun another morning brings,
I only wake to see care's piercing stings;
The soft moon comes with silent night and sleep,
And bringeth nought to me but time to weep.

My heart and conscience sorely wounded lie,
Struck by the arrows of Thy wrath, Most High!
From morn to eventide where'er I flee,
I find no hiding-place, great God, from Thee!

O Lord, be not so strict to mark my crimes!
Great God, dost thou remember yet those times
Of foolish thoughtlessness, when blind and young
My heart to vain delights of earth still clung?

Wilt Thou then always bear my sins in mind?
What offering, what atonement can I find!
Nought have I of mine own but sin and wrong,
But love and mercy, Lord, to Thee belong!

Oh therefore leave me not the wretched prey
Of those who seek to take my life away!
Yet though with streaming eyes to Thee I cry,
No answering voice comes from Thy throne on high.

Vain are my tears and prayers, vain all my woe,
While Thou dost fight against me as a foe;
The zeal of Thy just anger and Thy might
Have plunged my soul in blackest depths of night.

I sit alone; with tears I bathe my cheeks,
With bitter sighs and groans my spirit seeks,
For Him, who veils behind the clouds His face,

Catherine Winkworth

And hears not, as of old in happier days.

O that I had a dove's swift wings! I'd fly
Away to some far mountain lone and high,--
Yet could I not escape His mighty hand
Before whom all things bare and open stand.

Nay, rather let me suffer all His will,
Though His fierce anger beat upon me still,
A willing heart and patient mind, O God!
I bring to Thy sever but righteous rod.

Much have I sinned, I perish utterly
If my misdeeds be all avenged of Thee;
Yet, Lord of Hosts, doth not thy Word proclaim,
The Merciful is Thy most glorious name!

Second Sunday in Lent
And the disciples said, Send her away, for she crieth after us; . . . But He said, Great is thy faith, be it unto thee even as thou wilt.
    From the Gospel. [Matt. 15:23-28]
Wolfgang C. Deszler. 1692.
trans. by Catherine Winkworth, 1855

I will not let Thee go; Thou Help in time of need!
Heap ill on ill
I trust Thee still,
E'en when it seems that thou wouldst slay indeed!
Do as Thou wilt with me,
I yet will cling to Thee,
Hide Thou Thy face, yet, Help in time of need,
I will not let Thee go!

I will not let Thee go; should I forsake my bliss?
No, Lord, Thou'rt mine,
And I am Thine,
Thee will I hold when all things else I miss.
Though dark and sad the night,
Joy cometh with Thy light,
O Thou my Sun; should I forsake my bliss?
I will not let Thee go!

I will not let Thee go, my God, my Life, my Lord!
Not Death can tear
Me from His care,
Who for my sake His soul in death outpoured.
Thou diedst for love to me,
I say in love to Thee,
E'en when my heart shall break, my God, my Life, my Lord,
I will not let Thee go!

Third Sunday in Lent
Awake, thou that sleepest, and arise from the dead, and Christ shall give thee light.--
     From the Epistle. [Eph. 5:14]
Crasselius. 1697.
trans. by Catherine Winkworth, 1855

Awake, O man, and from thee shake
This heavy sleep of sin!
Soon shall the Highest vengeance take,
Soon shall His wrath begin
To smite the wretched sinner home;
In awful terrors He shall come,
To mete to all on earth their due reward,
Only the righteous spares our angry Lord.

Come then, ye sinners, great and small,
Weeping and mourning sore,
Low down before his footstool fall,
And vow to sin no more.
In faith and godliness array
Your souls against that final day,
So shall ye 'scape His wrath, and blessed die,
Heirs of the kingdom with your Lord on high.

Oh lay to heart this wondrous thought,
Through what sore agony
And death was your redemption bought,
And to your Saviour flee
Ere yet to late; the world disown,
And fix your love on Christ alone,
And do His will; for at the final doom,
Those who dishonoured Him shall wrath consume.

Turn Thou us, and we shall be turned,
Thou broughtest back of old
Thy straying people, when they yearned
After their proper fold;
Even so forgive what we have done,
Accept us in Thy blessed Son,
And let Thy Holy Spirit be our guide,
That we may spread Thy praises far and wide!

Fourth Sunday in Lent

Grant, we beseech Thee, Almighty God, that we, who for our evil deeds do worthily deserve to be punished, by the comfort of Thy grace may mercifully be relieved; through our Lord and Saviour, Jesus Christ.

From the Collect.
Anon.
trans. by Catherine Winkworth, 1855

Here, O my God, I cast me at Thy feet,
Ready to suffer what Thou thinkest meet;
Yet look on me, great God, with pitying eyes,
Reward me not for mine iniquities!

To oft, alas! my heart hath loved to stray
Downward along Sin's broad and easy way;
And worldly pride and carnal lusts most foul
Were shameless cherished in my inmost soul.

Thy Majesty have I offended, Lord,
And set at nought Thy law, Thy holy Word;
I had not learnt Thy righteous wrath to dread,
Nor saw the vengeance gathering o'er my head.

O wretched man, what evil have I wrought!
Who may these heavy chains of sin unbind?
Can man nor creature show me any place,
Where I may flee and hide me from God's face!

Nay, I must flee to God Himself, from whom
Our life and help, our hope and safety come;
What all the world must unaccomplished leave,
Thou, for Thou art Almighty, canst achieve.

Think on the covenant Thou hast never broken,
Think on the steadfast oath Thyself hast spoken,
Know that I am a God, Thy promise saith,
Who hath no pleasure in a sinner's death.

Then let the arms of love be round me thrown,
Have pity on me, hear my bitter moan,
Call back Thy sheep, that wandering far astray,
Was lost in sin, nor knew its homeward way.

Catherine Winkworth

Grant me to rule my inner life aright,
And act and speak as ever in Thy sight,
A friend to all true virtue, but a foe
To all Thou hatest, sins and follies low.

Thou Merciful! what thanks and praise shall be
For Thy great goodness offered unto Thee,
As is most meet, while here my days I spend,
And yonder in the world that shall not end!

Fifth Sunday in Lent
Out of the depths have I called unto Thee, O Lord; Lord, hear my voice. If Thou, Lord, wilt be extreme to mark what is done amiss, O Lord, who may abide it?--
    Ps. 130:1,3.
Luther. 1524.
trans. by Catherine Winkworth, 1855

Out of the depths I cry to thee,
Lord God! oh hear my prayer!
Incline a gracious ear to me,
And bid me not despair:
If Thou rememberest each misdeed,
If each should have its righteous meed,
Lord, who shall stand before Thee?

'Tis through Thy love alone we gain
The pardon of our sin;
The strictest life is but in vain,
Our works can nothing win,
That none should boast himself of aught,
But own in fear Thy grace hath wrought
What in him seemeth righteous.

Wherefore my hope is in the Lord,
My works I count but dust,
I build not there, but on His word,
And in His goodness trust.
Up to His care myself I yield,
He is my tower, my rock, my shield,
And for His help I tarry.

And though it linger till the night,
And round again till morn,
My heart shall ne'er mistrust Thy might,
Nor count itself forlorn.
Do thus, O ye of Israel's seed,
Ye of the Spirit born indeed,
Wait for your God's appearing.

Though great our sins and sore our wounds,
And deep and dark our fall,
His helping mercy hath no bounds,

Catherine Winkworth

His love surpasseth all.
Our trusty loving Shepherd He,
Who shall at last set Israel free
From all their sin and sorrow.

Palm Sunday

And the multitude that went before, and that followed, cried, saying, Hosanna to the Son of David; Blessed is He that cometh in the name of the Lord; Hosanna in the highest.
     Matt. 21:9.
Schmolck. 1704.
trans. by Catherine Winkworth, 1855

Hosanna to the Son of David! Raise
Triumphal arches to His praise,
For Him prepare a throne
Who comes at last to Zion--to His own!
Strew palms around, make plain and straight the way
For Him who His triumphal entry holds today!

Hosanna! Welcome above all Thou art!
Make ready each to lay his heart
Low down before His feet!
Come, let us hasten forth our Lord to meet,
And bid him enter in Zion's gates,
Where thousand-voiced welcome on His coming waits.

Hosanna! Prince of Peace and Lord of Might!
We hail Thee Conqueror in the fight!
All Thou with toil hast won,
Shall be our booty when the battle's done.
Thy right hand ever hath the rule and sway,
Thy kingdom standeth fast when all things else decay.

Hosanna! best-beloved and noble Guest!
Who makest us by thy behest
Heirs of Thy realm with Thee.
Oh let us therefore never weary be
To stand and serve before Thy righteous throne,
We know no king but Thee, rule Thou o'er us alone!

Hosanna! Come, the time draws on apace,
We long Thy mercy to embrace,
This servant's form can ne'er
Conceal the majesty Thy acts declare:
Too well art Thou here in Thy Zion known,
Who art the Son of God, and yet art David's Son.

Catherine Winkworth

Hosanna! Lord, be Thou our help and friend,
Thy aid to us in mercy send,
That each may bring his soul
An offering unto Thee, unstained and whole.
Thou wilt have none for Thy disciples, Lord,
But those who truly keep, not only hear Thy word.

Hosanna! Let us in Thy footsteps tread,
Not that sad Mount of Olives dread
Where we must weep and watch,
Until the far-off song of joy we catch
From Heaven our Bethphage, where we shall sing
Hosanna in the highest to our God and King!

Hosanna! Let us sound it far and wide!
Enter Thou in and here abide,
Thou Blessed of the Lord!
Why standest Thou without, why roam'st abroad!
Hosanna! Make Thy home with us for ever!
Thou comest, Lord! and nought us from Thy love shall sever.

Hallelujah.

Monday in Passion Week

And when He was come near, He beheld the city and wept over it.
    Luke 19:14
Heermann. 1630.
trans. by Catherine Winkworth, 1855

Thou weepest o'er Jerusalem,
Lord Jesus, bitter tears;
But deepest comfort lies in them
For us, whose sins have filled our soul with tears:
Since they that tell,
When sinners turn to Thee Thou lov'st it well,
And surely wilt efface, of Thy unbounded grace,
All the misdeeds that on our conscience dwell.

When God's just wrath and anger burn
Against me for my sin,
To these sad tears of Thine I turn,
And watching them fresh hope and courage win;
For God doth prize
These drops so greatly, that before His eyes
Who sprinkles o'er his soul with them is clean and whole,
And from his sorrows' depth new joy shall rise.

Earth is the home of tears and woe,
Where we must often weep,
Fighting the world our mighty foe,
Whose enmity to Thee doth never sleep;
My heart is torn
Afresh each day by her fierce rage and scorn,
But in my saddest hours, I think upon those showers
That tell how Thou hast all our sorrows borne.

Thou countest up my tears and sighs,
E'en were they numberless;
Not one is hidden from thy eyes,
Thou ne'er forgettest me in my distress,
But when they rain
Before Thee, Thou dost quickly turn again,
Hast pity on my woe, and makest me to know
What sweetest joy lies hid in sorest pain.

We sow in tears; but let us keep
Our faith in God, and trust Him still,
Yonder our harvest we shall reap,

Catherine Winkworth

Where gladness every heart and voice shall fill.
Such joy is there
No mortal tongue its glory can declare,
A joy that shall endure, unchanging deep and pure,
That shall be ours, if here the cross we bear.

O Christ, I thank Thee for Thy tears;
Those tears have won for me
That I shall wear, through endless years,
A crown of joy before my God and Thee.
All weeping o'er,
Up to Thy chosen saints I once shall soar,
And there Thy pity praise, in more befitting lays,
Thou glory of Thy Church, for evermore.

For these things I weep, Mine eye runneth down with water, because the comfort that should relieve my soul, is for ever from me; my children are desolate because the enemy prevailed.
      Lament. 1:16

Tuesday in Passion Week

By the which will we are sanctified, through the offering of the body of Jesus Christ once for all.
     Heb. 10:10
Heermann. 1644.
trans. by Catherine Winkworth, 1855

Lord! Thy death and passion give
Strength and comfort at my need,
Every hour while here I live
On Thy love my soul shall feed.
Doth some evil thought upstart?
Lo, Thy cross defends my heart,
Shows the peril, and I shrink
Back from loitering on the brink.

Doth my carnal nature yearn
After wanton joys? again
Quickly to Thy cross I turn,
And her voice is heard in vain.
Cometh strong temptation's hour,
When my foe puts forth his power?
Sheltered by this holy shield,
Soon I drive him from the field.

Would the world my steps entice
To yon wide and level road,
Filled with mirth and pleasant vice?
Lord, I think upon the load
Thou didst once for me endure,
And I fly all thoughts impure;
Thinking on Thy bitter pains,
Hushed in prayer my heart remains.

Yes, Thy cross hath power to heal
All the wounds of sin and strife,
Lost in Thee my heart doth feel
Sudden warmth and nobler life.
In my saddest, darkest grief,
Let Thy sweetness bring relief,
Thou who camest but to save,
Thou who fearedst not the grave!

Catherine Winkworth

Lord, in Thee I place my trust,
Thou art my defence and tower;
Death Thou treadest in the dust,
O'er my soul he hath no power.
That I may have part in Thee,
Help and save and comfort me,
Give me of Thy grace and might,
Resurrection, life and light.

Fount of Good, within me dwell,
For the peace Thy presence sheds
Keeps us safe in conflict fell,
Charms the pain from dying beds.
Hide me close within Thine arm,
Where no foe can hurt or harm;
Whoso, Lord, in Thee doth rest,
He hath conquered, he is blest.

Wednesday in Passion Week

Now once in the end of the world hath He appeared, to put away sin by the sacrifice of Himself.
   From the Epistle. [Heb. 9:26]
Gesenius. 1646.
trans. by Catherine Winkworth, 1855

When sorrow and remorse
Prey at my heart, to Thee
I look, who on the holy cross
Was slain for me.
Ah Lord, Thy precious blood was spilt
For me, O most unworthy,
To take away my guilt.

Oh wonder past belief!
Behold the Master spares
His servants, and sore pain and grief
For them He bears.
God stoopeth from His throne on high,
For me His guilty creature,
He deigns as man to die.

Thou countless were the sins
That weighed me to the dust,
Christ's death for me the favour wins
Of God most just.
His precious blood my debts hath paid,
Of hell and all its torments
I am no more afraid.

My heart is filled with ruth,
Thinking on all Thou'st borne,
How mighty love and tender truth
Were crowned with thorn.
In songs of thanks I'll spend my breath
For Thy sad cry, Thy sufferings,
Thy wrongs, Thy guiltless death.

Thy Passion, Lord, inspires
My spirit day by day,
With strength from all low dark desires
To flee away.
This thought I fain would cherish most,
What pain my soul's redemption

Catherine Winkworth

To Thee, O Saviour, cost.

Whate'er the burden be,
The cross upon me laid,
Or want or shame, I look to Thee,
Be Thou mine aid.
Give patience, give me strength to take
Thee for my bright example,
And all the world forsake.

Let me to others do,
As thou hast done to me,
Love them with love unfeigned and true,
Their servant be
Of willing heart, nor seek my own,
But as Thou, Lord, hast helped us,
From purest love alone.

And let Thy sorrows cheer
My soul when I depart;
Give strength to cast away all fear,
And tell my heart
That since my trust is in Thy grace,
Thou wilt accept me yonder,
Where I shall see Thy face.

Thursday in Passion Week

Pilate therefore, willing to release Jesus, spake again to them. But they cried saying, Crucify Him, crucify Him. And he said unto them the third time, Why, what evil hath He done?

     From the Gospel. [Lk. 23:20-22]
Heermann. 1630.
trans. by Catherine Winkworth, 1855

Alas dear Lord, what evil hast Thou done,
That such sharp sentence from Thy judge hath won?
What are His crimes, and what the guilt, oh, tell
Wherein He fell!

They scourge Him, crown Him with a crown of thorn,
They smite His face with bitter mock and scorn,
They give Him gall to drink, they pierce His side,
The Crucified!

From head to foot was there no spot in me
Unscarred by sin, from taint of evil free;
My sins had weighed me down that I should dwell
For aye in Hell.

Whence come these sorrows, whence this cruel woe?
It was my sins that struck the fatal blow;
Mine were the wrath and anguish, dearest Lord,
On Thee outpoured.

What strangest punishment! The Shepherd good
For erring sheep here pours His own heart's blood,
The servants' debts are on the Master laid,
Who all hath paid.

Oh wondrous love, love that no measure knows,
That brought Thee, Christ, to drink this cup of woes!
Full of the world's vain joys and hopes was I,
While Thou must die!

O mighty King! mighty beyond all time!
Fain would I sound Thy praise through every clime!
A gift were meet for Thee, my anxious thought
Long time hath sought.

Catherine Winkworth

But human wisdom searches, Lord, in vain
To find aught like Thy pity, or Thy pain.
How shall my works, though toiling day and night,
Thy love requite?

Yet have I somewhat that my Lord can please;
I can renounce sweet sins and selfish ease,
And quench the unhallowed fires that back would lure
To thoughts impure.

But since my strength, alas, will ne'er prevail
My strong desires upon the cross to nail,
Oh let Thy Spirit rule my heart, who leads
To all good deeds.

Then shall Thy mercy fill my every thought,
I love Thee so, the world to me is nought;
My sole endeavour, Lord, is to fulfil
Thy holy will.

My all I risk to magnify Thy name,
No cross shall daunt me, no reproach or shame;
Man's fiercest threats I will not lay to heart,
Nor Death's worst smart.

In truth my sacrifice is nothing worth,
Yet Thou in mercy wilt not cast it forth;
Thou'lt put me not to shame but for love's sake
My offering take.

Lord Jesus, once on high amongst Thine own,
Shall I stand crowned with light before Thy throne!
Where sweetest hymns are ever ringing round,
My voice shall sound.

Good Friday. Morning

He was wounded for our transgressions, He was bruised for our iniquities; the chastisement of our peace was upon Him, and with His stripes we are healed.
From the Lesson. [Is. 53:5]
Paul Gerhardt. 1659.
trans. by Catherine Winkworth, 1855

Ah wounded Head! Must Thou
Endure such shame and scorn!
The blood is trickling from Thy brow
Pierced by the crown of thorn.
Thou who wast crowned on high
With light and majesty,
In deep dishonour here must die,
Yet here I welcome Thee!

Thou noble countenance!
All earthly lights are pale
Before the brightness of that glance,
At which a world shall quail.
How is it quenched and gone!
Those gracious eyes how dim!
Whence grew that cheek so pale and wan?
Who dared to scoff at Him?

All lovely hues of life,
That glowed on lip and cheek,
Have vanished in that awful strife;
The Mighty One is weak.
Pale Death has won the day,
He triumphs in this hour
When Strength and Beauty fade away,
And yield them to his power.

Ah Lord, Thy woes belong,
Thy cruel pains, to me,
The burden of my sin and wrong
Hath all been laid on Thee.
Behold me where I kneel,
Wrath were my rightful lot,
One glance of love yet let me feel!
Redeemer, spurn me not!

Catherine Winkworth

My Guardian, own me Thine;
My Shepherd, bear me home:
O Fount of mercy, Source Divine,
From Thee what blessings come!
How oft Thy mouth has fed
My soul with angels' food,
How oft Thy Spirit o'er me shed
His stores of Heavenly good!

Ah would that I could share
Thy cross, Thy bitter woes!
All true delight lies hidden there,
Thence all true comfort flows.
Ah well were it for me
That I could end my strife,
And die upon the cross with Thee,
Who art my Life of life!

My soul is all o'erfraught,
O Jesus, dearest Friend,
With thankful love to Him who sought
Such woe for such an end.
Grant me as true a faith,
As Thou art true to me,
That so the icy sleep of death
Be but a rest in Thee.

Yes, when I must depart,
Depart Thou not from me;
When Death is creeping to my heart,
Bear Thou mine agony.
When faith and courage sink,
O'erwhelmed with dread dismay,
Come Thou who ne'er from pain didst shrink,
And chase my fears away.

Come to me ere I die,
My comfort and my shield;
Then gazing on Thy cross can I
Calmly my spirit yield.
On Thee, when life is past,
My darkening eyes shall dwell,
My heart in faith shall hold Thee fast;
Who dieth thus, dies well.

Good Friday. Evening

But God commended His love toward us, in that, while we were yet sinners, Christ died for us.
    Rom 5:8
Angelus. 1657.
trans. by Catherine Winkworth, 1855

Thou Holiest Love, whom most I love,
Who art my longed-for only bliss,
Whom tenderest pity erst did move
To fathom woe and death's abyss
Who once didst suffer for my good,
And die my guilty debts to pay,
Thou Lamb of God, whose precious blood
Can take a world's misdeeds away;

Thou Love, who didst such anguish bear
Upon the Mount of agony,
And yet with ceaseless watchful care
Dost yearn o'er us so tenderly;
Thou camest not Thy will to seek,
But all Thy Father's will obey,
Bearing the cross in patience meek,
That Thou might'st take our curse away.

O Love, who with unflinching heart
Enduredst all disgrace and shame;
O Love, who mid the keenest smart
Of dying pangs wert still the same;
Who didst Thy changeless virtue prove
E'en with Thy latest parting breath,
And spakest words of gentlest love
When soul and body sank in death;

O Love, through sorrows manifold
Hast Thou betrothed me as a bride,
By ceaseless gifts, by love untold,
Hast bound me ever to Thy side;
Oh let the weary ache, the smart,
Of life's long tale of pain and loss,
Be gently stilled within my heart
At thought of Thee, and of Thy cross!

Catherine Winkworth

O Love, who dying thus for me,
Hast won me an eternal good
Through sorest anguish on the tree,
I ever think upon Thy blood;
I ever thank Thy sacred wounds,
Thou wounded Love, Thou Holiest,
But most when life is near its bounds,
And in Thy bosom safe I rest.

O Love, who unto death hast grieved
For this cold heart, unworthy Thine,
Whom once the chill dark grave received,
I thank Thee for that grief divine;
I give Thee thanks that Thou didst die
To win eternal life for me,
To bring salvation from on high;
Oh draw me up through love to Thee!

Easter Even

And Joseph wrapped the body in a clean linen cloth, and laid it in his own new tomb, which he had hewn out in the rock.
    From the Gospel. [Matt. 27:59-60]
Salomo Franck (1659-1725). 1711.
trans. by Catherine Winkworth, 1855

Rest of the weary! Thou
Thyself art resting now,
Where lowly in Thy sepulchre Thou liest:
From out her deathly sleep
My soul doth start, to weep
So sad a wonder, that Thou Saviour diest!

Thy bitter anguish o'er,
To this dark tomb they bore
Thee, Life of Life--Thee, Lord of all creation!
The hollow rocky cave
Must serve Thee for a grave,
Who wast Thyself the Rock of our Salvation!

O Prince of Life! I know
That when I too lie low,
Thou wilt at last my soul from death awaken;
And thus I will not shrink
From the grave's awful brink;
The heart that trusts in Thee shall ne'er be shaken.

To me the darksome tomb
Is but a narrow room,
Where I may rest in peace from sorrow free;
Thy death shall give me power
To cry in that dark hour,
O Death, O Grave, where is your victory?

The grave can nought destroy,
Only the flesh can die,
And e'en the body triumphs o'er decay:
Clothed by Thy wondrous might
In robes of dazzling light,
This flesh shall burst the grave at that last Day.

Catherine Winkworth

My Jesus, day by day,
Help me to watch and pray,
Beside the tomb where in my heart Thou'rt laid.
Thy bitter death shall be
My constant memory,
My guide at last into Death's awful shade.

Easter Day. Morning

Christ being raised from the dead dieth no more: death hath no more dominion over Him.
　　From the Anthem [Rom. 6:9]
Luther. 1524.
trans. by Catherine Winkworth, 1855

In the bonds of Death He lay,
Who for our offense was slain,
But the Lord is risen today,
Christ hath brought us life again.
Wherefore let us all rejoice,
Singing loud with a cheerful voice
Hallelujah!

Of the sons of men was none
Who could break the bonds of Death,
Sin this mischief dire had done,
Innocent was none on earth;
Wherefore Death grew strong and bold,
Death would all men captive hold.
Hallelujah!

Jesus Christ, God's only Son,
Came at last our foe to smite,
All our sins away hath done,
Done away Death's power and right,
Only the form of Death is left,
Of his sting he is bereft;
Hallelujah.

'Twas a wondrous war, I trow,
When Life and Death together fought;
But life hath triumphed o'er his foe,
Death is mocked and set at nought;
Yea, 'tis as the Scripture saith,
Christ through death has conquered Death.
Hallelujah.

Now our Paschal Lamb is He,
And by Him alone we live,
Who to death upon the tree,
For our sake Himself did give.
Faith His blood strikes on our door,
Death dares never harm us more.

Catherine Winkworth

Hallelujah.

On this day most blest of days,
Let us keep high festival,
For our God hath showed His grace,
And our Sun hath risen on us all,
And our hearts rejoice to see
Sin and night before Him flee.
Hallelujah.

To the supper of the Lord,
Gladly we will come today,
The word of peace is now restored,
The old leaven is put away;
Christ will be our food alone,
Faith no life but His doth own.
Hallelujah.

Easter Day. Evening

If ye then be risen with Christ, seek those things which are above, where Christ sitteth on the right hand of God.
     From the Epistle. [Col. 3:1]
Gerhard Tersteegen. 1731.
trans. by Catherine Winkworth, 1855

O Glorious Head, Thou livest now!
Let us Thy members share Thy life;
Canst Thou behold their need, nor bow
To raise Thy children from the strife
With self and sin, with death and dark distress,
That they may live to Thee in holiness?

Earth knows Thee not, but evermore
Thou liv'st in Paradise, in peace;
Oh fain my soul would thither soar,
Oh let me from the creatures cease:
Dead to the world, but to Thy spirit known,
I live to Thee, O Prince of life, alone.

Break through my bonds whate'er it cost,
What is not Thine within me slay,
Give me the lot I covet most,
To rise as Thou hast risen today.
I nought can do, a slave to death I pine,
Work Thou in me, O Power and Life Divine!

Work Thou in me, and heavenward guide
My thoughts and wishes, that my heart
Waver no more nor turn aside,
But fix for ever where Thou art.
Thou art not far from us; who loves Thee well,
While yet on earth in heaven with Thee may dwell.

Monday in Easter Week

And they told what things were done in the way, and how he was known to them in breaking of bread. And as they thus spake, Jesus Himself stood in the midst of them, and saith unto them, Peace be unto you.
     From the Gospel. [Lk 24:35-36]
Schmolck. 1712.
trans. by Catherine Winkworth, 1855

Welcome Thou victor in the strife,
Now welcome from the cave!
Today we triumph in Thy life
Around Thine empty grave.

Our enemy is put to shame,
His short-lived triumph o'er;
Our God is with us, we exclaim,
We fear our foe no more.

The dwellings of the just resound
With songs of victory;
For in their midst, Lord, Thou art found,
And bringest peace with Thee.

O share with us the spoils, we pray,
Thou diedst to achieve;
We meet within Thy house today
Our portion to receive:

And let Thy conquering banner wave
O'er hearts Thou makest free,
And point the path that from the grave
Leads heavenward up to Thee.

We bury all our sin and crime
Deep in our Saviour's tomb,
And seek the treasure there, that time
Nor change can e'er consume.

We die with Thee; oh let us live
Henceforth to Thee aright;
The blessings Thou hast died to give,
Be daily in our sight.

Fearless we lay us in the tomb,
And sleep the night away,
If Thou art there to break the gloom,
And call us back to day.

Death hurts us not; his power is gone,
And pointless all his darts;
Now hath God's favour on us shone,
And joy fills all our hearts.

Tuesday in Easter Week
I know that my Redeemer liveth .. and though after my skin worms destroy this body, yet in my flesh shall I see God.
    Job 19:25,26

For this corruptible must put on incorruption, and this mortal must put on immortality.
    From the Lesson. [1 Cor. 15:53]
Louisa Henrietta, Electress of Brandenburgh. 1653.
trans. by Catherine Winkworth, 1855

Jesus my Redeemer lives,
Christ my trust is dead no more;
In the strength this knowledge gives
Shall not all my tears be o'er,
Though the night of Death be fraught
Still with many an anxious thought?

Jesus my Redeemer lives,
And His life I once shall see;
Bright the hope this promise gives,
Where He is I too shall be.
Shall I fear then? Can the Head
Rise and leave the members dead?

Close to Him my soul is bound
In the bonds of Hope enclasped;
Faith's strong hand this hold hath found,
And the Rock hath firmly grasped:
And no ban of death can part
From our Lord the trusting heart.

I shall see Him with these eyes,
Him whom I shall surely know;
Nort another shall I rise,
With His love this heart shall glow;
Only there shall disappear
Weakness in and round me here.

Ye who suffer, sigh, and moan,
Fresh and glorious there shall reign;
Earthly here the seed is sown,
Heavenly it shall rise again;
Natural here the death we die,
Spiritual our life on high.

Body, be thou of good cheer,
In thy Saviour's care rejoice,
Give not place to gloom and fear,
Dead, thou yet shalt know His voice,
When the final trump is heard,
And the deaf cold grave is stirred.

Laugh to scorn then death and hell,
Laugh to scorn the gloomy grave;
Caught into the air to dwell
With the Lord who comes to save,
We shall trample on our foes,
Mortal weakness, fear and woes.

Only see ye that your heart
Rise betimes from earthly lust;
Would ye there with Him have part,
Here obey your Lord and trust,
Fix your hearts beyond the skies,
Whither ye yourselves would rise.

First Sunday after Easter

God hath given to us eternal life, and this life is in His Son.
   From the Epistle. [1 Jn. 5:11]
After Novalis. about 1795.
trans. by Catherine Winkworth, 1855

What had I been if Thou wert not?
What were I now if Thou wert gone?
Ah, fear and anguish were my lot,
In this wide world I stood alone;
Whate'er I love were safe no more,
The future were a dark abyss;
To whom could I my sorrows pour,
If Thee my laden heart should miss?

Longing for love through lonely years,
The gloom of night came o'er my day;
I followed, yet with secret tears,
The world's wild joys, and owned her sway;
Till restless from her turmoil driven,
I turned within,--and grief was there:
Ah, had we not a Friend in heaven,
Who, who his lot on earth could bear!

But when Thou mak'st Thy presence felt,
And when the soul hath grasped Thee right,
How fast the dreary shadows melt
Beneath Thy warm and living light!
In Thee I find a nobler birth,
A glory o'er the world I see,
And paradise returns to earth,
And blooms again for us in Thee.

Thou strong and loving Son of Man,
Redeemer from the bonds of sin,
'Tis Thou the living spark dost fan
That sets my heart on fire within.
Thou openest heaven once more to men,
The soul's true home, Thy Kingdom, Lord,
And I can trust and hope again,
And feel myself akin to God.

Brethren, go forth beside all ways,
The wanderer greet with outstretched hand,
And call him back who darkly strays,

And bid him join our gladsome band.
That Heaven hath stooped to earth below,
Proclaim the glad news everywhere,
That all may learn our faith, and know
They too may find an entrance there.

Second Sunday after Easter

Jesus said, I am the Good Shepherd: the Good Shepherd giveth His life for His sheep.
    From the Gospel. [Jn. 10:11]
Angelus. 1657.
trans. by Catherine Winkworth, 1855

Loving Shepherd, kind and true,
Wilt Thou not in pity come
To Thy Lamb? As shepherds do,
Bear me in Thy bosom home;
Take me hence from earth's annoy
To Thy home of endless joy.

See how I have gone astray
In this earthly wilderness;
Come and take me soon away
To Thy flock who dwell in bliss,
And Thy glory, Lord, behold,
Safe within Thy heavenly fold.

For I fain would gaze on Thee,
With the lambs to whom 'tis given
That they feed, from danger free,
In the happy fields of heaven;
Praising Thee, all terrors o'er,
Never can they wander more.

Here I live in sore distress,
Fearing, watching, hour by hour;
For my foes around me press,
And I know their craft and power:
Lord, Thy lamb can never be
Safe one moment, but with Thee.

O Lord Jesus, let me not
'Mid the ravening wolves e'er fall,
Help me as a shepherd ought,
That I may escape them all:
Bear me homeward in Thy breast,
To Thy fold of endless rest.

Third Sunday After Easter

And ye now have sorrow; but I will see you again, and your heart shall rejoice, and your joy no man taketh from you.
　　　From the Gospel. [Jn. 16:22]
Paul Gerhardt. 1659.
trans. by Catherine Winkworth, 1855

Cometh sunshine after rain,
After mourning joy again,
After heavy bitter grief
Dawneth surely sweet relief!
And my soul, who from her height
Sank to realms of woe and night,
Wingeth now to heaven her flight.

He whom this world dares not face
Hath refreshed me with His grace,
And His mighty hand unbound
Chains of hell about me wound;
Quicker, stronger, leaps my blood,
Since His mercy, like a flood,
Poured o'er all my heart for good.

Bitter anguish have I borne,
Keen regret my heart hath torn,
Sorrow dimmed my weeping eyes,
Satan blinded me with lies;
Yet at last am I set free,
Help, protection, love to me
Once more true companions be.

None was ever left a prey,
None was ever turned away,
Who had given himself to God,
And on Him had cast his load.
Who in God his hope hath placed
Shall not life in pain outwaste,
Fullest joy he yet shall taste.

Though today may not fulfil
All thy hopes, have patience still,
For perchance tomorrow's sun
Sees thy happier days begun;
As God willeth march the hours,
Bringing joy at last in showers,

Catherine Winkworth

When whate'er we asked is ours.

Once a pain that would not cease
Gnawed my heart without release,
Sorrow bowed me 'neath her yoke,
Then in sadness oft I spoke:
Now no hope is left for me,
And no rest, until I be
Whelmed beneath Death's sunless sea.

But when I was worn with care,
Filled with dread well-nigh despair;
When with watching many a night,
On me fell pale sickness' blight;
When my courage failed me fast,
Camest Thou, my God, at last,
And my woes were quickly past.

Yea, Thou God didst make an end,
Thou such help and strength did send,
That I nevermore can praise
As I ought, Thy matchless grace;
When I shought with anxious fear,
And could see no refuge here,
Lo! I found Thy help was near.

Now as long as here I roam,
On this earth have house and home,
Shall this wondrous gleam from Thee
Shine through all my memory.
To my God I yet will cling.
All my life the praises sing
That from thankful hearts outspring.

Every sorrow, every smart,
That the Eternal Father's heart
Hath appointed me of yore,
Or hath yet for me in store,
As my life flows on I'll take
Calmly, gladly, for His sake,
No more faithless murmurs make.

I will meet distress and pain
I will greet e'en Death's dark reign,
I will lay me in the grave,
With a heart still glad and brave;
Whom the Strongest doth defend,
Whom the Highest counts His friend,
Cannot perish in the end.

Lyra Germanica: Hymns for the Sundays & Chief Festivals of The Christian Year - Book I & II
For I know that my Redeemer liveth, and that He shall stand at the latter day upon the earth: and though after my skin worms destroy this body, yet in my flesh shall I see God.
  Job 19:25,26

Fourth Sunday After Easter

It is expedient for you that I go away, for if I go not away, the Comforter will not come unto you.
       From the Gospel. [Jn. 16:7]
Translation of the 17th century after King Robert of France. About A.D. 1000.
trans. by Catherine Winkworth, 1855

Holy Ghost! my Comforter!
Now from highest heaven appear,
Shed Thy gracious radiance here.

Come to them who suffer dearth,
With Thy gifts of priceless worth,
Lighten all who dwell on earth!

Thou the heart's most precious guest,
Thou of comforters the best,
Give to us, the o'er-laden, rest.

Come, in Thee our toil is sweet,
Shelter from the noon-day heat,
From whom sorrow flieth fleet.

Blessed Sun of Grace! O'er all
Faithful hearts who on Thee call,
Let Thy joy and solace fall.

What without Thy aid is wrought,
Skilful deed or wisest thought,
God will count but vain and nought.

Cleanse us, Lord, from sinful stain,
O'er the parchèd heart oh rain,
Heal the wounded from its pain.

Bend the stubborn will to Thine,
Melt the cold with fire divine,
Erring hearts aright incline.

Grant us, Lord, who cry to Thee,
Steadfast in the faith to be,
Give Thy gifts of charity.

May we live in holiness,
And in death find happiness,
And abide with Thee in bliss!

Fifth Sunday after Easter

These things have I spoken unto you, that ye might have peace. In the world ye shall have tribulation; but be of good cheer, I have overcome the world.
    From the Gospel. [Jn. 16:33]
Läpwenstern. During the Thirty Years' War.
trans. by Catherine Winkworth, 1855

Christ Thou the champion of that war-worn host
Who bear Thy cross, haste, help, or we are lost;
The schemes of those who long our blood have sought
Bring Thou to nought.

Do Thou Thyself for us Thy children fight,
Withstand the devil, quell his rage and might,
Whate'er assails Thy members left below
Do Thou o'erthrow.

And give us peace; peace in the church and school,
Peace to the powers who o'er our country rule,
Peace to the conscience, peace within the heart,
Do Thou impart.

So shall Thy goodness here be still adored,
Thou guardian of Thy little flock, dear Lord,
And heaven and earth through all eternity
Shall worship Thee.

Ascension Day

This same Jesus which is taken up from you into heaven, shall so come, in like manner as ye have seen Him go into heaven.
     From the Epistle. [Acts 1:11]
Neumann. 1700.
trans. by Catherine Winkworth, 1855

Lord, on earth I dwell in pain;
Here in anguish I must lie;
Wherefore leav'st Thou me again,
Why ascendest Thou on high?
Take me, take me hence with Thee,
Or abide, Lord, still in me;
Let Thy love and gifts be left,
That I be not all bereft.

Leave Thy heart with me behind,
Take mine hence with Thee away;
Let my sighs an entrance find
To Thy heaven whene'er I pray.
When I cannot pray, oh plead
With Thy Father in my stead;
Seated now at God's right hand,
Help us here Thy faithful band.

Help me earthly toys to spurn,
Raise my thoughts from things below;
Mortal am I, yet I yearn
Heavenly like my Lord to grow,
That my time through faith may be
Ordered for eternity;
Till we meet, all perils o'er,
Whither Thou hast gone before.

In due season come again,
As was promised us of old;
Raise the members that have lain
Gnawed of death beneath the mould,
Judge the evil world that deems
Thy sure words but empty dreams;
Then for all our sorrows past,
Let us know Thy joy at last.

Sunday After Ascension Day

These all confessed that they were strangers and pilgrims on the earth. . . . For they desired a better country, that is, an heavenly; wherefore God is not ashamed to be called their God; for He hath prepared for them a city.
      Heb. 11:13,16
Schmolck. 1731.
trans. by Catherine Winkworth, 1855

Heavenward doth our journey tend,
We are strangers here on earth,
Through the wilderness we wend
Towards the Canaan of our birth.
Here we roam a pilgrim band,
Yonder is our native land.

Heavenward stretch, my soul, thy wings,
Heavenly nature canst thou claim,
There is nought of earthly things
Worthy to be all thine aim;
Every soul that God inspires
Back to Him, its Source, aspires.

Heavenward! doth His Spirit cry,
When I hear Him in His Word,
Showing thus the rest on high,
Where I shall be with my Lord:
When His Word fills all my thought,
Oft to heaven my soul is caught.

Heavenward ever would I haste,
When Thy table, Lord, is spread;
Heavenly strength on earth I taste,
Feeding on the Living Bread;
Such is e'en on earth our fare,
Who Thy marriage feast shall share.

Heavenward! Faith discerns the prize
That is waiting us afar,
And my heart would swiftly rise,
High o'er sun and moon and star,
To that Light behind the veil
Where all earthly splendours pale.

Heavenward Death shall lead at last,
To the home where I would be,
All my sorrows overpast,
I shall triumph there with Thee,
Jesus, who hast gone before,
That we too might Heavenward soar.

Heavenward! Heavenward! Only this
Is my watchword on the earth;
For the love of heavenly bliss
Counting all things little worth.
Heavenward all my being tends,
Till in Heaven my journey ends.

Whit Sunday

I will pray the Father, and He shall give you another Comforter, that He may abide with you for ever, even the Spirit of Truth.
     From the Gospel. [Jn. 14:16-17]
Schmolck. 1715.
trans. by Catherine Winkworth, 1855

Come, deck our feast today
With flowers and wreaths of May,
And bring an offering pure and sweet;
The Spirit of all grace
Makes earth His dwelling-place,
Prepare your hearts your Lord to meet;
Receive Him, and He shall outpour
Such light, all hearts with joy run o'er,
And sound of tears is heard no more.

Thou harbinger of peace,
Who makest sorrows cease,
Wisdom in word and deed is Thine;
Strong hand of God, Thy seal
The loved of Jesus feel;
Pure light, o'er all our pathway shine!
Give vigorous life and healthy powers,
O let Thy sevenfold gifts be ours,
Refresh us with Thy gracious showers!

O touch our tongues with flame,
When speaking Jesu's name!
And lead us up the heavenward road.
Give us the power to pray,
Teach us what words to say,
Whene'er we come before our God.
O Highest Good, our spirits cheer,
When raging foes are strong and near,
Give us brave hearts undimmed by fear.

O golden rain from heaven!
Thy precious dews be given
To bless the churches' barren field!
And let Thy waters flow,
Where'er the sowers sow,
The seed of truth, that it may yield
A hundred-fold its living fruit,
O'er all the land may take deep root,

And mighty branches heavenward shoot.

Thou fiery glow of Love!
Let us Thy ardours prove,
Consume our hearts with quenchless fire!
Come, O Thou trackless Wind!
Breathe gently o'er our mind!
Nor let the flesh to rule aspire;
Help us our free-born right to take,
The heavy yoke of sin to break,
And all her tempting paths forsake.

Be it Thine to stir our will;
Our good intents fulfil;
Be with us when we go and come;
Deep in our spirits dwell,
And make their inmost cell
Thy temple pure, Thy holy home!
Teach us to know our Lord, that we
May call His Father ours through Thee,
Thou Pledge of glories yet to be!

Oh make our crosses sweet,
And let Thy sunshine greet
Our longing eyes in clouded hours!
Wing Thou our upward flight
Toward yonder mountain bright,
Girded about with Zion's golden towers!
Forsake us not when our last foe
Puts forth his stength to lay us low,
Then joyful victory bestow!

Let us, while here we dwell,
This one thought ponder well,
That in God's likeness we are made.
As o'er a fruitful land
Rich harvests waving stand,
We, serving Him, bear fruits that never fade,
Till Thou in whom all comfort lies,
Lift us to fields above the skies,
And bid us bloom in Paradise!

Monday in Whitsun-Week
Would God that all the Lord's people were prophets, and that the Lord would put His Spirit upon them!
     From the Lesson. [Num. 11:29]
Paul Gerhardt. During the 30 Years' War.
trans. by Catherine Winkworth, 1855

Come to Thy temple here on earth,
Be Thou my spirit's guest,
Who givest us of mortal birth
A second birth more blest;
Spirit beloved, Thou mighty Lord,
Who with the Father and the Son
Reignest upon an equal throne,
Art equally adored!

Oh enter, let me feel and know
Thy mighty power within,
That can alone our help bestow,
And rescue us from sin.
Oh cleanse my soul and make it white,
That I with heart unstained and true,
May daily render service due,
And honour Thee aright.

I was a wild unfruitful vine
Which Thou shouldst prune and train;
Death pierced through all this life of min,
But Thou my foe hast slain.
Thy holy baptism is his grave,
He perishes beneath the flood
Of His most precious death and blood,
Who died our life to save.

Thou art the Spirit who dost teach
To pray aright, for all
Our prayers are heard if Thou beseech,
Thy songs have sweetest fall.
They soar on tireless wings to heaven,
They fail not from before God's throne,
Till all His goodness we have known
By whom all help is given.

Thou art the Spirit of all joy,
Sadness Thou lovest not;
Thy comfort beaming from on high,
Lights up the darkest lot.
Ah yes, how many a time of old
Thy voice hath rapt my soul away,
To yon bright halls of endless day,
And oped the gates of gold!

Thou art the Spirit of all love,
The Friend of all kindly life,
Thou wouldst not that our hearts should prove
The pangs of wrath and strife.
Thou hatest hatred's withering reign,
In souls that discord maketh dark
Dost Thou rekindle love's bright spark,
And make them one again.

On Thee is all this world upstaid,
And in Thy hands doth rest;
And Thou canst wayward hearts persuade
To turn as seems Thee best:
Oh therefore give Thy love and peace,
That they may join in strongest bands
Long parted foes, and through our lands
These sad divisions cease.

Thou art the true, the only Source
Whence concord comes to men;
Oh that Thy power might have free course
And bring us peace again!
Oh hear, and stem this mighty flood
That o'er us death and sorrow spreads;
Alas! each day afresh it sheds
Like water human blood.

And let our nation learn to know
What, and how deep, our sin;
Nay, let God's judgments come, if so
A fire be lit within
The hearts that loved themselves to please;
In bitter shame now let them burn,
And loving Thee, repentant spurn
Their selfish worldly ease.

Grace for the contrite heart abounds,
Joy to the sad is given;
To serve God's truth will heal our wounds,
And bring us help from heaven;
Lord, for Thine honour's sake, make known

Catherine Winkworth

Thy power, convert the wicked now,
And teach the hard to weep, for Thou
Canst soften steel and stone!

Arise and make an end of all
Our heartache, and our pain;
Thy wandering flock at last recall
And grant them joy again;
To peace and wealth the land restore,
Wasted with fire or plague or sword;
Come to Thy ruined churches, Lord,
And bid them bloom once more!

The rulers of our land defend,
Our sovereign's throne uphold;
That he and we may prosper, send
True wisdom to the old;
With piety the young men bless,
And through the nation shed abroad
True virtue and the fear of God,
A nation's happiness.

Fill every heart with holy zeal
To keep the faith unstained;
Let house and land Thy blessing feel,
Whence all true wealth is gained.
Him who resists Thy inward powers,
The Evil Spirit, make Thou flee;
Whate'er delights Thy heart, would he
Fain root from out of ours.

Give strong and cheerful hearts to stand
Undaunted in the wars
That Satan's fierce and mighty band
Is waging with Thy cause.
Help us to fight as warriors brave,
That we may conquer in the field,
And not one Christian man may yield
His soul to sin a slave.

Order according to Thy mind
Our life from day to day,
And when this life must be resigned,
And death has seized his prey,
When all our days have fleeted by,
Help us to die with fearless spirit,
And let us after death inherit
Eternal life on high.

Tuesday in Whitsun-Week
Hereby know ye the Spirit of God. Every spirit that confesseth that Jesus Christ is come in the flesh is of God.
    From the Lesson. [1 Jn. 4:2]
Luther. 1524.
trans. by Catherine Winkworth, 1855

Come, Holy Spirit, God and Lord,
Be all Thy graces now outpoured
On the believer's mind and soul,
And touch our hearts with living coal.
Thy Light this day shone forth so clear,
All tongues and nations gathered near,
To learn that faith, for which we bring
Glad praise to Thee, and loudly sing,
Hallelujah, Hallelujah!

Thou Strong Defence, Thou Holy Light,
Teach us to know our God aright,
And call Him Father from the heart:
The Word of life and truth impart,
That we may love not doctrines strange,
Nor e'er to other teachers range,
But Jesus for our Master own
And put our trust in Him alone.
Hallelujah, Hallelujah!

Thou Sacred Ardour, Comfort Sweet,
Help us to wait with ready feet
And willing heart at Thy command,
Nor trial fright us from Thy band.
Lord, make us ready with Thy powers,
Strengthen the flesh in weaker hours,
That as good warriors we may force
Through life and death to Thee our course.
Hallelujah, Hallelujah!

Trinity Sunday

And God said, Let us make man in our image.
　　From the Lesson. [Gen. 1:26]
Angelus. 1657.
trans. by Catherine Winkworth, 1855

Most High and Holy Trinity!
Who of Thy mercy mild
Hast formed me here in Time, to be
Thy image and Thy child:
Oh let me love Thee day and night
With all my soul, with all my might;
Oh come, Thyself my soul prepare,
And make Thy dwelling ever there!

Father! replenish with Thy grace
This longing heart of mine,
Make it Thy quiet dwelling-place,
Thy sacred inmost shrine!
Forgive that oft my spirit wears
Her time and strenght in trivial cares,
Enfold her in Thy changeless peace,
So she from all but Thee may cease!

Oh God the Son! Thy wisdom's light
On my dark reason pour;
Forgive that things of sense and sight
Were all her joy of yore;
Henceforth let every thought and deed
On Thee be fixed, from Thee proceed,
Draw me to Thee, for I would rise
Above these earthly vanities!

Oh Holy Ghost! Thou fire of love,
Enkindle with Thy flame my will;
Come with Thy strength, Lord, from above,
Help me Thy bidding to fulfil:
Forgive that I so oft have done
What I as sinful ought to shun;
Let me with pure and quenchless fire
Thy favour and Thyself desire!

Most High and Holy Trinity!
Draw me away far hence,
And fix upon eternity

All powers of soul and sense!
Make me at one within; at one
With Thee on earth; when life is done
Take me to dwell in light with Thee,
Most High and Holy Trinity!

Catherine Winkworth

First Sunday after Trinity
God is love . . . and herein is love, not that we loved God, but that He loved us.
    From the Epistle. [1 Jn. 4:10]
J. G. Hermann. 1747.
trans. by Catherine Winkworth, 1855

O wings of faith, ye thoughts, fly hence,
Roam o'er Eternity's vast field,
Surpass the bounds of time and sense,
And rise to Him, who hath revealed
That He is Love: there pause, and awestruck view
That ancient love with every morning new!

Ere earth's foundations yet were laid,
Or heaven's fair roof was spread abroad,
Ere man a living soul was made,
Love stirred within the heart of God;
Love filled the long futurity with good,
And grace to help at need beside her stood.

'Twas Love whose counsel gave to me
True life in Christ Thy only son,
Whom Thou hast made our Way to Thee,
From whom all grace flows ever down;
Whose sacrifice can make us pure and whole,
And bless and hallow all our inmost soul.

'Twas Love, that long ere time began,
That precious name of child bestowed;
That opened Heaven on earth to man,
And called us sinners sons of God;
Whose gracious promptings move the Father's hand,
That on the page of life our names may stand!

Ah happy hours, whene'er upsprings
My soul to yon Eternal Source,
Whence the glad river downward sings,
Watering with goodness all my course,
So that each passing day anew I prove
How tender and how true my Father's love!

For what am I? At His command
The million creatures of His power
Start to life on sea and land;
Oh why should God such blessings shower

On me, who am a leaf that fadeth fast,
A little shifting dust before the blast!

I am not worthy, Lord, that Thou
Shouldst such compassion on me show;
That He who made the world should bow
To cheer with love a wretch so low.
O Father, I would utterly resign
Myself to Thee; take me, and make me Thine.

When strength and heart grow faint and sad,
From battling long with heavy pain,
Thy smile shines forth to make me glad,
Thou crownest me with joy again;
Then I behold Thy Spirit's wondrous power,
Whose work is mightiest in our weakest hour.

Forth from Thy rich and bounteous store
Life's common blessings daily flow;
More than we dare to ask, far more
That we deserve, dost Thou bestow.
My heart dissolves in tears of thankfulness,
To see how true Thy care, how quick to bless.

Nor here alone: hope pierces far
Through all the shades of earth and time;
Faith mounts beyond the farthest star,
Yon shining heights she loves to climb,
And gazing on eternity behold
The promised land, our heritage of old.

Can I with loveless heart receive
Tokens of love that never cease?
Can I be thankless still, and grieve
Him who is all my joy and peace?
Ah Friend of Man, were I to turn from Thee,
Myself were sure my own worst enemy.

Could I but honour Thee aright,
Noble and sweet my song should be,
That earth and heaven should learn Thy might,
And what my God hath done for me.
There is no music sweet as is Thy name,
No joy so deep as pondering o'er Thy fame.

Catherine Winkworth

O heart redeemed! thou think'st it long
Till the appointed hour be come,
When thou shalt join the angels' song
To that Fair Love that brought thee home.
Have patience, heart; time hurries fast away,
Soon shalt thou reach the one Eternal Day.

Second Sunday after Trinity

And this is His commandment; That we should believe on the name of His Son Jesus Christ, and love one another, as He gave us commandment.
    From the Epistle. [1 Jn. 3:23]
After Zinzendorf. About 1731.
trans. by Catherine Winkworth, 1855

Heart and heart together bound,
Seek in God your true repose,
In your love the price be found
Of your Saviour's love and woes;
We the members, He the Head,
He the sun, we beams He showers,
Brethren by one Master led,
We are His, and he is ours.

Children of His realm draw near,
Make your covenant stronger still,
From your hearts allegiance swear
Unto Him who conquered ill.
If your bonds are yet too weak,
If but fragile yet they prove,
Help from His good Spirit seek
Who can steel the chains of love.

Only such love will suffice,
As the love that dwells in Him,
Love that from the cross ne'er flies,
Love that spares not life or limb;
'Twas for sinners He was slain,
'Twas for foes He shed His blood,
That His death for all might gain
Endless life--the Highest Good.

Thus, O truest Friend, unite
All Thy consecrated band,
That their hearts be set aright
To fulfil Thy last command.
Each must onward urge his friend,
Helping him in word and deed,
Love's blest pathway to ascend,
Following on where Thou dost lead.

Catherine Winkworth

Thou who dost command that all
Practise love who bear Thy name,
Wake the dead, new followers call,
Touch the slothful with Thy flame.
Let us live, O Lord, at one,
As Thou with the Father art,
That through all the world be none
Of Thy members left apart.

Then were given what Thou hast sought,
In the Son were all men freed,
And the world at last were taught
That Thy rule is blest indeed.
Father of all souls, we praise
Thee who shinest in the Son;
Lord, to Thee our hymns we raise,
Who hast all men to Thee drawn!

Third Sunday after Trinity

Cast all your care upon Him, for He careth for you.
    From the Epistle. [1 Pet. 5:7]
after A. H. Franke (1663-1727).
trans. by Catherine Winkworth, 1855

What within me and without,
Hourly on my spirit weighs,
Burdening heart and soul with doubt,
Darkening all my weary days:
In it I behold Thy will,
God, who givest rest and peace,
And my heart is calm and still,
Waiting till Thou send release.

God! Thou art my rock of strength,
And my home is in Thine arms,
Thou wilt send me help at length,
And I feel no wild alarms.
Sin nor Death can pierce the shield
Thy defence has o'er me thrown,
Up to Thee myself I yield,
And my sorrows are Thine own.

Thou my shelter from the blast,
Thou my strong defence art ever;
Though my sorrows thicken fast,
Yet I know Thou leav'st me never;
When my foe puts forth his might,
And would tread me in the dust,
To this rock I take my flight,
And I conquer him through trust.

When my trials tarry long,
Unto Thee I look and wait,
Knowing none, though keen and strong,
Can my faith in Thee abate.
And this faith I long have nurst,
Comes alone, O Lord, from Thee;
Thou my heart didst open first,
Thou didst set this hope in me.

Christians! cast on Him your load,
To your tower of refuge fly;
Know He is the Living God,

Catherine Winkworth

Ever to His creatures nigh.
Seek His ever-open door
In your hours of utmost need;
All your hearts before Him pour,
He will send you help with speed.

But hast thou some darling plan,
Cleaving to the things of earth?
Leanest thou for aid on man?
Thou wilt find him nothing worth.
Rather trust the One alone
Whose is endless power and love,
And the help He gives His own,
Thou in very deed shalt prove.

Yea, on Thee, my God, I rest,
Letting life float calmly on,
For I know the last is best,
When the crown of joy is won.
In Thy might all things I bear,
In Thy love find bitters sweet,
And with all my grief and care
Sit in patience at Thy feet.

O my soul, why art thou vexed?
Let things go as e'en they will;
Though to thee they seem perplexed,
Yet His order they fulfil.
Here He is thy strength and guard,
Power to harm thee here has none;
Yonder will He each reward
For the works he here has done.

Let Thy mercy's wings be spread
O'er me, keep me close to Thee,
In the peace Thy love doth shed,
Let me dwell eternally.
Be my All; in all I do
Let me only seek Thy will,
Where the heart to Thee is true,
All is peaceful, calm, and still.

Fourth Sunday after Trinity

I reckon that the sufferings of this present time are not worthy to be compared with the glory that shall be revealed in us.
     From the epistle. [Rom. 8:18]
Simon Dach. 1640.
trans. by Catherine Winkworth, 1855

Wouldst thou inherit life with Christ on high?
Then count the cost, and know
That here on earth below
Thou needs must suffer with thy Lord and die.
We reach that gain to which all else is loss,
But through the cross.

Oh think what sorrows Christ himself has known!
The scorn, and anguish sore,
The bitter death He bore,
Ere He ascended to His heavenly throne;
And deemest thou, thou canst with right complain,
Whate'er thy pain?

Not e'en the sharpest sorrows we can feel,
Nor keenest pangs, we dare
With that great bliss compare
When God His glory shall in us reveal,
That shall endure when our brief woes are o'er
For evermore!

Fifth Sunday after Trinity

And who is he that will harm you, if ye be followers of that which is good? But and if ye suffer for righteousness' sake, happy are ye; and be not afraid of their terror, neither be troubled; but sanctify the Lord God in your hearts.
    From the Epistle. [1 Pet. 3:13-14]
Paul Gerhardt. 1650.
trans. by Catherine Winkworth, 1855

If God be on my side,
Then let who will oppose,
For oft ere now to Him I cried,
And he hath quelled my foes.
If Jesus be my Friend,
If God doth love me well,
What matters all my foes intend,
Though strong they be and fell?

Here I can firmly rest,
I dare to boast of this,
That God the Highest and the Best,
My Friend and Father is.
From dangerous snares He saves,
Where'er He bids me go
He checks the storms and calms the waves,
That nought can work me woe.

I rest upon the ground
Of Jesus and His blood,
For 'tis through Him that I have found
The True Eternal Good.
Nought have I of mine own,
Nought in the life I lead,
What Christ hath given me, that alone
Is worth all love indeed.

His Spirit in me dwells,
O'er all my mind He reigns,
All care and sadness He dispels,
And soothes away all pains.
He prospers day by day
His work within my heart,
Till I have strength and faith to say,
Thou God my Father art!

When weakness on me lies,
And tempts me to despair,
He speaketh words and utters sighs
Of more than mortal prayer;
But what no tongue can tell,
Thou God canst hear and see,
Who readest in the heart full well
If aught there pleaseth Thee.

He whispers in my breast
Sweet words of holy cheer,
How he who seeks in God his rest
Shall ever find Him near;
How God hath built above
A city fair and new,
Where eye and heart shall see and prove
What faith has counted true.

There is prepared on high
My heritage, my lot;
Though here on earth I sink and die,
My heaven shall fail me not.
Though here my days are dark,
And oft my tears must rain,
Whene'er my Saviour's Light I mark,
Lo, all is bright again.

Who joins him to that Lord
Whom Satan flies and hates,
Shall find himself despised, abhorred,
For him the burden waits
Of mockery and shame,
Heaped on his guiltless head;
And crosses, trials, cruel blame,
Shall be his daily bread.

I knew it long ere now,
Yet am I not afraid;
The God to whom I pledged my vow,
Will surely send His aid.
At cost of all I have,
At cost of life and limb,
I cling to God who yet shall save,
I will not turn from Him.

The world may fail and flee,
Thou standest fast for ever,
Nor fire, nor sword, nor plague, from Thee
My trusting soul shall sever.
No hunger, and no thirst,

Catherine Winkworth

No poverty or pain,
Let mighty princes do their worst,
Shall fright me back again.

No joys that angels know,
No throne or wide-spread fame,
No love or loss, no fear or woe,
No grief of heart or shame--
Man cannot aught conceive
Of pleasure or of harm
That e'er could tempt my soul to leave
Her refuge in Thine arm.

My heart for gladness springs,
It cannot more be sad,
For very joy it laughs and sings,
Sees nought but sunshine glad.
The sun that glads mine eyes
Is Christ the Lord I love,
I sing for joy of that which lies
Stored up for us above.

Sixth Sunday after Trinity

Know ye not, that so many of us as were baptized into Christ, were baptized into His death?

From the Epistle. [Rom. 6:3]
Anon.
trans. by Catherine Winkworth, 1855

Well for him who all things losing,
E'en himself doth count as nought,
Still the one thing needful choosing
That with all true bliss is fraught!

Well for him who nothing knoweth
But his God, whose boundless love
Makes the heart wherein it gloweth,
Calm and pure as saints above!

Well for him who all forsaking
Walketh not in shadows vain,
But the path of peace is taking
Through this vale of tears and pain!

Oh that we our hearts might sever
From earth's tempting vanities,
Fixing them on Him for ever
In whom all our fulness lies!

Oh that we might Him discover
Whom with longing love we've sought,
Joining us to Him for ever,
For without Him all is nought!

Oh that ne'er our eyes might wander
From our God, so might we cease
Ever o'er our sins to ponder,
And our conscience be at peace!

Thou abyss of love and goodness,
Draw us by Thy cross to Thee,
That our senses, soul, and spirit
Ever one with Christ may be!

Seventh Sunday after Trinity

O Lord, how manifold are Thy works; in wisdom hast Thou made them all; the earth is full of Thy riches.
     Psalm 104:24
Paul Gerhardt. 1659.
trans. by Catherine Winkworth, 1855

Go forth, my heart, and seek delight
In all the gifts of God's great might,
These pleasant summer hours:
Look how the plains for thee and me
Have decked themselves most fair to see,
All bright and sweet with flowers.

The trees stand thick and dark with leaves,
And earth o'er all here dust now weaves
A robe of living green;
Nor silks of Solomon compare
With glories that the tulips wear,
Or lilies' spotless sheen.

The lark soars singing into space,
The dove forsakes her hiding-place,
And coos the woods among;
The richly-gifted nightingale,
Pours forth her voice o'er hill and dale,
And floods the fields with song.

Here with her brood the hen doth walk,
There builds and guards his nest the stork,
The fleet-winged swallows pass;
The swift stag leaves his rocky home,
And down the light deer bounding come
To taste the long rich grass.

The brooks rush gurgling through the sand,
And from the trees on either hand,
Cool shadows o'er them fall;
The meadows at their side are glad
With herds; and hark! the shepherd lad
Sends forth his mirthful call.

And humming, hovering to and fro,
The never-wearied swarms no go
To seek their honey'd food;

And through the vine's yet feeble shoots
Stream daily upwards from her roots
New strength and juices good.

The corn springs up, a wealth untold,
A sight to gladden young and old,
Who now their voices lift
To Him who gives such plenteous store,
And makes the cup of life run o'er
With many a noble gift.

Thy mighty working, mighty God,
Wakes all my powers; I look abroad
And can no longer rest:
I too must sing when all things sing,
And from my heart the praises ring
The Highest loveth best.

I think, Art Thou so good to us,
And scatterest joy and beauty thus
O'er this poor earth of ours;
What nobler glories shall be given
Hereafter in Thy shining heaven,
Set round with golden towers!

What thrilling joy when on our sight
Christ's garden beams in cloudless light,
Where all the air is sweet,
Still laden with the unwearied hymn
From all the thousand seraphim
Who God's high praise repeat!

Oh were I there! Oh that I now,
Dear God, before Thy throne could bow,
And bear my heavenly palm!
Then like the angels would I raise
My voice, and sing Thy endless praise
In many a sweet-toned psalm.

Nor can I now, O God, forbear,
Though still this mortal yoke I wear,
To utter oft Thy name;
But still my heart is bent to speak
Thy praises; still, though poor and weak,
Would I Thy love proclaim.

But help me; let Thy heavenly showers
Revive and bless my fainting powers,
And let me thrive and grow
Beneath the summer of Thy grace,

Catherine Winkworth

And fruits of faith bud forth apace
While yet I dwell below.

And set me, Lord, in Paradise
When I have bloomed beneath these skies
Till my last leaf is flown;
Thus let me serve Thee here in time,
And after, in that happier clime,
And Thee, my God, alone!

Eighth Sunday after Trinity

Brethren, we are debtors, not to the flesh, to live after the flesh. For if ye live after the flesh, ye shall die; but if ye through the Spirit do mortify the deeds of the body, ye shall live.
    From the Epistle. [Rom. 8:12-13]
Gerhard Tersteegen. 1731.
trans. by Catherine Winkworth, 1855

O God, O Spirit, Light of all that live,
Who dost on us that sit in darkness shine,
Our darkness ever with Thy Light dost strive,
In vain Thou lur'st us with Thy beams divine;
Yet none, O Spirit, from Thine eye can hide,
Gladly [will] I Thy searching glance abide.

Search all my hidden parts, whate'er impure
Thy Light discovers there, do Thou destroy;
The bitterst pain I willingly endure,
Such pain is followed by eternal joy;
Thou'lt cleanse me from my stains of darkest hue,
And in Christ's image form my soul anew.

I cannot stay the venomed power of sin,
'Tis Thy anointing only can avail;
Oh make my spirit new and right within,
Without Thee all my utmost efforts fail.
Life to my cold dead soul I cannot give,
Be Thou my life, so only shall I live.

O Breath from out the Eternal Silence, blow
All softly o'er my spirit's barren ground,
The precious fulness of my God bestow,
That where erst sin and shame alone were found,
Faith, love, and holy reverence may upspring,
In spirit and in truth to worship God our King.

Oh let my thoughts, my actions and my will
Obedient solely to Thy impulse move,
My heart and senses keep Thou blameless still,
Fixed and absorbed in God's unuttered love.
Thy praying, teaching, striving, in my heart,
Let me not quench, nor make Thee to depart.

Catherine Winkworth

O Fount, O Spirit, who dost take and show
Things of the Son to us, who crystal clear
From God's throne and the Lamb's doth ceaseless flow
Into the quiet hearts that seek Thee here,
I open wide my mouth, and thirsting sink
Beside Thy stream, its living waves to drink.

I give myself to Thee, to Thee alone,
From all else sundered, Thou art ever near,
The creature and myself I all disown,
Trusting with inmost faith that God is here!
O God, O Spirit, Light of Life, we see
None ever wait in vain, who wait for Thee.

Ninth Sunday after Trinity

How long halt ye between two opinions? If the Lord be God, follow Him; but if Baal, then follow him.
     From the Lesson. [1 Kings 18:21]
Lehr. 1733.
trans. by Catherine Winkworth, 1855

Why halt thus, O deluded heart,
Why waver longer in thy choice?
Is it so hard to choose the part
Offered by Heaven's entreating voice?
Oh look with clearer eyes again,
Nor strive to enter in, in vain.
Press on!

Remember, 'tis not Caesar's throne,
Nor earthly honour, wealth or might
Whereby God's favour shall be show
To him who conquers in the fight;
Himself and an eternity
Of bliss and rest he offers thee.
Press on!

God crowneth no divided heart;
To Him oh hallow all thy life!
Who loveth Jesus but in part,
he works himself much pain and strife,
And gains what he deserveth well,
Here conflict, and hereafter hell.
Press on!

Who wrestling long, with many a cry
Can bid farewell at last to all,
Yet ever loves the Lord most High,
Loves Him alone whate'er befall,
Is counted worthy of the crown,
And on a kingly throne set down.
Press on!

Then break the rotten bonds away
That hinder you your race to run,
That make you linger oft and stay;
Oh be your course afresh begun!
Let no false rest your soul deceive,
Up! 'tis a Heaven ye must receive!

Catherine Winkworth

Press on!

Omnipotence is on your side,
And Wisdom watches o'er your heads,
And God Himself will be your guide
So ye but follow where He leads;
How many guided by His hand,
Have reached ere now their father-land!
Press on!

Nor let the body dull the soul,
Its weakness, fears, and sloth despise;
Man toils and roams from pole to pole
To gain some earthly fleeting prize,
The Highest Good he little cares
To win, or striving soon despairs.
Press on!

Oh help each other, hasten on,
Behold the goal is nigh at hand;
The battle-field shall soon be won,
Your King shall soon before you stand!
To calmest rest He leads you now,
And sets His crown upon your brow.
Press on!

Tenth Sunday after Trinity
As the hart panteth after the water brooks, even so panteth my soul after Thee, O God.
     Psalm 47:1
Anton Ulrich, Duke of Brunswick. 1667.
trans. by Catherine Winkworth, 1855

O God, I long Thy Light to see,
My God, I hourly think on Thee;
Oh draw me up, nor hide Thy face,
But help me from Thy holy place.

As toward her sun the sunflower turns,
Towards Thee, my Sun my spirit yearns;
Oh would that free from sin I might
Thus follow evermore Thy Light!

But sin hath so within me wrought,
Such deadly sickness on me brought,
My languid soul sits drooping here
And cannot reach the heavenly sphere.

Ah how shall I my freedom win?
How break this heavy yoke of sin?
My fainting spirit thirsts for Thee,
Come, Lord, to help and set me free.

My heart is set to do Thy will,
But all my deeds are faulty still;
My best attempts are nothing worth,
But soiled with cleaving taint of earth.

Remember that I am Thy child,
Forgive whate'er my soul defiled,
Blot out my sins, that I may rise
Freely to Thee beyond the skies.

Help me to love the world no more,
Be Master of my house and store,
The shield of faith around me throw,
And break the arrows of my foe.

Fain would my heart henceforward be
Fixed, O my God, alone on Thee,
That heart and soul by Thee possest,

Catherine Winkworth

May find in Thee their perfect rest.

Begone, ye pleasures false and vain,
Untasted, undesired remain!
In heaven alone those joys abound,
Where all my true delight is found.

Oh take away whate'er has stood
Between me and the Highest Good;
I ask no better boon than this,
To find in God my only bliss.

Eleventh Sunday after Trinity
In Thy presence is fulness of joy; at Thy right hand there are pleasures for evermore.
    Psalm 16:12
Wolfgang C. Deszler. 1692.
trans. by Catherine Winkworth, 1855

O Friend of Souls, how well is me,
Whene'er Thy love my spirit calms!
From sorrow's dungeon forth I flee,
And hide me in Thy shelt'ring arms.
The night of weeping flies away
Before the heart-reviving ray
Of love, that beams from out Thy breast;
Here is my heaven on earth begun;
Who were not joyful had he won
In Thee, O God, his joy and rest!

The world may call herself my foe,
So be it; for I trust her not,
E'en though a friendly face she show,
And with her bounties heap my lot.
In Thee alone will I rejoice,
Thou art the Friend, Lord, of my choice,
For Thou art true when friendships fail;
'Mid storms of woe Thy truth is still
My anchor; hate me as it will,
The world shall o'er me ne'er prevail.

Through deserts of the cross Thou leadest,
I follow leaning on Thy hand;
From out the clouds Thy child Thou feedest,
And giv'st him water from the sand.
I know Thy wondrous ways will end
In love and blessing, Thou true Friend,
Enough if Thou art ever near!
I know, whom Thou wilt glorify,
And raise o'er sun and stars on high,
Thou lead'st through depths and darkness here.

To others Death seems dark and grim,
But not, Thou Life of life, to me;
I know Thou ne'er forsakest him
Whose heart and spirit rest in Thee.
Oh who would fear his journey's close,

Catherine Winkworth

If from dark woods and lurking foes,
He then found safety and release?
Nay, rather with a joyful heart
From this dark region I depart
To Thy eternal light and peace.

O Friend of souls, then well indeed
Is me, when on Thy love I lean!
The world, nor pain, nor death I heed,
Since Thou, my God, my joy hast been.
Oh let this peace that Thou hast given
Be but a foretaste of Thy heaven,
For goodness infinite is Thine.
Hence, world, with all thy flattering toys!
In God alone be all my joys;
Oh rich delight, my Friend is mine!

Twelfth Sunday after Trinity

Not that we are sufficient of ourselves to think anything as if of ourselves, but our sufficiency is of God.
     From the Epistle. [2 Cor. 3:5]
Marperger. 1713.
trans. by Catherine Winkworth, 1855

Who seeks in weakness an excuse,
His sins will vanquish never;
Unless he heart and mind renews,
He is deceived for ever.
The strait and narrow way,
That shines to perfect day,
He hath not found, hath never trod;
Little he knows, I ween,
What prayer and conflict mean
To one who hath the light of God.

In what the world calls weakness lurks
The very strength of evil,
Full mightily it helps the works
Of our great foe the devil.
Awake, my soul, awake,
Thy refuge quickly take
With Him, the Almighty, who can save;
One look from Christ thy Lord
Can sever every cord
That binds thee now, a wretched slave.

Know, the first step in Christian lore
Is to depart from sin;
True faith will leave the world no more
A place thy heart within.
Thy Saviour's Spirit first
The heavy bonds must burst,
Wherein Death bound thee in thy need;
Then the freed spirit know
What strength He gives to those
Who with their Lord are risen indeed.

And why Thy Spirit, Lord, began
Help Thou with inner might!
Earth has no better gift for man
Than strength and love of right.
Oh make Thy followers just

Catherine Winkworth

Who look to Thee in trust,
Thy strength and justice let us know;
Our souls through Thee would wear
The power of grace, most fair
Of all the jewels faith can show.

Strong Son of God, break down Thy foes,
So shall we conquer ours;
Strong in the might from Thee that flows,
We mourn not lack of powers,
E'er since that from above,
The witness of Thy love
Thy Spirit cam, and doth abide
With us, dispelling fear
And falsehood, that we here
May fight and conquer on Thy side.

Give strength, whene'er our strength must fail;
Give strength the flesh to curb;
Give strength when craft and sin prevail
To weaken and disturb.
The world doth lay her snares
To catch us unawares,
Give strength to sweep them all away;
So in our utmost need,
And when death comes indeed,
Thy strength shall be our perfect stay.

Thirteenth Sunday after Trinity
Then Hezekiah received the letter of the hands of the messengers, and read it, and Hezekiah went up into the house of the Lord, and spread it before the Lord.
    From the Lesson. [Is. 37:14]
Neumarck. 1653.
trans. by Catherine Winkworth, 1855

Leave God to order all thy ways,
And hope in Him whate'er betide,
Thou'lt find Him in the evil days
Thy all-sufficient strength and guide;
Who trusts in God's unchanging love,
Builds on the rock that nought can move.

What can these anxious cares avail,
These never-ceasing moans and sighs?
What can it help us to bewail
Each painful moment as it flies?
Our cross and trials do but press
The heavier for our bitterness.

Only thy restless heart keep still,
And wait in cheerful hope; content
To take whate'er His gracious will,
His all-discerning love hath sent;
Nor doubt our inmost wants are known
To Him who chose us for His own.

He knows when joyful hours are best,
He sends them as He sees it meet;
When thou hast borne the fiery test,
And now art freed from all deceit,
He comes to thee all unaware,
And makes thee own His loving care.

Nor in the heat of pain and strife,
Think God hath cast thee off unheard,
And that the man, whose prosperous life
Thou enviest, is of Him preferred;
Time passes and much change doth bring,
And sets a bound to everything.

All are alike before His face;
'Tis easy to our God most High
To make the rich man poor and base,

Catherine Winkworth

To give the poor man wealth and joy.
True wonders still by Him are wrought,
Who setteth up, and brings to nought.

Sing, pray, and swerve not from His ways,
But do thine own part faithfully,
Trust His rich promises of grace,
So shall they be fulfilled in thee;
God never yet forsook in need
The soul that trusted Him indeed.

Fourteenth Sunday after Trinity
And they that are Christ's have crucified the flesh with the affections and lusts.
    From the Epistle. [Gal. 5:24]
Gotter. 1697.
trans. by Catherine Winkworth, 1855

O Cross, we hail thy bitter reign,
O come, thou well-beloved guest!
Whose sorest sufferings work not pain,
Whose heaviest burden is but rest.

For is not our Redeemer bound
In closest ties of love to those
Who faithful to the cross are found,
Through ceaseless tears, through saddest woes?

Hark, the confessors of the faith
Yet of their cross and fetters boast;
All saints have borne it to the death,
With all the martyrs' radiant host.

Pledge of our glorious home afar!
Thee, Holy Sign, with joy we take,
Sign of a peace life could not mar,
Of just content death could not shake:

The Sign how Truth, once crucified,
Now throned in majesty doth reign,
How Love is bless'd and glorified,
That here on earth was mocked and slain.

Their names are writ in words of light
Who here on earth their Lord confest;
They hear the bridegroom's cry at night,
Come to my marriage feast, ye blest!

Who then would faint, nor join to share
In Christ's reproach, in want or pain?
The bitterest death who would not dare?
Who fears a martyr's crown to gain?

Up, Brethren of the Cross! and haste
Where Christ our Head hath gone before!
We hymn His praise the while we taste
The shame and death He sometime bore.

Catherine Winkworth

In bonds and stripes, in falsest blame,
Our crown, our dearest wealth we see,
A dungeon were a throne, and shame
Our chiefest glory, borne for Thee.

What though the world on us may fling
Its scorn, and oft we strive with death,
The holy angels speed to bring
Our help and strength, our victor's wreath.

Up, quit the gates where sin abides,
From earth's doomed cities quickly come,
Yon eastern Star full surely guides
All pilgrims to their Father's home.

Fifteenth Sunday after Trinity

Therefore take no thought, saying, What shall we eat, or what shall we drink..
for your Heavenly Father knoweth that ye have need of all these things.
     From the Gospel. [Matt. 6:31-32]
Paul Gerhardt. 1657.
trans. by Catherine Winkworth, 1855

Be thou content; be still before
His face, at whose right hand doth reign
Fulness of joy for evermore,
Without whom all thy toil is vain.
He is thy living spring, thy sun, whose rays
Make glad with life and light thy dreary days.
Be thou content.

In Him is comfort, light and grace,
And changeless love beyond our thought;
The sorest pang, the worst disgrace,
If He is there, shall harm thee not.
He can lift off thy cross, and loose thy bands,
And calm thy fears, nay, death is in His hands.
Be thou content.

Or art thou friendless and alone,
Hast none in whom thou canst confide?
God careth for thee, lonely one,
Comfort and help will He provide.
He sees thy sorrows and thy hidden grief,
He knoweth when to send thee quick relief;
Be thou content.

Thy heart's unspoken pain He knows,
Thy secret signs He hears full well,
What to none else thou dar'st disclose,
To Him thou mayst with boldness tell;
He is not far away, but ever nigh,
And answereth willingly the poor man's cry.
Be thou content.

Be not o'er-mastered by thy pain,
But cling to God, thou shalt not fall;
The floods sweep over thee in vain,
Thou yet shalt rise above them all;
For when thy trial seems to hard to bear,
Lo! God, thy King, hath granted all thy prayer:

Catherine Winkworth

Be thou content.

Why art thou full of anxious fear
How thou shalt be sustained and fed?
He who hath made and placed thee here,
Will give the needful daily bread;
Canst thou not trust His rich and bounteous hand,
Who feeds all living things on sea and land?
Be thou content.

He who doth teach the little birds
To find their meat in field and wood,
Who gives the countless flocks and herds
Each day their needful drink and food,
Thy hunger too will surely satisfy,
And all thy wants in His good time supply.
Be thou content.

Sayst thou, I know not how or where,
No help I see where'er I turn;
When of all else we most despair,
The riches of God's love we learn;
When thou and I His hand no longer trace,
He leads us forth into a pleasant place.
Be thou content.

Though long His promised aid delay,
At last it will be surely sent:
Though thy heart sink in sore dismay,
The trial for thy good is meant.
What we have won with pains we hold more fast,
What tarrieth long is sweeter at the last.
Be thou content.

Lay not to heart whate'er of ill
Thy foes may falsely speak of thee,
Let man defame thee as he will,
God hears, and judges righteously.
Why shouldst thou fear, if God be on thy side,
Man's cruel anger, or malicious pride?
Be thou content.

We know for us a rest remains,
When God will give us sweet release
From earth and all our mortal chains,
And turn our sufferings into peace.
Sooner or later death will surely come
To end our sorrows, and to take us home:
Be thou content.

Home to the chosen ones, who here
Served their Lord faithfully and well,
Who died in peace, without a fear,
And there in peace for ever dwell;
The Everlasting is their joy and stay,
The Eternal Word Himself to them doth say,
Be thou content!

Sixteenth Sunday after Trinity
And when the Lord saw her, He had compassion on her, and said unto her, Weep not!
     From the Gospel. [Lk. 7:13]
Anton Ulrich, Duke of Brunswick. 1667.
trans. by Catherine Winkworth, 1855

Leave all to God,
Forsaken one, and stay thy tears;
For the Highest knows thy pain,
Sees thy sufferings and thy fears
Thou shalt not wait His help in vain,
Leave all to God.

Be still and trust!
For His strokes are strokes of love,
Thou must for thy profit bear;
He thy filial fear would move,
Trust thy Father's loving care,
Be still and trust!

Know, God is near!
Though thou think Him far away,
Though His mercy long have slept,
He will come and not delay,
When His child enough hath wept,
For God is near!

O teach Him not
When and how to hear thy prayers;
Never doth our God forget,
He the cross who longest bears
Finds his sorrows' bounds are set,
Then teach Him not.

If thou love Him,
Walking truly in His ways,
Then no trouble, cross or death,
E'er shall silence faith and praise;
All things serve thee here beneath,
If thou love God!

Seventeenth Sunday after Trinity

I beseech you that ye walk worthy of the vocation wherewith ye are called, with all lowliness and meekness, with long suffering, forbearing one another in love; endeavouring to keep the unity of the spirit in the bond of peace.
        From the Epistle. [Eph. 4:1-3]
Gerhard Tersteegen. 1731.
trans. by Catherine Winkworth, 1855

Come, brethren, let us go!
The evening closeth round,
'Tis perilous to linger here
On this wild desert ground.
Come, towards eternity
Press on from strength to strength,
Nor dread your journey's toils nor length,
For good its end shall be.

We shall not rue our choice,
Though straight our path and steep,
We know that He who called us here
His word shall ever keep.
Then follow, trusting; come,
And let each set his face
Toward yonder fair and blessed place,
Intent to reach our home.

The body and the house
Deck not, but deck the heart
With all your powers; we are but guests,
Ere long we must depart.
Ease brings disease; content
Howe'er his lot may fall,
A pilgrim bears and bows to all,
For soon the time is spent.

Come, children, let us go!
Our Father is our guide;
And when the way grows steep and dark,
He journeys at our side.
Our spirits He would cheer,
The sunshine of His love
Revives and helps us as we rove,
Ah, blest our lot e'en here!

Catherine Winkworth

Each hasten bravely on,
Not yet our goal is near;
Look to the fiery pillar oft,
That tells the Lord is here.
Your glances onward send,
Love beckons us, nor think
That they who following chance to sink
Shall miss their journey's end.

Come, children, let us go!
We travel hand in hand;
Each in his brother finds his joy
In this wild stranger land.
As children let us be,
Nor by the way fall out,
The angels guard us round about,
And help us brotherly.

The strong be quick to raise
The weaker when they fall;
Let love and peace and patience bloom
In ready help for all.
In love yet closer bound,
Each would be least, yet still
On love's fair path most pure from ill,
Most loving, would be found.

Come, wander on with joy,
For shorter grows the way,
The hour that frees us from the flesh
Draws nearer day by day.
A little truth and love,
A little courage yet,
More free from earth, more apt to set
Your hopes on things above.

It will not last for long,
A little farther roam;
It will not last much longer now
Ere we shall reach our home;
There shall we ever rest,
There with our Father dwell,
With all the saints who served Him well,
There truly, deeply blest.

For this all things we dare,--
'Tis worth the risk I trow,--
Renouncing all that clogs our course,
Or weighs us down below.
O world, thou art too small,

We seek another higher,
Whither Christ guides us ever nigher,
Where God is all in all.

Friend of our perfect choice,
Thou joy of all that live,
Being that know'st not chance or change,
What courage dost Thou give!
All beauty, Lord, we see,
All bliss and life and love,
In Him in whom we love and move,
And we are glad in Thee!

Eighteenth Sunday after Trinity
Waiting for the coming of our Lord Jesus Christ, who shall also confirm you unto the end.
    From the Epistle. [1 Cor. 1:7-8]

Now faith is the substance of things hoped for, the evidence of things not seen.
    Heb. 11:1
After Novalis. about 1795.
trans. by Catherine Winkworth, 1855

Though all to Thee were faithless,
I yet were true, my Head,
To show that love is deathless,
From earth not wholly fled.
Here didst Thou live in sadness,
And die in pain for me,
For this I give with gladness
My heart and soul to Thee.

I could weep night and morning
That Thou hast died, and yet
So few will heed Thy warning,
So many Thee forget.
O loving and true-hearted,
How much for us didst Thou!
Yet is Thy fame departed,
And none regards it now.

But still Thy love befriends us,
Of every heart the guide;
Unfailing help it lends us,
Thou all had turned aside.
Oh! such love soon or later
Must conquer, must be felt,
Then at Thy feet the traitor
In bitter tears shall melt.

Lord, I have inly found Thee,
Depart Thou not from me,
But wrap Thy love around me,
And keep me close to Thee.
Once too my brethren, yonder
Upgazing where Thou art,
Shall learn Thy love with wonder,
And sink upon Thy heart.

Nineteenth Sunday after Trinity

But ye have not so learned Christ, if so be that ye have heard Him, and have been taught by Him, as the truth is in Jesus: that ye put off, concerning the former conversation, the old man, which is corrupt according to the deceitful lusts; and be renewed in the spirit of your mind; and that ye put on the new man, which after God is created in righteousness and true holiness.

From the Epistle. [Eph. 4:20-24]
Anon.
trans. by Catherine Winkworth, 1855

Oh well for him who all things braves,
A soldier of the Lord to be,
Whom vice counts not among her slaves,
From envy, pride, and passion free;
Who wars against the world of sin
Without him, and self-will within.

Who follows Christ whate'er betide,
Is worthy of a soldier's name;
Is He thy Way, thy Light, thy Guide,
'Tis meet thou also bear His shame;
Who shrinks from dark Gethsemane,
Shall Tabor's glories never see.

What profits it that Christ hath deigned
To wear our mortal nature thus,
If we ourselves have ne'er attained
That God reveal Himself in us?
The pure and virgin soul alone
He chooseth for His earthly throne.

What profits it that Christ is born,
And bringeth childhood back to men,
Unless our long-lost right we mourn,
And win through penitence again,
And lead a God-like life on earth,
As children of the second birth?

What profits all that Christ hath taught,
If man is slave to reason still,
And worldly wisdom, honour, thought,
Rule all his acts, and move his will?
He follows what his Lord doth teach
Who true denial of self would reach.

Catherine Winkworth

What profit us His deeds and life,
His meekness, love so quick to bless,
If we give place to pride and strife,
Dishonouring thus His holiness?
What profits it, if for reward,
And not in faith, we call Him Lord?

What profits us His agony,
If we endure not pain and scorn?
'Tis combat brings forth victory,
Of sorrow sweetest joys are born;
And ne'er to him Christ's crown is given,
Who hath not here with Adam striven.

What profit ye His death and cross,
Unless to self ye also die?
Ye love your life to find it loss,
Afraid the flesh to crucify.
Wouldst live to this world still? Then know,
His death to thee is barren show.

What profit that He loosed and broke
All bonds, if ye in league remain
With earth? Who weareth Satan's yoke
Shall call Him Master but in vain.
Count ye the soul for reconciled,
Yet slave to earth, by sin defiled?

What profits it that He is risen,
If dead in sins thou yet dost lie?
If yet thou cleavest to thy prison,
What profit that He dwells on high?
His triumph will avail thee nought
If thou hast ne'er the battle fought.

Then live and suffer, do and bear,
As Christ thy pattern here hath done,
And seek His innocence to wear,
That he may count thee of His own.
Who loveth Christ cares but to win
New triumphs o'er the world of sin.

Twentieth Sunday after Trinity
Singing and making melody in your heart unto the Lord; giving thanks always for all things unto God and the Father, in the name our Lord Jesus Christ.
    From the Epistle. [Eph. 5:19-20]
Mentzer, 1704.
trans. by Catherine Winkworth, 1855

Oh would I had a thousand tongues,
To sound Thy praise o'er land and sea!
Oh! rich and sweet should be my songs,
Of all my God has done for me!
With thankfulness my heart must often swell,
But mortal lips Thy praises faintly tell.

Oh that my voice could far resound
Up to yon stars that o'er me shine!
Would that my blood for joy might bound
Through every vein while life is mine!
Would that each pulse were gratitude, each breath
A song to Him who keeps me safe from death!

O all ye powers of soul and mind,
Arise, keep silence thus no more;
Put forth your strength, and ye shall find
Your noblest work is to adore.
O soul and body, make ye pure and meet,
With heartfelt praise your God and Lord to greet.

Ye little leaves so fresh and green,
That dance for joy in summer air,
Ye slender grasses, bright and keen,
Ye flowers so wondrous sweet and fair;
Ye only for your Maker's glory live,
Help me, for all His love, meet praise to give.

O all ye living things that throng
With breath and motion earth and sky,
Be ye companions in my song,
Help me to raise His praises high;
For my unaided powers are far too weak
The glories of His mighty works to speak.

And first, O Father, praise to Thee
For all I am and all I have,
It was Thy merciful decree

Catherine Winkworth

That all those blessings richly gave,
Which o'er the earth are scattered far and near,
To help and gladden us who sojourn here.

And, dearest Jesus, blest be Thou,
Whose heart with pity overflows,
Thou rich in help! who deign'dst to bow
To earth, and taste her keenest woes;
Thy death has burst my bonds and set me free,
Has made me Thine; henceforth I cling to Thee.

Nor less to Thee, O Holy Ghost,
Be everlasting honours paid,
For all Thy comfort, Lord, and most
That I a child of life am made
By Thy deep love; my good deeds are not mine,
Thou workest them through me, O Light Divine.

Yes, Lord, through all my changing days,
With each new scene afresh I mark
How wondrously Thou guid'st my ways,
Where all seems troubled, wilder'd, dark;
When dangers thicken fast, and hopes depart,
Thy light beams comfort on my sinking heart.

Shall I not then be filled with joy,
Shall I not praise Thee evermore?
Triumphant songs my lips employ,
E'en when my cup of woe runs o'er;
Nay, though the heavens should vanish as a scroll,
Nothing shall shake or daunt my trusting soul.

But of Thy goodness will I sing
As long as I have life and breath,
Offerings of thanks I'll daily bring
Until my heart is still in death;
And when at last my lips grow pale and cold,
Yet in my sighs Thy praises shall be told.

Father, do Thou in mercy deign
To listen to my earthly lays;
Once shall I learn a nobler strain,
Where angels ever hymn Thy praise,
There in the radiant choir I too shall sing
Loud hallelujahs to my glorious Kings.

Twenty-first Sunday after Trinity

Be strong in the Lord, and in the power of His might. Put on the whole armour of God, that ye may be able to stand against the wiles of the devil. For we wrestle not against flesh and blood, but against principalities, against powers, against the rulers of the darkness of this world, against spiritual wickedness in high places.
    From the Epistle. [Eph. 6:10-12]
    [Psalm 46]
Luther. 1530.
Hymn composed on the road to Worms.
trans. by William Gaskell, 1855

A sure stronghold our God is He,
A trusty shield and weapon;
Our help He'll be and set us free
From every ill can happen.
That old malicious foe
Intends us deadly woe;
Armed with the strength of hell
And deepest craft as well,
On earth is not his fellow.

Through our own force we nothing can,
Straight were we lost forever;
But for us fights the proper Man,
By God sent to deliver.
Ask ye who this may be?
Christ Jesus named is He,
Of Sabaoth the Lord;
Sole God to be adored;
'Tis he must win the battle.

And were the world with devils filled,
All eager to devour us,
Our souls to fear should little yield,
They cannot overpower us.
Their dreaded Prince no more
Can harm us as of yore;
Look grim as e'er he may,
Doomed is his ancient sway;
A word can overthrow him.

Still shall they leave that Word His might,
And yet no thanks shall merit;
Still is He with us in the fight,

Catherine Winkworth

By His good gifts and Spirit.
E'en should they take our life,
Goods, honour, children, wife--
Though all of these be gone,
Yet nothing have they won,
God's kingdom ours abideth!

Twenty-second Sunday after Trinity.
Trust in the Lord with all thine heart, and lean not unto thine own understanding.
　　　From the Lesson. [Prov. 3:5]
Gottfried Arnold. 1666-1714.
trans. by Catherine Winkworth, 1855

How blest to all Thy followers, Lord, the road
By which Thou lead'st them on, yet oft how strange!
But Thou in all dost seek our highest good,
For Truth were true no longer, couldst Thou change.
Though crooked seem the paths, yet are they straight,
By which Thou draw'st Thy children up to Thee,
And passing wonders by the way they see,
And learn at last to own Thee wise and great.

No human laws can bind Thy Spirit, Lord,
That reason or opinion frame for us;
The knot of doubt is severed by Thy sword,
Or falls unravelled if Thou willest thus.
The strongest bonds are weak to Thee, O God,
All sinks and fails that would Thy course oppose;
Thy lightest word can quell Thy stoutest foes,
And desert paths are by Thy footsteps trod.

What human prudence fondly strives to bind,
Thy wisdom sunders far as east to west;
Who long beneath the yoke of man have pined,
Thy hand exalteth high above the rest.
The world would scatter, Thou dost union give;
She breaks, Thou buildest; what she builds is made
A ruined heap; her light is nought but shade;
Her dead Thy Spirit calls to rise and live.

Is there an act our reason would applaud?
Lo! in Thy book hast Thou the example given;
But him whom none as wise and pious laud,
Thou often lead'st in secret up to Heaven,
As Thou didst leave the Pharisee, to go
And eat with sinners whom all else forsook.
Who can search out Thy purposes, or look
Into the abyss of wisdom whence they flow?

Catherine Winkworth

Our all, O God, is nothing in Thine eyes,
Our nothing Thou regardest oft with love;
Glory and pomp of words Thou dost not prize,
Thy impulse only gives them power to move.
Thy noblest works awaken not man's praise,
For they are hidden, and he blindly turns
Away, nor though he see, their light discerns,
Too gross his sense, too keen their dazzling rays.

O Ruler! We would bless Thee and adore,
At whose command we live or turn to dust;
When Thou dost give us of Thy wisdom's store,
We see how true Thy care, and learn to trust.
Thy wisdom plays with us as with a child,
Who playing learns his Father loves him well;
'Tis love that brings Thee down with man to dwell,
Love guides our faltering footsteps through the wild.

Now seems to us o'er harsh and strict Thy school,
Now dost Thou greet us mild and tenderly,
Now when our wilder passions break Thy rule,
Thy judgments fright us back again to Thee.
With downcast eyes we seek Thy face again,
Thou kissest us, we promise fair amends,
Once more Thy Spirit rest and pardon sends,
And curbs our passions with a stronger rein.

Thou know'st, O Father, all our weakness well,
Our impotence, our foolishness of mind;
Almost a passing glance may serve to tell
How weak are we, how ignorant, how blind,
And so Thou comest with Thy help and stay,
A father's rule, a mother's love are Thine;
The lamb, on whom none else discern Thy sign,
Thou carriest in Thy bosom day by day.

The common ways are trodden not of Thee,
Thy steps are seldom traced by mortal eyes,
Yet art Thou near us, and unseen, dost see
All hopes and wishes that within us rise.
The bright reflection of Thy inner thought
Is day by day before our eyes outspread;
Who thinks he quickest hath Thy meaning read,
Is oft another deeper lesson taught.

O Eye, whose glance no falsehood can endure,
Grant me to wisely judge, and well discern
Nature from grace--Thy Light serene and pure
From grosser fires that in and round me burn.
Let no strange fire be kindled on the shrine

Within my heart, lest I should madly bring
The hated offering unto Thee, O King.
Ah, blest the soul whose light is born of Thine!

When reason contradicts Thy law, or climbs
So high, she weeneth to know more than Thou,
Break down her confidence, great God, betimes,
And teach her lowly at Thy feet to bow.
Nor let my proud heart dictate, Lord, to Thee,
But tame the wayward will that seeks its own,
And wake the love that clings to Thee alone,
And takes Thy judgments in humility.

Absorb my will in Thine; support and bear
Onward in loving arms Thy timid child;
Thy Spirit's voice dispels all doubt, all fear,
And quells the passions erst so fierce and wild.
Thou art mine All, since that Thy Son is mine;
Oh let Thy Spirit work with power in me,
With strong desire I thirst, I pant for Thee,
Oh joy whene'er Thy glories round me shine!

So shall the creature ever serve me here,
Nor angels blush to bear me company;
The perfect spirits to Thy throne most near,
They are my brethren, waiting there for me;
And oft my spirit joys to meet a heart,
That loveth Thee and me and every saint.
Is aught then left can make me sad and faint?
Come, Fount of Joy! vain sorrows, all depart!

Twenty-third Sunday after Trinity

For our conversation is in heaven; from whence also we look for the Saviour, the Lord Jesus Christ; who shall change our vile body, that it may be fashioned like unto His glorious body, according to the working whereby He is able even to subdue all things unto Himself.

    From the epistle. [Philip. 3:20-21]
Johann Franck. 1653.
trans. by Catherine Winkworth, 1855

Let who will in thee rejoice,
O thou fair and wondrous earth!
Ever anguished sorrow's voice
Pierces through thy seeming mirth;
Let thy vain delights be given
Unto them who love not Heaven,
My desire is fixed on Thee,
Jesus, dearest far to me!

Weary souls with toil outworn,
Drooping 'neath the glaring light,
Wish that soon the coming morn
Might be quenched again in night,
That their toils might find a close
In a soft and deep repose;
I but wish to rest in Thee,
Jesus, dearest far to me!

Others dare the treacherous wave,
Hidden rock and shifting wind--
Storm and danger let them brave,
Earthly good or wealth to find;
Faith shall wing my upward flight
Far above yon starry height,
Till I find myself with Thee,
Jesus, dearest Friend to me!

Many a time ere now I said,
Many a time again shall say,
Would to God that I were dead,
Would that in my grave I lay!
Rest were mine, and sweet my lot
Where the body hindereth not,
And the soul can ever be,
Jesus, dearest Lord, with Thee!

Come, O Death, thou twin of Sleep,
Lead me hence,--I pray thee come,
Loose my rudder, through the deep
Guide my vessel safely home.
Thy approach who will may fly,
'Twere a joy to me to die,
Death but opes the gates to Thee,
Jesus, dearest Friend to me!

Would that I today might leave
This my earthly prison here,
And my crown of joy receive
Waiting me in yon bright sphere!
In that home of joy, where dwell
Hosts of angels, would I tell
How the Godhead shines in Thee,
Jesus, dearest Lord to me!

But not yet the gates of gold
I may see nor enter in,
Nor the heavenly fields behold,
But must sit and mourning spin
Life's dark thread on earth below;
Let my thoughts then hourly go
Whither I myself would be,
Jesus, dearest Lord, with Thee!

Twenty-fourth Sunday after Trinity

Jesus answered and said unto her, Martha, Martha, thou art careful and troubled about many things; but one thing is needful, and Mary hath chosen that good part which shall not be taken away from her.
     Luke 10:41,42
SchrÃpder. 1697.
trans. by Catherine Winkworth, 1855

One thing is needful! Let me deem
Aright of that whereof He spoke;
All else, how sweet soe'er it seem,
Is but in truth a heavy yoke,
'Neath which the toiling spirit frets and pants,
Yet never finds the happiness it wants:
This one can make amends, whate'er I miss,
Who hath it finds in all his joy through this!

My soul, wouldst thou this one thing find?
Seek not amid created things;
Leave what is earthly far behind,
O'er Nature heavenward stretch thy wings,
Where God and man are One, in whom appear
All truth and fulness, thou hast found it here,--
The better part, the One thing needful He,
My One, my All, my Joy, who saveth me.

As Mary once devoutly sought
The eternal truth, the better part,
And sat, enwrapt in holy thought,
At Jesu's feet with burning heart,
For nought else caring, yearning for the word
That should be spoken by her Friend, her Lord,
Losing her All in Him, His word believing,
And through the One all things again receiving:

Even so is all my heart's desire
Fixed, dearest Lord, on Thee alone;
Oh make me true and draw me nigher,
And make Thyself, O Christ, my own.
Though many turn aside to join the crowd,
To follow Thee in love my heart is vowed,
Thy word is life and spirit, whither go?
What joy is there in Thee we cannot know?

All perfect wisdom lies in Thee
As in its primal hidden source;
Oh let my will submissive be,
And hold henceforth its even course,
Controlled by truth and meekness, for high Heaven
To lowly simple hearts hath wisdom given;
Who knoweth Christ aright, and in Him lives,
Hath won the highest prize that wisdom gives.

Oh that my soul from sleep might wake,
And ever, Lord, Thine image bear!
Thee for my portion I will take,
Thy holiness Thou bidd'st us share,
Whate'er we need for God-like walk and life
Is given to us in Thee; oh end this strife,
And free me from the love of passing things,
To know alone the life from Thee that springs!

What can I ask for more? Behold
Thy mercy is a very flood;
I know that Thou hast passed of old
Into the Holiest through Thy blood,
And there redeemed for ever those who lay
Beneath the rule of Satan; now are they
Made free by Thee, who erst were slaves and weak,
And childlike hearts the name of Father speak.

Deep joy and peace and holy calm
Fill my once restless spirit now;
O'er verdant pastures free from harm,
She follows Thee, her shepherd Thou;
Whate'er rejoices or consoles us here,
Is not so sweet as feeling Thou art near;
This One is needful, but all else is dross,
Let me win Christ, all other gain is loss.
One thing have I desired of the Lord, that will I seek after; that I
may dwell in the house of the Lord all the days of my life, to behold
the beauty of the Lord, and to enquire in His temple.
Psalm 27:4

Twenty-fifth Sunday after Trinity
Behold, the days come, saith the Lord, that I will raise unto David a righteous Branch, and a King shall reign, and prosper, and shall execute judgment and justice in the earth.
　　　From the Passage for the Epistle. [Jer. 23:5]
Johann Franck.
After St. Ambrose.
trans. by Catherine Winkworth, 1855

Redeemer of the nations, come!
Ransom of earth, here make Thy home!
Bright Sun, oh dart Thy flame to earth,
For so shall God in Christ have birth!

Thou comest from Thy kingly throne,
O Son of God, the Virgin's Son!
Thou Hero of a twofold race,
Dost walk in might earth's darkest place.

Thou stoopest once to suffer here,
And risest o'er the starry sphere;
Hell's gates at Thy descent were riven,
Thy ascent is to highest Heaven.

One with the Father! Prince of might!
O'er nature's realm assert Thy right,
Our sickly bodies pine to know
Thy heavenly strength, Thy living glow.

How bright Thy lowly manger beams!
Down earth's dark vale its glory streams,
The splendour of Thy natal night
Shines through all Time in deathless light.

St. Andrew's Day

And Jesus saith unto them, Follow me... And they straightway left their nets, and followed Him.
    From the Gospel. [Mk 1:17-18]
Rist. 1644.
trans. by Catherine Winkworth, 1855

Follow me, in me ye live,
What ye ask I freely give,
Only heed ye lest ye stray,
Follow me, the Living Way;
Follow me with all your hearts,
I will ward off sorrow's darts;
Learn from Christ your Lord to be
Rich in meek humility.

Yea, Lord, meet it is indeed
We should all thy bidding heed;
Who in fear of this earth's blame,
Counts Thy lowly yoke a shame,
To Thy name, Lord, hath no right,
Is no Christian, in Thy sight.
Ah too well I know that we,
Hear on earth, should follow Thee.

Where is strength, Lord, to fulfil,
Glad at heart, Thy works and will,
Following on where Thou hast trod?
All too weak am I, O God;
If awhile Thy paths I keep,
Soon I pine for rest and sleep;
E'en to love Thee, Lord, aright,
Passeth far my feeble might.

Yet I will not turn from Thee,
Yet my joy in Christ shall be;
Help me, make me strong and bold,
Firm and fast Thy grace to hold;
This world and her lusts I leave,
Only to my Lord I cleave;
All their promises are lies,
But who follows Thee is wise.

Catherine Winkworth

Thou hast gone before us, Lord,
Not with anger, strife, or sword,
Not with kingly pomp and pride,
But with mercy at Thy side.
Moved by wondrous love divine
For our life Thou gavest Thine,
And Thy precious outpoured blood,
Won for us the highest good.

Let us follow in such sort,
Christ-like every deed and thought,
That Thy love most true and kind
All our hearts henceforth may bind;
None may look behind him now,
Who to Christ hath pledged his vow;
Jesus leads, no longer stand,
Follow me, is His command.

Draw me up, my God, from hence,
Raise me high o'er earth and sense,
That I lose not Thee from sight,
Nor in life nor death, my Light!
In my soul's most deep recess
Let me cherish holiness,
Not for show or human praise,
But for Thy sake, all my days.

Grant me, Lord, my heart's desire,
So my course to run nor tire,
That my practised soul may prove
What Thy meekness, what Thy love.
Grant me here to trust Thy grace,
There with joy to see Thy face,
This in time my portion be,
That through all eternity!

St. Thomas the Apostle

And Thomas answered and said unto Him, My Lord and my God. Jesus saith unto Him, Thomas, because thou hast seen me thou hast believed; blessed are they that have not seen, and yet have believed.

From the Gospel. [Jn. 20:29]
Albertini. 1821.
trans. by Catherine Winkworth, 1855

Long in the spirit-world my soul had sought
Some friendly being, close to her akin;
Long had prepared a dwelling in her thought
And heart for such an one; for she could win
Through Him alone her strength, for Him she yearned,
Toward Him her fervent longing ever burned.

And rich the world in things invisible,
In heathen gods, and spirits great and small,
And bright and dark; yet ever did she dwell
Alone, for One was wanting 'mid them all;
One having might and glory, rich in love,
God, who as man could shame and weakness prove.

Then came the Word, and took on Him our flesh,
And dwelt with men, here in the world of sight,
And made an end of strife, and linked afresh
Our sinful earth unto the throne of light;
Into His ancient glory He is gone,
And yet He dwells with us till time be done.

Thus, O my soul, hast thou received thy will;
The glory of the world of ghosts is dim
Before the One, who is and was, and still
Shall ever be; all hearts are fixed on Him,
And spirit worlds, since He is there, become
Hallowed and safe to thee, thy proper home.

Thou soarest now through all their heights sublime,
And not as once dost empty back return,
But gazing on Thy God, forgettest time
Beneath His loving glance, whence thou wouldst learn
How thou shouldst love, and know His Word aright:
Ah, blest the love and faith that ask not sight!

Presentation in the Temple
Lord, now lettest Thou Thy servant depart in peace, according to Thy word; for mine eyes have seen Thy salvation.
    From the Gospel. [Lk. 2:29-30]
Johann Franck. 1653.
trans. by Catherine Winkworth, 1855

Light of the Gentile world!
Thy people's joy and love!
Drawn by Thy Spirit we are come
Thy presence, Lord, to prove.
Within Thy temple walls
We wait with earnest mind,
As Simeon waited long of old
His Saviour God to find.

Thou wilt be found of us,
O Lord, in every place,
Where Thou hast promised faithfully
We should behold Thy face.
Thou yet dost suffer us,
Who oft are gathered here,
To bear Thee in the arms of faith
As once that aged seer.

Be Thou our bliss, our light
Shining 'mid pain and loss,
Our Sun of strength in time of fear,
The glory round our cross;
A glow in sinking hearts,
A sunbeam in distress,
Physician, nurse, in sickness' hours,
In death our happiness.

Oh let us, Lord, prevail
With Simeon at the last;
May we take up his dying song
When life is waning fast!
"Let me depart in peace,
Since that mine aged eyes
Have seen the Saviour here on earth,
Have seen His day arise."

Yes, with the eye of faith
My Jesus I behold;
No foe can rob me of my Lord,
Though fierce his threats and bold.
I dwell within Thy heart,
Thou dost in mine abide,
Not sorrow, pain nor death itself,
Can tear me from Thy side.

Catherine Winkworth

St. Matthias' Day
Come unto Me, all ye that labour and are heavy laden, and I will give you rest.
    From the Gospel. [Matt. 10:28]
Kunth. 1733.
trans. by Catherine Winkworth, 1855

Yes, there remaineth yet a rest!
Arise, sad heart, who now dost pine,
By heavy care and pain opprest,
On whom no sun of joy can shine;
Look to the Lamb! in yon bright fields
Thou'lt know the joy His presence yields;
Cast off thy load and thither haste;
Soon shalt thou fight and bleed no more,
Soon, soon thy weary course be o'er,
And deep the rest thou then shalt taste:

The rest appointed thee of God,
The rest that nought shall break or move,
That ere this earth by man was trod
Was set apart for thee by Love.
Our Saviour gave His life to win
This rest for thee; oh enter in!
Here how His voice sounds far and wide:
Ye weary souls, no more delay,
Nor loiter faithless by the way,
Here in my peace and rest abide!

Ye heavy-laden, come to Him!
Ye who are bent with many a load,
Come from your prisons drear and dim,
Toil not thus sadly on your road!
Ye've borne the burden of the day,
And hear ye not your Saviour say,
I am your refuge and your rest?
His children ye, of heavenly birth,
Howe'er may rage sin, hell, or earth,
Here are ye safe, here calmly blest.

Yonder in joy the sheaves we bring,
Whose seed was sown on earth in tears;
There in our Father's house we sing
The song too sweet for mortal ears.
Sorrow and sighing all are past,
And pain and death are fled at last,

There with the Lamb of God we dwell,
He leads us to the crystal river,
He wipes away all tears for ever;
What there is ours no tongue can tell.

Hunger nor thirst can pain us there,
The time of recompense is come,
Nor cold nor scorching heat we bear,
Safe sheltered in our Saviour's home.
The Lamb is in the midst; and those
Who followed Him through shame and woes,
Are crowned with honour, joy, and peace.
The dry bones gather life again,
One Sabbath over all shall reign,
Wherein all toil and labour cease.

There is untroubled calm and light,
No gnawing care shall mar our rest;
Ye weary, heed this word aright,
Come, lean upon your Saviour's breast.
Fain would I linger here no more,
Fain to yon happier world upsoar,
And join that bright expectant band.
Oh raise, my soul, the joyful song
That rings through yon triumphant throng;
Thy perfect rest is nigh at hand.

The Annunciation

Behold the handmaid of the Lord; be it unto me according to Thy word.
         From the Gospel. [Lk. 1:38]
Winkler. 1713.
trans. by Catherine Winkworth, 1855

Yea my spirit fain would sink
In Thy heart and hands, my God,
Waiting till Thou show the end
Of the ways she here hath trod;
Stripped of self, how calm her rest
On her loving Father's breast!

And my soul repineth not,
Well content whate'er befall;
Murmurs, wishes, of self-will,
They are slain and vanquished all,
Restless thoughts, that fret and crave,
Slumber in her Saviour's grave.

And my soul is free from care,
For her thoughts from all things cease
That can pierce like sharpest thorns
Wounding sore the inner peace.
He who made her careth well,
She but seeks in peace to dwell.

And my soul despaireth not,
Loving God amid her woe;
Grief that wrings and breaks the heart
Only they who hate Him know:
They who love Him still possess
Comfort in their worst distress.

And my soul complaineth not,
For she knows not pain or fear,
Clinging to her God in faith,
Trusting though He slay her here.
'Tis when flesh and blood repine,
Son of joy, Thou canst not shine.

Thus my soul before her God
Lieth still, nor speaketh more,
Conqueror thus o'er pain and wrong,
That once smote her to the core;
Like a silent ocean, bright
With her God's great praise and light.

St. Barnabas' Day

We preach unto you that ye should turn from these vanities unto the living God which made heaven, and earth, and the sea, and all things that are therein: who in time past suffered all nations to walk in their own ways. Nevertheless He left not Himself without witness, in that He did good, and gave us rain from heaven, and fruitful seasons, filling our hearts with food and gladness.

    From the Lesson. [Acts 14:15]
Paul Gerhardt. 1659.
trans. by Catherine Winkworth, 1855

Shall I not sing praise to Thee,
Shall I not give thanks, O Lord?
Since for us in all I see
How Thou keepest watch and ward;
How the truest tenderest love
Ever fills Thy heart, my God,
Helping, cheering, on their road,
All who in Thy service move.
All things else have but their day,
God's love only lasts for aye.

As the eagle o'er her nest
Spreads her sheltering wings abroad,
So from all that would molest,
Doth Thine arm defend me, Lord;
From my youth up e'en till now
Of the being Thou didst give,
And the earthly life I live,
Faithful Guardian still wert Thou.
All things else have but their day,
God's love only lasts for aye.

Nay, He kept not back His Son,
But hath given Him for our good,
And our safety He hath won
By the shedding of His blood.
O Thou fathomless abyss!
My weak powers but strive in vain,
Knowledge of Thy depths to gain,
Man knows not such love as this.
All things else have but their day,
God's love only lasts for aye.

And His Spirit, blessed Guide,
In His holy Word doth teach,
How on earth we may abide,
So that heaven at last we reach;
Every longing heart doth fill
With the pure light of faith,
That can break the bonds of death,
And control the powers of ill.
All things else have but their day,
God's love only lasts for aye.

Truly hath He cared indeed
For my soul's health, and no less
If my body suffer need,
Will He help in my distress.
When my strength and courage fail,
When my powers can do no more,
Doth my God such strength outpour,
That I rise up and prevail.
All things else have but their day,
God's love only lasts for aye.

All the hosts of heaven and earth,
Hath He placed at my command,
Nowhere is there lack or dearth,
But I find in sea and land
All things ordered for my wants,
Living things in fields and woods,
On the heights or in the floods,
And the earth brings forth her plants.
All things else have but their day,
God's love only lasts for aye.

When I sleep my Guardian wakes,
And revives my wearied mind;
Every morning on me breaks
With some mark of love most kind;
Had my God not stood my Friend,
Had His countenance not been
Here my guide, I had not seen
Many a trial reach its end.
All things else have but their day,
God's love only lasts for aye.

Often hath my crafty Foe
Threatened to bring down on me
Many a sore and heavy woe,
From which yet my life is free;
For the angel whom God sends,
Wards off every threatened hurt,

Catherine Winkworth

Every evil doth avert
That mine Enemy intends.
All things else have but their day,
God's love only lasts for aye.

As a father ne'er withdraws
From a child his all of love,
Though it often break his laws,
Though it careless, wilful, prove:
Even so my loving Lord
Doth my faults with pity see,
With His rod He chastens me,
Not avenging with His sword.
All things else have but their day,
God's love only lasts for aye.

When His strokes upon me light,
Bitterly I feel their smart,
Yet are they, if seen aright,
Tokens that my Father's heart
Yearns to bring me back again
Through these crosses to His fold,
From the world that fain would hold
Soul and body in its chain.
All things else have but their day,
God's love only lasts for aye.

All my life I still have found,
And I will forget it never,
Every sorrow hath its bound,
And no cross endures for ever.
After all the winter's snows
Comes sweet summer back again,
Patient souls ne'er wait in vain,
Joy is given for all their woes.
All things else have but their day,
God's love only lasts for aye.

Since then neither change nor end
In Thy love can e'er have place,
Father! I beseech Thee send
Unto me Thy loving grace.
Help Thy feeble child, and give
Strength to serve Thee day and night,
Loving Thee with all my might,
While on earth I yet must live;
So shall I when Time is o'er,
Praise and love Thee evermore.

St. Michael and all Angels.

Are they not all ministering spirits, sent forth to minister for those that shall be heirs of salvation?
     Heb. 1:14
Rist. 1655.
trans. by Catherine Winkworth, 1855

Praise and thanks to Thee be sung,
Mighty God, in sweetest tone!
Lo! from every land and tongue,
Nations gather round Thy Throne,
Praising Thee, that Thou dost send,
Daily from Thy Heaven above,
Angel-messengers of love,
Who Thy threatened Church defend,
Who can offer worthily,
Lord of angels, praise to Thee!

'Tis your office, Spirits bright,
still to guard us night and day,
And before your heavenly might,
Powers of darkness flee away;
Ever doth your unseen host
Camp around us, and avert
All that seeks to do us hurt,
Curling Satan's malice most.
Lord, who then can worthily
For such goodness honour Thee!

And ye come on ready wing,
When we drift toward sheer despair,
Seeing nought where we might cling,
Suddenly, lo, ye are there!
And the wearied heart grows strong,
As an angel strengthened Him,
Fainting in the garden dim,
'Neath the world's vast woe and wrong.
Lord, who then can worthily
For such mercy honour Thee!

Right and seemly is it then
We should glory, that our God
Hath such honour put on men,
That He sends o'er earth abroad
Princes of the realm above,

Catherine Winkworth

Champions, who by day and night,
Shield us with His holy might;
Come, behold how great His love!
Lord, who then can worthily
For such favour honour Thee!

Praise and thanks to Thee be sung,
Mighty God, in sweetest tone.
Lo! from every land and tongue,
Nations gather round Thy throne,
Praising Thee that Thou dost send,
Hourly from Thy glorious sphere,
Angels down to help us here,
And Thy threatened Church defend.
Let us henceforth worthily,
Lord of angels, honour Thee.

All Saint's Day

Lo, a great multitude which no man could number, of all nations, and kindreds and people, and tongues, stood before the throne and before the Lamb, clothed with white robes, and palms in their hands; and cried with a loud voice, saying, Salvation to our God which sitteth upon the throne and unto the Lamb.
     From the Epistle. [Rev. 7:9-10]
Schenk. d. 1727.
trans. by Catherine Winkworth, 1855

Who are those before God's throne,
What the crownÃ"d host I see?
As the sky with stars thick-strown
Is their shining company:
Hallelujahs, hark, they sing,
Solemn praise to God they bring.

Who are those that in their hands
Bear aloft the conqueror's palm,
As one o'er his foeman stands,
Fallen beneath his mighty arm?
What the war and what the strife,
Whence came such victorious life?

Who are those arrayed in light,
Clothed in righteousness divine,
Wearing robes most pure and white,
That unstained shall ever shine,
That can nevermore decay;
Whence came all this bright array?

They are those who, strong in faith,
Battled for the mighty God;
Conquerors o'er the world and death,
Following not Sin's crowded road;
Through the Lamb who once was slain,
Did they such high victory gain.

They are those who much have borne,
Trial, sorrow, pain, and care,
Who have wrestled night and morn
With the mighty God in prayer;
Now their strife hath found its close,
God hath turned away their woes.

Catherine Winkworth

They are branches of that Stem,
Who hath our Salvation been,
In the blood He shed for them,
Have they made their raiment clean;
Hence they wear such radiant dress,
Clad in spotless holiness.

They are those who hourly here
Served as priests before their Lord,
Offering up with gladsome cheer
Soul and body at His word.
Now within the Holy Place,
They behold Him face to face.

As the harts at noonday pant
For the river fresh and clear,
Did they ofttimes long and faint
For the Living Fountain here.
Now their thirst is quenched, they dwell
With the Lord they loved so well.

Thitherwards I stretch my hands;
O Lord Jesus, day by day,
In Thy house in these strange lands,
Compassed round with foes, I pray,
Let me sink not in the war,
Drive for me my foes afar.

Cast my lot in earth and heaven
With Thy saints made like to Thee,
Let my bonds be also riven,
Make Thy child who loves Thee free;
Near the throne where Thou dost shine,
May a place at last be mine!

Ah! that bliss can ne'er be told,
When with all that army bright,
Thee, my Sun, I shall behold,
Shining star-like, with Thy light.
Amen! Thanks be brought to Thee,
Praise through all eternity.

Morning Hymns[1]

My voice shalt Thou hear in the morning, O Lord; in the morning will I direct my prayer unto Thee, and will look up.
      Psalm 5:3

I.

Gott dess Himmels und der Erden
Heinrich Albert. 1644.
trans. by Catherine Winkworth, 1855

God who madest earth and heaven,
Father, Son, and Holy Ghost,
Who the day and night has given,
Sun and moon and starry host,
All things wake at Thy command,
Held in being by Thy hand:

God, I thank Thee from my heart,
That through all the livelong night,
Thou hast kept me safe apart
From all danger, pain, affright,
And the cunning of my foe
Hath not wrought my overthrow.

Let the night of sin depart,
As this earthly night hath fled;
Jesus, take me to Thy heart,
In the blood that Thou hast shed
Is my help and hope alone,
For the evil I have done.

Help me as each morn shall break,
In the Spirit to arise,
Let my soul from sin awake,
That when o'er the aged skies,
Shall the morn of Doom appear,
I may see it free from fear.

Ever lead me, ever guide
All my wanderings by Thy Word;
As Thou hast been, still abide
My defence, my refuge, Lord.
Never safe except with Thee,
Ever Thou my Guardian be!

Mighty God, I now commend
Soul and body unto Thee,
All the powers that Thou dost lend,
By Thy hand directed be;
Thou my boast, my strength divine,
Keep me with Thee, I am Thine.

Let Thine angel guard my soul
From the Evil One's dark power,
All his thousand wiles control,
Warning, guiding me each hour,
Till my final rest be come,
And Thine angel bear me home.

II
Paul Gerhardt.
trans. by Catherine Winkworth, 1855

The golden sunbeams with their joyous gleams,
Are kindling o'er earth, her life and mirth,
Shedding forth lovely and heart-cheering light;
Through the dark hours' chill I lay silent and still,
But risen at length to gladness and strength,
I gaze on the heavens all glowing and bright.

Mine eyes now behold Thy works, that of old
And ever are telling to all men here dwelling,
How great is Thy glory, how wondrous Thy power;
They tell of the home where the faithful shall come,
Who depart to that peace that can change not or cease,
From earth where all passeth as passes the hour.

O come let us raise our voices, and praise
The Maker of all, at His feet let us fall,
Offering to Him again all He hath given,
The best that is ours, our hearts and our powers;
Glad songs that we sing Him, thanks that we bring Him,
These are the incense most grateful to Heaven.

Evening and morning thus ever he cares for us,
Blessing, renewing, warding off ruin,
These are His works, thus His goodness we prove;
When we are sleeping, watch He is keeping,
Whe we arise, He gladdens our eyes
With the sunshine of mercy, the glow of His love.

All passeth away, but God liveth aye,
And changeth in nought; eternal His thought,
His Word and His Will are steadfast and sure;

Never His grace nor His mercy decays,
It heals the sad heart from its deadliest smart,
Giving it life that shall ever endure.

God, Thou my crown! forgiving look down,
And hide from Thy face through Thy pitying grace,
All my transgressions against Thy command;
Henceforth oh rule me, guide me and school me,
As Thou seest fit; my ways I commit
All to Thy pleasure, Thy merciful hand.

Crosses and sorrow may end with the morrow,
Stormiest seas shall sink into peace,
The wild winds are hushed, and the sunshine returns;
So fulness of rest, and the calm of the blest,
Are waiting me there, in that garden most fair,
That home for which daily my spirit here yearns.

III
Von Canitz. 1654-1699.
trans. by Catherine Winkworth, 1855

Come, my soul, awake, 'tis morning,
Day is dawning
O'er the earth, arise and pray;
Come, to Him who made this splendour,
Thou must render
All thy feeble powers can pay.

From the stars now learn thy duty,
See their beauty
Paling in the golden air;
So God's light thy mists should banish,
Thus should vanish
What to darkened sense seemed fair.

See how everything that liveth,
Gladly striveth
On the pleasand light to gaze;
Stirs with joy each thing that groweth,
As it knoweth
Darkness smitten by these rays.

Soul, thy incense also proffer;
Thou shouldst offer
Praise to Him, who from thy head
Kept afar the storms of sorrow,
And the morrow
Finds the night in peace hath fled.

Catherine Winkworth

Bid Him bless what thou art doing,
If pursuing
Some good aim; but if there lurks
Ill intent in thine endeavour,
May He ever
Thwart and turn thee from Thy works.

Think that he, the All-discerning,
Knows each turning
Of thy path, each sinful stain;
Nay what shame would fain gloss over,
Can discover;
All thou dost to Him is plain.

Bound unto the flying hours
Are our powers;
Earth's vain good floats down their wave,
That thy ship, my soul, is hasting,
Never resting,
To its haven in the grave.

Pray that when thy life is closing,
Calm reposing,
Thou mayst die, and not in pain;
That, the night of death departed,
Thou glad-hearted,
Mayst behold the Sun again.

From God's glances shrink thou never,
Meet them ever;
Who submits him to His grace,
Finds that earth no sunshine knoweth
Such as gloweth
O'er his pathway all his days.

Wakenest thou again to sorrow,
Oh! then borrow
Strength from Him, whose sun-like might
On the mountain-summit tarries,
And yet carries
To the vales their mirth and light.

Round the gifts He on thee showers,
Fiery towers
Will he set, be not afraid,
Thou shalt dwell 'mid angel legions,
In the regions
Satan's self dares not invade.

IV
Von Rosenroth. 1684.
trans. by Catherine Winkworth, 1855

Dayspring of eternity!
Dawn on us this morning-tide.
Light from Light's exhaustless sea,
Now no more Thy radiance hide,
But dispel with glorious might
All our night.

Let the morning dew of love
On our sleeping conscience rain;
Gentle comfort from above
Flow through life's long parchÃ"d plain;
Water daily us Thy flock
From the rock.

Let the glow of love destroy
Cold obedience faintly given;
Wake our hearts to strength and joy
with the flushing eastern heaven,
Let us truly rise ere yet
Life hath set.

Brightest Star of eastern skies,
Let that final morn appear,
When our bodies too shall rise
Free from all that pained them here,
Strong their joyful course to run
As the sun.

To yon world be Thou our light,
O Thou glorious Sun of grace;
Lead us through the tearful night,
To yon fair and blessed place,
Where to joy that never dies
We shall rise.

V
Anton Ulrich, Duke of Brunswick. 1667.
trans. by Catherine Winkworth, 1855

Once more from rest I rise again,
To greet a day of toil and pain,
My Heaven-appointed lot;
Unknowing what new grief may be
With this new day in store for me,
But it shall harm me not
I know full well; my loving God

Catherine Winkworth

Will send me not a hurtful load.

My burden every day is new,
But every day my God is true,
And all my cares hath borne;
Ere eventide can no man know
What Day shall bring of joy or woe,
And though it seem each morn
To some new path of suffering call,
With God I can surmount it all.

Since this I know, oh wherefore sink,
My faithless heart? And why thus shrink
To take thy load again?
Bear what thou canst, God bears thy lot,
The Lord of All, He stumbleth not;
Pure blessing shalt thou gain,
If thou with Him right onward go,
Nor fear'st to tread the path of woe.

My heart grows strong, all terrors fly
Whene'er I feel Thy love Most High,
Doth compass me around;
But would I have Thee for my shield,
No more to sin my soul must yield,
But in Thy ways be found;
Thou, God, wilt never walk my way
If from Thy paths my feet should stray.

But let me feel Thou guidest me,
And humbly I will follow Thee,
Lord, make me true and pure;
Then strong and dauntless in Thy might
Against a world of sin I'll fight,
And know my triumph sure;
Then bravely I can meet each day,
And fear it not, come what come may.

My God and Lord, I cast on Thee
The load that weighs too sore on me,
The yoke 'neath which I bow;
I lay my rank, my high command,
In my Almighty Father's hand,
Well knowing, Lord, that Thou
Wilt ne'er withdraw it, for Thy truth
Hath let me onward from my youth.

To Thee my kindred I commend,
For they are safe if Thou defend,
Oh guard them round about;

My sinful soul would shelter take
In Jesu's bosom, for whose sake
Thou wilt not cast her out;
When soul and body part at last,
Then all myself on Thee I cast.

Evening Hymns[2]

Evening and morning and at noon will I pray and cry aloud! and He shall hear my voice.
     Psalm 141:2

I
N. Hermann. 1560.
trans. by Catherine Winkworth, 1855

The happy sunshine all is gone,
The gloomy night comes swiftly on;
But shine Thou still, O Christ our Light,
Nor let us lose ourselves in night.

We thank Thee, Father, that this day
Thy angels watched around our way,
And free from harm and vexing fear,
Have led us on in safety here.

Lord, have we angered Thee today,
Remember not our sins, we pray,
But let Thy mercy o'er them sweep,
And give us calm and restful sleep.

Thy angels guard our sleeping hours,
And keep afar all evil Powers;
And Thou all pain and mischief ward
From soul and body, faithful Lord!

II
Paul Gerhardt. 1653.
trans. by Catherine Winkworth, 1855

Now all the woods are sleeping,
And night and stillness creeping
O'er field and city, man and beast;
But thou, my heart, awake thee,
To prayer awhile betake thee,
And praise thy Maker ere thou rest.

O Sun, where art thou vanished?
The Night thy reign hath banished,
Thy ancient foe, the Night.
Farewell, a brighter glory
My Jesus sheddeth o'er me,
All clear within me shines His light.

The last faint beam is going,
The golden stars are glowing
In yonder dark-blue deep;
And such the glory given
When called of God to heaven,
On earth no more we pine and weep.

The body hastes to slumber,
These garments now but cumber;
And as I lay them by
I ponder how the spirit
Puts off the flesh t'inherit
A shining robe with Christ on high.

Now thought and labour ceases,
For Night the tired releases
And bids sweet rest begin:
My heart, there comes a morrow
Shall set thee free from sorrow
And all the dreary toil of sin.

Ye aching limbs! now rest you,
For toil hath sore oppressed you,
Lie down my weary head;
A sleep shall once o'ertake you
From which earth ne'er shall wake you,
Within a narrower, colder bed.

My heavy eyes are closing,
When I lie deep reposing--
O soul and body, where are ye?
To helpless sleep I yield them,
Oh let Thy mercy shield them,
Thou sleepless Eye, their guardian be!

My Jesus, stay Thou by me,
And let no foe come nigh me,
Safe sheltered by Thy wing;
But would the foe alarm me,
O let him never harm me,
But still Thine angels round me sing!

My loved ones, rest securely,
From every peril surely
Our God will guard your heads;
And happy slumbers send you,
And bid His hosts attend you,
And golden-armed watch o'er your beds.

III
Freylinghausen. 1704.
trans. by Catherine Winkworth, 1855

The day expires;
My soul desires
And pants to see that day,
When the vexing cares of earth
Shall be done away.

The night is here;
Oh! be Thou near,
Christ, make it light within;
Drive away from out my heart
All the night of sin.

The sunbeams pale,
And flee and fail;
O uncreated Sun!
Let Thy light now shine on us,
Then our joy were won.

All things that move
Below, above,
Now with sleep are blest,
Work Thou still in me, while I
Calmly in Thee rest.

When shall the sway
Of night and day
Cease to rule man thus?
When that brightest day of days
Once shall dawn on us.

Ah! never then
Her light again
Jerusalem shall miss,
For the Lamb shall be her Light,
Filling her with bliss.

Oh were I there!
Where all the air
With lovely sounds is ringing;
Where the saints Thee, Holy Lord,
Evermore are singing!

Lord Jesus, Thou
My rest art now,
Oh help me that I come,
Radient with Thy light to shine

In Thy glorious home!

IV
Claudius. 1782.
trans. by Catherine Winkworth, 1855

The moon hath risen on high,
And in the clear dark sky
The golden stars all brightly glow;
And black and hushed the woods,
While o'er the fields and floods
The white mists hover to and fro.

How still the earth! how calm!
What dear and home-like charm
From gentle twilight doth she borrow!
Like to some quiet room,
Where wrapt in still soft gloom,
We sleep away the daylight's sorrow.

Look up; the moon tonight
Shows us but half her light,
And yet we know her round and fair.
At other things how oft
We in our blindness scoffed,
Because we saw not what was there.

We haughty sons of men
Have but a narrow ken,
We are but sinners poor and weak,
Yet airy dreams we build,
And deem us wise and skilled,
And come not nearer what we seek.

Thy mercy let us see,
Nor find in vanity
Our joy; nor trust in what departs;
But true and simple grow,
And live to Thee below
With sunny pure and childlike hearts.

Let Death all gently come
At last to take us home,
And let us meet him fearlessly;
And when these bonds are riven,
O take us to Thy heaven,
Our Lord and God, to dwell with Thee.

Catherine Winkworth

Now in His name most blest
My brethren sink to rest;
The wind is cold, chill falls the dew.
Spare us, O God, and keep
Us safe in quiet sleep,
And all the sick and suffering too.

For the Sick & Dying[3]
I was sick and ye visited me.
    Matthew 25:36

The Lord will strengthen him upon the bed of languishing; Thou wilt make all this bed in his sickness.
    Psalm 41:3

I
Luther. 1524.
trans. by Catherine Winkworth, 1855

In the midst of life, behold
Death has girt us round.
Whom for help then shall we pray,
Where shall grace be found?
In Thee, O Lord, alone!
We rue the evil we have done,
That Thy wrath on us hath drawn.
Holy Lord and God!
Strong and Holy God!
Merciful and Holy Saviour!
Eternal God!
Leave us not to sink beneath
These dark pains of bitter death;
Kyrie eleison!

In the midst of death the jaws
Of hell against us gape.
Who from peril dire as this
Openeth us escape?
'Tis Thou, O Lord, alone!
Our bitter suffering and our sin
Pity from Thy mercy win,
Holy Lord and God!
Strong and Holy God!
Merciful and Holy Saviour!
Eternal God!
Let not dread our souls o'erwhelm
Of the dark and burning realm,
Kyrie Eleison!

In the midst of hell would Sin
Drive us to despair;
Whither shall we flee away?

Catherine Winkworth

Where is refuge, where?
With Thee, Lord Christ, alone!
For Thou hast shed Thy precious blood,
All our sins Thou makest good,
Holy Lord and God!
Strong and Holy God!
Merciful and Holy Saviour!
Eternal God!
Leave us not to fall in death
From the hope of Thy true Faith,
Kyrie Eleison!

II
Richter. 1713.
trans. by Catherine Winkworth, 1855

God whom I as love have known,
Thou hast sickness laid on me,
And these pains are sent of Thee,
Under which I burn and moan;
Let them burn away the sin,
That too oft hath checked the love
Wherewith Thou my heart wouldst move,
When Thy Spirit works within!

In my weakness be Thou strong,
Be Thou sweet when I am sad,
Let me still in Thee be glad,
Though my pains be keen and long.
All that plagues my body now,
All that wasteth me away,
Pressing on me night and day,
Love ordains, for Love art Thou!

Suffering is the work now sent,
Nothing I can do but lie
Suffering as the hours go by;
All my powers to this are bent.
Suffering is my gain; I bow
To my heavenly Father's will,
And receive it hushed and still;
Suffering is my worship now.

God! I take it from Thy hand
As a sign of love, I know
Thou wouldst perfect me through woe,
Till I pure before Thee stand.
All refreshment, all the food
Given me for the body's need,
Comes from Thee, who lov'st indeed,

Comes from Thee, for Thou art good.

Let my soul beneath her load
Faint not, through the o'erwearied flesh;
Let her hourly drink afresh
Love and peace from Thee, my God.
Let the body's pain and smart
Hinder not her flight to Thee,
Nor the calm Thou givest me;
Keep Thou up the sinking heart.

Grant me never to complain,
Make me to Thy will resigned,
With a quiet, humble mind,
Cheerful on my bed of pain.
In the flesh who suffers thus,
Shall be purified from sin,
And the soul renewed within;
Therefore pain is laid on us.

I commend to Thee my life,
And my body to the cross;
Never let me think it loss
That I thus am freed from strife--
Wholly Thine; my faith is sure
Whether life or death be mine,
I am safe if I am Thine;
For 'tis Love that makes me pure.

III
Anon.
trans. by Catherine Winkworth, 1855

When the last agony draws nigh,
My spirit sinks in bitter fear:
Courage! I conquer though I die,
For Christ with Death once wrestled here.
Thy strife, O Christ, with Death's dark power
Upholds me in this fearful hour.

In faith I hide myself in Thee,
I shall not perish in the strife;
I share Thy war, Thy victory,
And Death is swallowed up in Life.
Thy strife, O Christ, with Death of yore
Hath conquered, and I fear no more.

IV
Paul Eber. 1557.
trans. by Catherine Winkworth, 1855

Lord Jesus Christ, true Man and God,
Who borest anguish, scorn, the rod,
And diedst at last upon the tree,
To bring Thy Father's grace to me;
I pray Thee through that bitter woe,
With me, a sinner, mercy know.

When comes the hour of failing breath,
And I must wrestle, Lord, with death,
When from my sight all fades away,
And when my tongue no more can say,
And when mine ears no more can hear,
And when my heart is racked with fear;

When all my mind is darkened o'er,
And human help can do no more,
Then come, Lord Jesus, come with speed,
And help me in my hour of need,
Lead me from this dark vale beneath,
And shorten then the pangs of death.

All evil spirits drive away,
But let Thy Spirit with me stay
Until my soul the body leave;
Then in Thy hands my soul receive,
And let the earth my body keep,
Till the Last day shall break its sleep.

Joyful my resurrection be,
Thou in the Judgment plead for me,
And hide my sins, Lord, from Thy face,
And give me Life of Thy dear grace!
I trust Thee utterly, my Lord,
For Thou hast promised in Thy Word:

"In truth I tell you, who receives
My word, and keeps it, and believes,
Shall never fall God's wrath beneath,
Shall never taste eternal death;
Though here on earth, in time, he die,
He is not therefore lost; for I

Will come, and with a mighty hand
Will break away Death's strongest band,
And lift him hence that he shall be
For ever in my realm with Me,

For ever living there in bliss."
Ah let us not that glory miss!

Dear Lord, forgive us all our guilt,
Help us to wait until Thou wilt
That we depart; and let our faith
Be brave and conquer e'en in death,
Firm resting on Thy sacred Word,
Until we sleep in Thee, our Lord.

V
Ernst Moritz Arndt.
trans. by Catherine Winkworth, 1855

Go and dig my grave today!
Weary of my wanderings all,
Now from earth I pass away,
For the heavenly peace doth call;
Angel voices from above
Call me to their rest and love.

Go and dig my grave today!
Homeward doth my journey tend,
And I lay my staff away
Here where all things earthly end,
And I lay my weary head
In the only painless bed.

What is there I yet should do,
Lingering in this darksome vale?
Proud and mighty, fair to view,
Are our schemes, and yet they fail,
Like the sand before the wind,
That no power of man can bind.

Farewell, earth, then; I am glad
That in peace I now depart,
For thy very joys are sad,
And thy hopes deceive the heart;
Fleeting is thy beauty's gleam,
False and changing as a dream.

And to you a last good night,
Sun and moon, and stars so dear;
Farewell all your golden light;
I am travelling far from here,
To the splendours of that day
Where ye all must fade away.

Catherine Winkworth

Farewell, O ye much-loved friends!
Grief hath smote you as a sword,
But the Comforter descends
Unto them that love the Lord.
Weep not o'er a passing show,
To th' eternal world I go.

Weep not that I take my leave
Of the world; that I exchange
Errors that too closely cleave,
Shadows, empty ghosts that range
Through this world of nought and night,
For a land of truth and light.

Weep not, dearest to my heart,
For I find my Saviour near,
And I know that I have part
In the pains He suffered here,
When He shed His sacred blood
For the whole world's highest good.

Weep not, my Redeemer lives;
Heavenward springing from the dust,
Clear-eyed Hope her comfort gives;
Faith, Heaven's champion, bids us trust;
Love eternal whispers nigh,
"Child of God, fear not to die!"

VI
Sacer. 1665.
trans. by Catherine Winkworth, 1855

Then I have conquered; then at last
My course is run, good night!
I am well pleased that it is past;
A thousand times, good night!
But ye, dear friends, whom I must leave,
Look not thus anxiously;
O wherefore thus lament and grieve?
It standeth well with me.

Farewell, O anguish, pain, and fear,
Farewell, farewell for ever!
It glads my heart to leave you here,
Redeemed from you for ever!
Henceforth a life of joy I share,
In my Creator's hand;
None of the griefs can touch me there,
That haunt this lower land.

Who yet o'er earth in time must roam,
Not yet from error free,
Scarce lisp the language of our home,
The glad eternity.
Far better is a happy death,
Than worldly life, I trow;
The weakness once I sank beneath,
I nevermore shall know.

Lay on my coffin many a wreath,
For conquerors wreathed are seen;
And lo! my soul attains through death
The crown of evergreen,
That blooms in fadeless groves of heaven;
And this fair victor's crown,
That mighty Son of God hath given,
Who for my sake came down.

'Twas but a while that I was sent
To dwell among you here;
Now God resumes what He hath lent,
Oh grieve not o'er my bier;
But say, 'twas given at His command
Who takes it, He is just;
Our life and death are in His hand,
His servants can but trust.

That ye should see my grave, alas!
Shows we are frail indeed;
That it so soon should come to pass,
Our Father hath decreed,
And He your bitter grief shall still;
Think not too young am I,
For he who dies as God doth will,
Is old enough to die.

Farewell, thou dear, dear soul, farewell!
To those sweet pleasures go,
That we who mourning here must dwell,
Not yet, alas! can know.
Ah when shall that great day be come,
When these things fade away,
And Thou shalt bid us welcome home;
Would God it were today!

VII
Hiller. 1765.
trans. by Catherine Winkworth, 1855

My God, to Thee I now commend
My soul; for Thou, O Lord,
Dost live and love me without end,
And wilt perform Thy word.

To whom else should I make my plea,
That heavenly life be mine?
All souls, my God, belong to Thee,
My soul is also Thine.

Thou gav'st my spirit at my birth,
Take back what Thou hast given;
And with the Lord I served on earth,
Grant me to live in heaven.

Faith spreads her wings, she sees revealed
The shining walls above;
My spirit knows that she is sealed,
Redeemed from death by love.

Thou my Deliverer wast of yore,
From sin Thou mad'st me free,
Now, faithful God, dost Thou once more
In death deliver me.

Thou liv'st and lovest without end,
And dost perform Thy word;
My passing soul I now commend
To Thee, my God and Lord!

For the Burial of the Dead[4]
Blessed are the dead which die in the Lord.
   Rev. 14:13

For he that is dead is freed from sin; now if we be dead with Christ, we believe that we shall also live with Him.
   Rev. 14:13 [Rom. 6:7-8]

I
After Prudentius.
trans. by N. Hermann. 1560.
trans. by Catherine Winkworth, 1855

Now hush your cries, and shed no tear,
On such death none should look with fear;
He died a faithful Christian man,
And with his death true life began.

Coffin and grave we deck with care,
His body reverently we bear,
It is not dead but rests in God,
And softly sleeps beneath the sod.

It seems as all were over now,--
The heavy limbs, the soulless brow,--
Yet through these rigid limbs once more
A nobler life, ere long, shall pour.

These dead dry bones again shall feel
New warmth and vigour through them steal;
Reknit and living they shall soar
On high where Christ lives evermore.

This body, lying stiff and stark,
Shall rise unharmed from out the dark,
And swiftly mount up through the skies,
Even as the spirit heavenwards flies.

The buried grain of wheat must die,
Withered and worthless long must lie,
Yet springs to light all sweet and fair,
And proper fruits shall richly bear:

Even so this body made of dust,
To earth we once again entrust,
And painless it shall slumber here,
Until the Last Great Day appear.

God breathed into this house of clay
The spirit that hath passed away,
Christ gave the true courageous mind,
The noble heart, ye no more find.

Now earth has hid it from our eyes,
Till God shall bid it wake and rise,
Who ne'er the creature will forget,
On whom His image He hath set.

Ah, would that promised Day were here,
When Christ shall once again appear;
When He shall call, nor one be lost,
To endless life earth's buried host!

II
Allendorf. 1725.
trans. by Catherine Winkworth, 1855

Now rests her soul in Jesu's arms,
Her body in the grave sleeps well,
His heart her death-chilled heart re-warms,
And rest more deep than tongue can tell,
Her few brief hours of conflict passed,--
She finds with Christ, her Friend, at last;
She bathes in tranquil seas of peace,
God wipes away her tears, she feels
New life that all her languor heals,
The glory of the Lamb she sees.

She hath escaped all danger now,
Her pain and sighing all are fled;
The crown of joy is on her brow,
Eternal glories o'er her shed,
In golden robes, a queen, a bride,
She standeth at her Sovereign's side,
She sees His face unveiled and bright;
With joy and love He greets her soul,
She feels herself made inly whole,
A lesser light amid His light.

The child hath now its Father seen,
And feels what kindling love may be,
And knoweth what those words may mean,
"Himself, the Father, loveth thee."

A shoreless ocean, an abyss
Unfathomed, filled with good and bliss,
Now breaks on her enraptured sight;
She sees God's face, she learneth there
What this shall be, to be His heir,
Joint-heir with Christ, her Lord, in light.

The body rests, its labours over,
And sleeps till Christ shall bid it wake;
The dust that earth and darkness cover,
Then as a sun its tomb shall break.
Ah, with what joy it rises then
To meet the perfect soul again!
Redeemed from death, no more to sever,
At that great marriage feast shall they
With all the saints their homage pay,
And worship there the Lamb for ever.

We who yet wander through the waste,
In faith long after Thee on high;
While here the bread of tears we taste,
We think upon that home of joy,
Where we (who knows how soon?) shall meet
With all the saints at Jesu's feet,
And dwell with Him for ever there.
We shall see God; how deep the bliss
We know not yet that lies in this;
Lord Jesus, come, our hearts prepare!

III
Simon Dach. 1650.
trans. by Catherine Winkworth, 1855

Oh how blessed, faithful souls, are ye,
Who have passed through death; your God ye see,
Escaped at last
From all the sorrows that yet hold us fast!

Here as in a prison we are bound,
Care and fear, and terrors hem us round,
And all we know
It is but toil and grief of heart below.

While that ye are resting in your home,
Safe from pain, all misery o'ercome,
No grief or cross
Can mix with yonder joys to work you loss.

Catherine Winkworth

Christ doth wipe away your every tear,
Ye possess what we but long for here,
To you is sung
The song that ne'er through mortal ears hath rung.

Who is there that would not gladly die,
Changing earth for such a home on high,
Or who would stay
To toil amid these sorrows night and day!

Come, O Christ, release us from our post,
Lead us quickly hence to yonder host,
Whose battle won,
Now drink in joy and bliss from Thee our Sun.

Appendix I: Alternate Versions

[Psalm 46]
Luther. 1530.
trans. by Catherine Winkworth, 1855

God is our stronghold firm and sure,
Our trusty shield and weapon,
He shall deliver us, whate'er
Of ill to us may happen.
Our ancient Enemy
In earnest now is he,
Much craft and great might
Arm him for the fight,
On earth is not his fellow.

Our might is nought but weakness, soon
Should we the battle lose,
But for us fights the rightful Man,
Whom God Himself doth choose.
Asketh thou His name?
'Tis Jesus Christ, the same
Whom Lord of Hosts we call,
God only over all;
None from the field can drive Him.

What though the world were full of fiends,
That would us sheer devour!
We know we yet shall win the day,
We fear not all their power.
The Prince of this world still,
May struggle as he will,
He nothing can prevail,
A word shall make him quale,
For he is judged of heaven.

The word of God they cannot touch,
Yet have no thanks therefore,
God by His Spirit and His gifts,
Is with us in the war.
Then let them take our life,
Goods, honour, children, wife,
Though nought of these we save,
Small profit shall they have,
The kingdom ours abideth.

Catherine Winkworth

(This translation only appears in the first edition (1855) of Lyra Germanica, First Series: in all subsequent editions and, slightly altered, in The Chorale Book for England (No. 124) and again in Christian Singers of Germany (p. 110) the translation by W. Gaskell (1805 - 1884) was used - A sure stronghold our God is He. See Catherine Winkworth's footnote to the preface of second edition of Lyra Germanica, First Series in 1855).

Appendix II: Manuscript Addenda

[Note: this information, except for the book dedication and the text of the memorial tablet from Bristol Cathedral, was transcribed into this copy of the book by a grand-niece.]

Dedication
To Jane.
In remembrance of the 9th March 1861
from M. R. and A. M. R.

"M. R. & A. M. R" were Mary & Anna Maria Rawson, old school-friends of my great-aunt "Jane" - Jane Adair Atkins.

Mary Rawson married Dr. Burqhardt, an analytical chemist, & they went to live at Delamere, Meyes Lane, Alderley Edge, moving later to Fern Cottage, Macclesfield Road, Alderley Edge.

Biography

Catherine Winkworth was born in No. 20, Ely Place, Holborn, on the 13th September 1827. Her parents moved to Manchester while she was still very young as her father had a silk mill (at Macclesfield?); & Emily & Susanna were left with their grandmother Winkworth & her daughter, Eliza, who had lived with them in Ely Place, & they went to live at Islington where "Aunt Eliza" undertook their education. When they followed their parents to Manchester they had lessons from the Rev. William Gaskell, minister of Cross Street Chapel, Manchester, & husband of the well-known novelist. Later Catherine became very friendly with both Mr. & Mrs. Gaskell, & also knew the Martineaus, Miss Bronte, The Goldschmidts (Madame Goldschmidt was Jenny Lind before her marriage), Adelaide Procter, the Froudes, Mrs. Carlyle, etc., & it was through Mrs. Gaskell that she came to know Chevalier Bunson who started Catherine & Susanna in their literary work, & to whom Catherine dedicated her "Lyra Germanica."

"We were spending the spring & summer in a small cottage (Fern Cottage) which our father had taken at Alderley Edge, about fifteen miles from Manchester, a hill on the edge of Lord Stanley's Park, with a beautiful view over the Cheshire plain below. This led to his building a house there to which the family moved in June 1850 (Thornfield), but I remained behind in Manchester with my brother Stephen (removing to a little house in Nelson Street) until his marriage in 1861" (Susanna Winkworth) The home was then broken up, & Susanna returned to Alderley Edge.

"Tonight Mr. Heugh & Papa & some more gentlemen are to meat at Mr. Consterdine's to try & arrange plans for opening a Reading Room that shall be a counter-attraction to the public house," (a letter dated 1855, from Catherine to her sister Emily). Mr. Consterdine was the first vicar of the new church of St. Philip's Chorley, which was built in 1851-2. As soon as the vicar was settled at the new church Catherine untertook active work among the poor in the newly-established Sunday School & District Visiting Society. She was regarded with extreme affection by the poor, & long after she left the neighbourhood, she used to receive occasional letters from them. For nearly two years from January, 1848, Catherine had a long period of ill-health, & on this account went for several visits for her health. Most of the winter of 1859 was spent by her & her sister Susanna, at Malvern owing to illness; & catching a fresh chill Catherine had to stay on at Malvern till October, when they moved to Westen for a change of air. They arrived home at Alderley in time for Christmas. Again in 1861 Susanna had a serious illness which left her more or less of an invalid for some years. In spite of this ill-health, the sisters continued with their translations of German works & made several visits abroad. In February 1861, their father was tken ill; this was the beginning of his complete breakdown in health, which obliged him to give up his business, & ultimately led to the family leaving Thornfield, Alderley Edge, & settling at Clifton in October 1862. After the birth of Emily's youngest child, she was an invalid for many years & was the centre of all the family thoughts and plans. During the later part of her life Catherine's principal work was in connection with education, & in 1870 she was made secretary of the Committee to Promote the Higher Education of Women.

In 1878 Catherine went to Mornix near Geneva where she joined Annie Shaen to help her in the care of their nephew Frank Shaen, then an invalid. She arrived on June 17th, & on the 21st they proceeded to Monnetiex. On the morning of the 1st of July she was suddenly attacked by a pain at the heart, & in half-an-hour all was over. Susanna immediately started for Monnetiex, & in a few days Catherine was laid to rest in the corner of the churchyard set aside for Protestants. In her memory her friends raised a sum sufficient to endow two "Catherine Winkworth" scholarships for women at the Bristol University College, & also to erect a memorial tablet to her in Bristol Cathedral.

In Memory of CATHERINE WINKWORTH

Who, in her Lyra Germanica,
Rendering into English verse
The treasures of German sacred poetry,
Opened a new source of light, consolation, and strength
In many thousand homes.
Her works reveal a clear and harmonious intellect
A gift of true poetic insight and expression,
And the firm Christian faith
Which was the mainspring of a life
Rich in tender and affectionate ministration
And fruitful in various fields of active service.
Her loss is mourned by all who shared her labour,
And by the many friends whom death has bereft
Of her rare sympathy, her wise counsel,
Her bright companionship, and her unfailing help
In every time of need.
To commemorate her work, and to perpetuate
Her efforts for the better education of women,
A scholarship, bearing her name,
Has been founded in University College, Bristol
By friends who now dedicate this table
To her memory
Born in London, September 13th, 1827
Died in Monnetier, Savoy, July lst, 1878

"The child has now its Father seen,
And feels what kindling love may be,
And knoweth what those words may mean,
'Himself, the Father, loveth thee'."

Footnotes:

1. See also from Christian Singers of Germany, "A Morning Prayer"; "Make me Thine own and keep me Thine"; "O Light, who out of Light wast born"; "Morning Star in darksome night"; from Lyra Germanica, Second Series, Morning Prayer.

2. See also from Christian Singers of Germany, "Now God be with us, for the night is closing"; "Lord Jesu Christ, with us abide"; "At Evening;" from Lyra Germanica, Second Series, Evening Prayer; "True mirror of the Godhead! Perfect Light!"

3. See also from Christian Singers of Germany, "Sonnet"; "He Maketh all our Bed in our Sickness".

4 See also from Christian Singers of Germany, "I fall asleep in Jesu's arms", "Rise again! yes, rise again wilt thou"; from Lyra Germanica, Second Series, At the Burial of the Dead, and "Who puts his trust in God most just".

Book II: Lyra Germanica: Second Series: The Christian Life

Translated from the German By Catherine Winkworth
Originally Published by: London: Longman, Green, Longman, and Roberts, 1863.

PREFACE

Those who are best acquainted with the rich stores of German hymnology will feel the least surprise at the appearance of a second series of Translations from the same source. Many excellent and classical compositions were necessarily excluded from the plan of the former volume, which it was felt would still be no less acceptable to English Christians than those already translated. In this series therefore hymns are admitted of a more personal and individual character than in the former,--hymns adapted to particular circumstances or periods of life, and to peculiar states of feeling. At the same time many will be found of sufficiently comprehensive import to be suited for congregational singing and will be recognized by those familiar with the services of the German Church as constantly used there in public worship, especially those on pages 145, 146, 170, and 68. The first of these indeed holds in Germany, with its fine old tune, much the same place as the Old Hundredth with us. The second is remarkable as being, as far as we know, the only hymn of its author, a man of consideration and wealth in Frankfort. It was published without his name, and as it immediately became popular it was ascribed at first to Hugo Grötius, and other celebrated authors. The third is one of the well-known hymns of Joachim Neander, the most important hymnwriter of the German Reformed Church, whose productions are marked by great depth and tenderness of feeling.

Most of the hymns under the last two divisions of this series are popular in Protestant Germany in the truest sense of the word, to be found in the well-worn hymn-books of every cottage home, or heard as the village funeral passes on to the "court of peace." It will be observed that one of the hymns for the burial of the dead bears the name of Michael Weiss, and that some others are designated as belonging to the Bohemian Brethren. These are productions of that ancient Church which existed in Bohemia from the first introduction of Christianity into that country by two Greek monks of the eighth century. In the eleventh century it formed itself into a separate community, distinguished from the Roman Church in Bohemia, among other things, by the celebration of public worship, according to the native ritual and in the vulgar tongue. After suffering bitter persecutions under various Popes, in one of which John Huss was burnt in 1415, in 1453 its remaining members, including men of all classes, withdrew to a district assigned to them on the borders of Silesia and Moravia, where we find them, fifty years later, numbering about two hundred congregations, under the name of Brethren or United Brethren. But here too fierce persecutions followed them; their countrymen were incited from the pulpits to hunt them down like wild beasts; and in 1508, despairing of peace at home, they sent out four messengers to search whether anywhere a Christian people might be found, serving Christ truly, into whose communion they might ask admission. One of these brethren went to Russia, one to Greece, one to Bulgaria, and one to Palestine and Egypt; but they all returned unsuccessful, no such Christian people had they found. Two more were then sent to the Waldenses in France and Italy, but they too brought back nothing but admonitions to patience and steadfastness. The Brethren therefore remained in their own country, and occupied themselves in printing the Bible, no fewer than three editions having been publishied in Bohemian before the Reformation. The dawn of that great event filled them with joy, and in 1522 they sent two messengers to Luther to greet him and ask his advice, one of whom was Michael Weiss. In 1531 Michael Weiss published the hymns of the Bohemian Brethren translated into German, with the addition of several of his own. They passed through many editions, and some of them were introduced into Luther's hymn-book. They have great warmth of feeling, and directness of expression, (often with intricate metres,) and are marked by frequent pathetic reference to the troubles of this Church, and by a strong sense of the living union of Christians with each other and their Head. The subsequent settlement of the small remnant of this Church on Count Zinzendorf's estates in Saxony, and its rapid growth and spread into other countries are well known. That the spirit of Christian poetry still lives among them in modern times is proved by the names of Zinzendorf, Christian Gregor, L. von Hayn, Spangenberg, and Albertini.[1]

As the object of this work is chiefly devotional, the hymns are arranged according to their subjects, not in chronological order, and have been selected for their warmth of feeling and depth of Christian experience, rather than as specimens of a particular master or school. Still it is believed that these two series afford on the whole fair examples of most of the principal writers, not of course without omissions, since only about two hundred and twenty hymns are given from a literature containing several thousands. Of Luther none are given in this series, (unless the hymn known as "Queen Maria of Hungary's song" were written by him for that princess,) for those productions of his which no collection of German hymns could omit, had been already inserted in the previous volume, and there seemed the less necessity for introducing any of minor importance, as all his hymns are accessible to the English reader in the excellent translation of Mr. Massie.[2]

The writers perhaps the least fully represented, are Gellert, Klopstock, and others of the middle and latter half of the last century, whose productions constitute a large proportion of most of the collections made fifty or sixty years ago. But these hymns are, for the most part, either of a purely reflective or didactic character, or in very many instances are merely versions of more ancient hymns, smoothed down to a dead level of tame correctness in form, and robbed of their original fervour and strength. Gellert, however, appreciated the characteristic excellences of the ancient hymns, and his own have high merit, as lessons of Christian duty, or paraphrases of Scripture, expressed in simple, clear, and unaffected verse, sometimes with much true poetic feeling. Yet while they thus supplied a want among the hymns of his country,--which, during the last century especially, had lost that direct application to real life which makes a hymn speak to the hearts of all,--and have therefore become very popular in Germany, for the same reason they more nearly resemble what we already possess in our own language.

There is a very large school of hymn-writers springing up in Germany at the present day, whose works are distinguished by much thoughtful feeling and great fluency and sweetness of expression. In general, however, these hymns are suited rather to private reading, than congregational singing; the length of the lines, and the reflective tone of thought, deprive them of that strength and simple grandeur which many of the older hymns possess. Specimens are given here from Spitta, Puchta, Knapp, Hensel, and others; those hymns to which no dates are affixed being written by authors living or very recently deceased.

The hymns in this series have been chosen from various sources, most of them being such as would be found in any standard collection. The greater number, however, are taken from Bunsen's "Versuch eines allgemeinen Gesang und Gebet buchs," a collection distinguished above most others by its wide range of Christian experience and sympathy, and the poetic merit of the versions it gives. The short notices prefixed to some of these hymns are derived from the same source.

One or two verses have been omitted in several of the hymns, for in many instances even fine hymns are weakened by repetition, or disfigured by verses of decidedly inferior merit; this is especially the case with Paul Gerhardt, notwithstanding the remarkable beauty of his works. The original metre has been almost invariably maintained; in some hymns metres strange to our ears have been preserved with care for the sake of the fine chorales attached to them.

Alderley Edge,
May 19th, 1858

[*] From the frequent inquiries received from clergymen and others for tunes adapted to these hymns, it has been arranged to bring out an edition of the work, containing the fine old German chorales to which they are sung in their own country by vast congregations. This edition, which will shortly be completed, is now in progress, under the superintendence of Professor Sterndale Bennett and Mr. Otto Goldschmidt, and will be adapted for use in choirs and families.

Feb. 15, 1859

PART I. AIDS OF THE CHURCH
   I. HOLY SEASONS.
   II. SERVICES.

HOLY SEASONS
   Advent
   Christmas
   Epiphany
   Passion Week
   Easter
   Ascension
   Whitsuntide
   Trinity

ADVENT
   1. Ye heavens, oh haste your dews to shed
   2. Arise, the kingdom is at hand
   3. Wherefore dost Thou longer tarry
   4. Thank God that towards eternity

I. The Dayspring from on High
Johann Franck. 1653.

Ye heavens, oh haste your dews to shed,
Ye clouds, rain gladness on our head,
Thou earth, behold the time of grace,
And blossom forth in righteousness!

O living Sun, with joy break forth,
And pierce the gloomy clefts of earth;
Behold, the mountains melt away
Like wax beneath Thine ardent ray!

O Life-dew of the Churches, come,
And bid this arid desert bloom!

The sorrows of Thy people see,
And take our human flesh on Thee.

Refresh the parch'd and drooping mind,
The broken limb in mercy bind,
Us sinners from our guilt release,

And fill us with Thy heavenly peace.

O wonder! night no more is night!
Comes then at last the long'd-for light?
Ah yes, Thou shinest, O true Sun,
In whom are God and man made one!

II. The Deliverer
Rist. 1651.

Arise, the kingdom is at hand,
The King is drawing nigh;
Arise with joy, O faithful band,
To meet the Lord most high!
Ye Christians, hasten forth,
With holy ardours greet your King,
And glad Hosannas to Him sing,
Nought else your love is worth.

Look up, ye drooping hearts, to-day!
The King is very near,
Oh cast your griefs and fears away,
For lo! your Help is here;
And comfort rich and sweet
In many a place for us is stored,
Where in His sacraments and word
Our Saviour we can meet.

Look up, ye souls weigh'd down with care!
The Sovereign is not far.
Look up, faint hearts, from your despair,
Behold the Morning Star!
The Lord is with us now,
Who shall the sinking spirit feed
With strength and comfort at its need,
To whom e'en Death shall bow.

Hope, O ye broken hearts, at last!
The King comes on in might,
He loved us in the ages past
When we sat wrapp'd in night;
Now are our sorrows o'er,
And fear and wrath to joy give place,
Since God hath made us in His grace
His children evermore.

O rich the gifts Thou bringest us,
Thyself made poor and weak;
O love beyond compare that thus

Can foes and sinners seek!
For this to Thee alone
We raise on high a gladsome voice,
And evermore with thanks rejoice
Before Thy glorious throne.

III. The Heart longing for the inner advent
Paul Gerhardt. 1653.

Wherefore dost Thou longer tarry,
Blessed of the Lord, afar?
Would it were Thy will to enter
To my heart, O Thou my Star,
Thou my Jesus, Fount of power,
Helper in the needful hour!
Sharpest wounds my heart is feeling,
Touch them, Saviour, with Thy healing!

For I shrink beneath the terrors
Of the law's tremendous sway;
All my countless crimes and errors
Stand before me night and day.
Oh the heavy, fearful load
Of the righteous wrath of God!
Oh the awful voice of thunder
Cleaving heart and soul asunder!

While the foe my soul is telling,
"There is grace no more for thee,
Thou must make thy endless dwelling
In the pains that torture me."
Yes, and keener still thy smart,
Conscience, in my anguished heart,
By thy venomed tooth tormented,
Long-past sins are sore repented.

Would I then, to soothe my sorrow,
And my pain awhile forget,
From the world a comfort borrow,
I but sink the deeper yet;
She hath comforts that but grieve,
Joys that stinging memories leave,
Helpers that my heart are breaking,
Friends that do but mock its aching.

All the world can give is cheating,
Strengthless all, and merely nought;
Have I greatness, it is fleeting;
Have I riches, are they aught
But a heap of glittering earth?
Pleasure? Little is it worth

When it brings no joy or laughter
That we shall not rue hereafter.

All delight, all consolation
Lies in Thee, Lord Jesus Christ,
Feed my soul with Thy salvation,
O Thou Bread of Life unpriced.
Blessed Light, within me glow,
Ere my heart breaks in its woe;
Oh refresh me and uphold me,
Jesus, come, let me behold Thee.

Joy, my soul, for He hath heard thee,
He will come and enter in;
Lo! He turns and draweth toward thee,
Let thy welcome-song begin;
Oh prepare thee for such guest,
Give thee wholly to thy rest,
With an open'd heart adore Him,
Pour thy griefs and fears before Him.

Thy misdeeds are thine no longer,
He hath cast them in the sea,
And the love of God shall conquer
All the strength of sin in thee.
Christ is victor in the field,
Mightiest wrong to Him must yield,
He with blessing will exalt thee
O'er whatever would assault thee.

What would seem to hurt or shame thee
Shall but work thy good at last;
Since that Christ hath deign'd to claim thee,
And His truth stands ever fast;
And if thine can but endure,
There is nought so fixed and sure,
As that thou shalt hymn His praises
In the happy heavenly places.

IV. The New Year

Composed on his journey to Gotha after his unjust expulsion from Erfurt; as we are told in the oration delivered at his grave, "in the full experience of the unspeakable consolations of the Holy Spirit."
A. H. Francke. 1691

Thank God that towards eternity
Another step is won!
Oh longing turns my heart to Thee
As Time flows flowly on,
Thou Fountain whence my life is born,
Whence those rich streams of grace are drawn
That through my being run!

I count the hours, the days, the years,
That stretch in tedious line,
Until, O Life, that hour appears,
When, at Thy touch divine,
Whate'er is mortal now in me
Shall be consumed for aye in Thee,
And deathless life be mine.

So glows Thy love within this frame,
That, touch'd with keenest fire,
My whole soul kindles in the flame
Of one intense desire,
To be in Thee, and Thou in me,
And e'en while yet on earth to be
Still pressing closer, nigher!

Oh that I soon might Thee behold!
I count the moments o'er;
Ah come, ere yet my heart grows cold
And cannot call Thee more!
Come in Thy glory, for Thy Bride
Hath girt her for the holy-tide,
And waiteth at the door.

And since Thy Spirit sheds abroad
The oil of grace in me,
And Thou art inly near me, Lord,
And I am lost in Thee,
So shines in me the Living Light,
And steadfast burns my lamp and bright,
To greet Thee joyously.

Come! is the voice, then, of Thy Bride,
She loudly prays Thee come!
With faithful heart she long hath cried,
Come quickly, Jesus, come!
Come, O my Bridegroom, Lamb of God,
Thou knowest I am Thine, dear Lord;
Come down and take me home.

Yet be the hour that none can tell
Left wholly to Thy choice,
Although I know Thou lov'st it well,
That I with heart and voice
Should bid Thee come, and from this day
Care but to meet Thee on Thy way,
And at Thy sight rejoice!

I joy that from Thy love divine
No power can part me now,
That I may dare to call Thee mine,
My Friend, my Lord, avow,
That I, O Prince of Life, shall be
Made wholly one in heaven with Thee;
My portion, Lord, art Thou!

And therefore do my thanks o'erflow,
That one more year is gone,
And of this Time, so poor, so slow,
Another step is won;
And with a heart that may not wait,
Toward yonder distant golden gate
I journey gladly on.

And when the wearied hands grow weak,
And wearied knees give way,
To sinking faith, oh quickly speak,
And make Thine arm my stay;
That so my heart drink in new strength,
And I speed on, nor feel the length
Nor steepness of the way.

Then on, my soul, with fearless faith,
Let nought thy terror move;
Nor aught that earthly pleasure saith
E'er tempt thy steps to rove;
If slow thy course seem o'er the waste,
Mount upwards with the eagles' haste,
On wings of tireless love.

Catherine Winkworth

O Jesus, all my soul hath flown
Already up to Thee,
For Thou, in whom is love alone,
Hast wholly conquer'd me.
Farewell, ye phantoms, day and year,
Eternity is round me here,
Since, Lord, I live in Thee.

CHRISTMAS
1. All my heart this night rejoices
2. Thou fairest Child Divine
3. O blessed Jesus! This

I. A Song of Joy at Dawn
Paul Gerhardt. 1651

All my heart this night rejoices,
As I hear,
Far and near,
Sweetest angel voices;
"Christ is born," their choirs are singing,
Till the air
Everywhere
Now with joy is ringing.

For it dawns,--the promised morrow
Of His birth
Who the earth
Rescues from her sorrow.
God to wear our form descendeth,
Of His grace
To our race
Here His Son He lendeth:

Yea, so truly for us careth,
That His Son
All we've done
As our offering beareth;
As our Lamb who, dying for us,
Bears our load,
And to God
Doth in peace restore us.

Hark! a voice from yonder manger,
Soft and sweet,
Doth entreat,
"Flee from woe and danger;
Brethren come, from all doth grieve you
You are freed,
All you need
I will surely give you."

Catherine Winkworth

Come then, let us hasten yonder;
Here let all,
Great and small,
Kneel in awe and wonder.
Love Him who with love is yearning;
Hail the Star
That from far
Bright with hope is burning!

Ye who pine in weary sadness,
Weep no more,
For the door
Now is found of gladness.
Cling to Him, for He will guide you
Where no cross,
Pain or loss,
Can again betide you.

Hither come, ye heavy-hearted;
Who for sin
Deep within,
Long and sore have smarted;
For the poison'd wounds you're feeling
Help is near,
One is here
Mighty for their healing!

Hither come, ye poor and wretched;
Know His will
Is to fill
Every hand outstretched;
Here are riches without measure,
Here forget
All regret,
Fill your hearts with treasure.

Blessed Saviour, let me find Thee!
Keep Thou me
Close to Thee,
Cast me not behind Thee!
Life of life, my heart Thou stillest,
Calm I rest
On Thy breast,
All this void Thou fillest.

Thee, dear Lord, with heed I'll cherish,
Live to Thee,
And with Thee
Dying, shall not perish;
But shall dwell with Thee for ever,
Far on high,
In the joy
That can alter never.

II. We love Him for He first loved Us
Tersteegen. 1731.

Thou fairest Child Divine,
In yonder manger laid,
In whom is God Himself well pleased,
By whom were all things made,
On me art Thou bestow'd;
How can such wonders be!
The dearest that the Father hath
He gives me here in Thee!

I was a foe to God,
I fought in Satan's host,
I trifled all His grace away,
Alas! my soul was lost.
Yet God forgets my sin,
His heart, with pity moved,
He gives me, Heavenly Child, in Thee;
Lo! thus our God hath loved!

Once blind with sin and self,
Along the treacherous way,
That ends in ruin at the last,
I hasten'd far astray;
Then God sent down His Son
For with a love most deep,
Most undeserved, His heart still yearn'd
O'er me, poor wandering sheep!

God with His life of love
To me was far and strange,
My heart clung only to the world
Of sight and sense and change;
In Thee, Immanuel,
Are God and man made one;
In Thee my heart hath peace with God,
And union in the Son.

Oh ponder this, my soul,
Our God hath loved us thus,
That even His only dearest Son
He freely giveth us.
Thou precious gift of God,
The pledge and bond of love,

With thankful heart I kneel to take
This treasure from above.

I kneel beside Thy couch,
I press Thee to my heart,
For Thee I gladly all forsake
And from the creature part:
Thou priceless Pearl! lo, he
By whom Thou'rt loved and known,
Will give himself and all he hath
To win Thee for his own.

Oh come, Thou Blessed Child,
Thou Saviour of my soul,
For ever bound to Thee, my name
Among Thy host enrol.
Oh deign to take my heart,
And let Thy heart be mine,
That all my love flow out to Thee,
And lose itself in Thine.

III. God with Us
Paul Gerhardt.

O blessed Jesus! This
Thy lowly manger is
The Paradise where oft my soul would feed:
Here is the place, my Lord,
Where lies the Eternal Word
Clothed with our flesh, made like to us indeed.

For He whose mighty sway
The winds and seas obey,
Submits to serve, and stoops to those who sin;
The glorious Son of God
Doth bear the mortal load
Of earth and dust, like us and all our kin.

For thus, O Good Supreme,
Wilt Thou our flesh redeem,
And raise it to Thy throne o'er every height:
Eternal Strength, here Thou
To brotherhood dost bow
With transient things that pass like mists of night.

Thy glory and Thy joy
All woe and grief destroy;
Thou, Heavenly Treasure, dost all wealth restore!
Thou deep and living Well!
Thou great Immanuel
Dost conquer sin and death for evermore!

Then come, whoe'er thou art,
O poor desponding heart,
Take courage now, let this thy fears dispel,
That since His Son most dear
Thy God hath given thee here,
It cannot be but God doth love thee well.

How often dost thou think
That thou must surely sink,
That hope and comfort are no more for thee;
Come hither then and gaze
Upon this Infant's face,
And here the love of God incarnate see.

Ah now the blessed door
Stands open evermore
To all the joys of this world and the next:
This Babe will be our Friend,
And quickly make an end
Of all that faithful hearts long time hath vex'd.

Then, earth, we care no more
To seek thy richest store,
If but this treasure will be still our own;
And he who holds it fast,
Till all this life is past,
Our Lord will crown with joy before His throne.

EPIPHANY
    1. O King of Glory! David's Son!
    2. Christ, our true and only Light
    3. Is thy heart athirst to know
    4. Ever would I fain be reading

I. The King of Men
Behemb. 1606.

O King of Glory! David's Son!
Our Sovereign and our Friend!
In Heaven for ever stands Thy throne,
Thy kingdom hath no end:
Oh now to all men, far and near,
Lord, make it known, we pray.
That as in heaven all creatures here
May know Thee and obey.

The Eastern sages gladly bring
Their tribute-gifts to Thee;
They witness that Thou art their King,
And humbly bow the knee;
To Thee the Morning Star doth lead,
To Thee th' inspired Word,
We hail Thee, Saviour in our need,
We worship Thee, the Lord.

Ah look on me with pitying grace,
Though weak and poor I be,
Within Thy kingdom grant a place
Secure and blest to me.
Oh rescue me from all my woes,
And shield me with Thine arm
From Sin and Death, the mighty foes
That daily seek our harm.

And bid Thy Word, the fairest Star,
Within us clearly shine;
Keep sin and all false doctrine far,
Since Thou hast claim'd us Thine:
Let us Thy name aright confess,
And with Thy Christendom,
Our King and Saviour own and bless
Through all the world to come.

II. The Light of the World
J. Heermann. 1630.

Christ, our true and only Light,
Illumine those who sit in night,
Let those afar now hear Thy voice,
And in Thy fold with us rejoice.

Fill with the radiance of Thy grace
The souls now lost in error's maze,
And all whom in their secret minds
Some dark delusion hurts and blinds.

And all who else have stray'd from Thee,
Oh gently seek! Thy healing be
To every wounded conscience given,
And let them also share Thy heaven.

Oh make the deaf to hear Thy word,
And teach the dumb to speak, dear Lord,
Who dare not yet the faith avow,
Though secretly they hold it now.

Shine on the darken'd and the cold,
Recal the wanderers from Thy fold,
Unite those now who walk apart,
Confirm the weak and doubting heart.

So they with us may evermore
Such grace with wondering thanks adore,
And endless praise to Thee be given
By all Thy Church in earth and heaven.

III. Forsaking all for the True Light
Laurentius Laurenti. 1700.

Is thy heart athirst to know
That the King of heaven and earth
Deigns to dwell with man below,
Yea, hath stoop'd to mortal birth?
Search the Word with ceaseless care
Till thou find this treasure there.

With the sages from afar
Journey on o'er sea and land,
Till thou see the Morning Star
O'er thy heart unchanging stand,
Then shalt thou behold His face
Full of mercy, truth and grace.

For if Christ be born within,
Soon that likeness shall appear
Which the heart had lost through sin,
God's own image fair and clear,
And the soul serene and bright
Mirrors back His heavenly light.

Jesus, let me seek for nought
But that Thou shouldst dwell in me;
Let this only fill my thought,
How I may grow liker Thee,
Through this earthly care and strife,
Through the calm eternal life.

With the wise who know Thee right,
Though the world accounts them fools,
I will praise Thee day and night,
I will order by Thy rules
All my life, that it may be
Fill'd with praise and love of Thee.

IV. Christ our Example
Luise Hensel.

Ever would I fain be reading
In the ancient holy Book,
Of my Saviour's gentle pleading,
Truth in every word and look.

How when children came He bless'd them,
Suffer'd no man to reprove,
Took them in His arms, and press'd them
To His heart with words of love.

How to all the sick and tearful
Help was ever gladly shown;
How He sought the poor and fearful,
Call'd them brothers and His own.

How no contrite soul e'er sought Him,
And was bidden to depart,
How with gentle words He taught him,
Took the death from out his heart.

Still I read the ancient story,
And my joy is ever new,
How for us He left His glory,
How He still is kind and true.

How the flock He gently leadeth
Whom His Father gave Him here;
How His arms He widely spreadeth
To His heart to draw us near.

Let me kneel, my Lord, before Thee,
Let my heart in tears o'erflow,
Melted by Thy love adore Thee,
Blest in Thee 'mid joy or woe!

PASSION WEEK
1. Whenever again thou sinkest
2. Oh, world! behold upon the tree
3. Jesus, the merit
4. Him on yonder cross I love
5. Thou sore-oppress'd
6. Lord Jesus, who, our souls to save

I. In the Garden
W. Hey. 1828.

Whenever again thou sinkest,
My heart, beneath thy load,
Or from the battle shrinkest,
And murmurest at thy God;
Then I will lead thee hither,
To watch thy Saviour's prayer,
And learn from His endurance
How thou shouldst also bear.

Oh come, wouldst thou be like Him,
Thy Lord Divine, and mark
What sharpest sorrows strike Him,
What anguish deep and dark,--
That earnest cry to spare Him,
The trial scarce begun?
Yet still he saith: "My Father,
Thy will, not mine, be done."

Oh wherefore doth His spirit
Such bitter conflict know?
What sins, what crimes could merit
Such deep and awful woe?
So pure are not the heavens,
So clear the noonday sun,
And yet He saith: "My Father,
Thy will, not mine, be done!"

Oh mark that night of sorrow,
That agony of prayer;
No friend can watch till morrow
His grief to soothe and share;
Oh where shall He find comfort?
With God, with God alone;

And still He saith: "My Father,
Thy will, not mine, be done!"

Hath life for Him no gladness,
No joy the light of day?
Can He then feel no sadness,
When heart and hope give way?
That cup of mortal anguish
One bitter cry hath won,
That it might pass: "Yet, Father,
Thy will, not mine, be done!"

And who the cup prepared Him,
And who the poison gave?
'Twas one He loved ensnared Him,
'Twas those He came to save.
Oh sharpest pain, to suffer
Betray'd and mock'd--alone;
Yet still He saith: "My Father,
Thy will, not mine, be done!"

But what is joy or living,
What treachery or death,
When all His work, His striving,
Seems hanging on His breath?
Oh can it stand without Him,
That work but just begun?
Yet still He saith: "My Father,
Thy will, not mine, be done!"

He speaks; no more He shrinketh,
Himself He offers up,
He sees it all, yet drinketh
For us that bitter cup,
He goes to meet the traitor,
The cross He will not shun,--
He saith: "I come, My Father,
Thy will, not mine, be done!"

My Saviour, I will never
Forget Thy word of grace,
But still repeat it ever,
Through good and evil days;
And looking up to Heaven,
Till all my race is run,
I'll humbly say: "My Father,
Thy will, not mine, be done!"

II. At the Foot of the Cross
Paul Gerhardt. 1659.

Oh, world! behold upon the tree
Thy Life is hanging now for thee,
Thy Saviour yields His dying breath;
The mighty Prince of glory now
For thee doth unresisting bow
To cruel stripes, to scorn and death.

Draw near, O world, and mark Him well;
Behold the drops of blood that tell
How sore His conflict with the foe:
And hark! how from that noble heart,
Sigh after sigh doth slowly start
From depths of yet unfathom'd woe.

Alas! my Saviour, who could dare
Bid Thee such bitter anguish bear,
What evil heart entreat Thee thus?
For Thou art good, hast wronged none,
As we and ours too oft have done,
Thou hast not sinn'd, dear Lord, like us.

I and my sins, that number more
Than yonder sands upon the shore,
Have brought to pass this agony;
'Tis I have caused the floods of woe
That now Thy dying soul o'erflow,
And those sad hearts that watch by Thee.

'Tis I to whom these pains belong,
'Tis I should suffer for my wrong,
Bound hand and foot in heavy chains;
The scourge, the fetters, whatsoe'er
Thou bearest, 'tis my soul should bear,
For she hath well deserved such pains.

Yet Thou dost even for my sake
On Thee in love the burdens take
That weigh'd my spirit to the ground:
Yes, Thou art made a curse for me,
That I might yet be blest through Thee;
My healing in Thy wounds is found.

To save me from the monster's power,
From Death that all things would devour,
Thyself into his jaws dost leap;
My death Thou takest thus away,
And buriest in Thy grave for aye,
O love most strangely true and deep!

From henceforth there is nought of mine
But I would seek to make it Thine,
Since all myself to Thee I owe.
Whate'er my utmost powers can do,
To Thee to render service true,
Here at Thy feet I lay it low.

Ah! little have I, Lord, to give,
So poor, so base the life I live,
But yet, till soul and body part,
This one thing I will do for Thee--
The woe, the death endured for me,
I'll cherish in my inmost heart.

Thy cross shall be before my sight,
My hope, my joy, by day and night,
Whate'er I do, where'er I rove;
And, gazing, I will gather thence
The form of spotless innocence,
The seal of faultless truth and love.

And from Thy sorrows will I learn
How fiercely doth God's anger burn,
How terribly His thunders roll,
How sorely this our loving God
Can smite with His avenging rod,
How deep His floods o'erwhelm the soul.

And I will study to adorn
My heart with meekness under scorn,
With gentle patience in distress,
With faithful love, that yearning cleaves
To those o'er whom to death it grieves,
Whose sins its very soul oppress.

When evil tongues with stinging blame
Would cast dishonour on my name,
I'll curb the passions that upstart;
And take injustice patiently,
And pardon, as Thou pardon'st me,
With an ungrudging generous heart.

Catherine Winkworth

And I will nail me to Thy cross,
And learn to count all things but dross
Wherein the flesh doth pleasure take;
Whate'er is hateful in Thine eyes,
With all the strength that in me lies,
Will I cast from me and forsake.

Thy heavy groans, Thy bitter sighs,
The tears that from Thy dying eyes
Were shed when Thou wast sore oppress'd,
Shall be with me, when at the last
Myself on Thee I wholly cast,
And enter with Thee into rest.

III. Our Heritage
Anon.

Jesus, the merit
Of all that Thou hast borne
Maketh me inherit
The crown that hath no thorn!

Ah then, teach me duly
To worship at Thy cross,
Owning inly, truly,
The Love that bore our loss.

There to sin, oh let me
From henceforth daily die;
Nor in death forget me,
Then grant me life on high.

Catherine Winkworth

IV. Our Requital
Greding. Born 1676.

Him on yonder cross I love,
Nought beside on earth count dear!
May He mine for ever prove,
Who is now so inly near!
Here I stand: whate'er may come,
Days of sunshine or of gloom,
From this word I will not move;
Him upon the cross I love!

'Tis not hidden from my heart,
What true love must often bring;
Want and grief have sorest smart,
Care and scorn can sharply sting;
Nay, but if Thy will were such,
Bitterest death were not too much!
Dark though here my course may prove:
Him upon the cross I love!

Rather sorrows such as these,
Rather love's acutest pain,
Than without Him days of ease,
Riches false and honours vain.
Count me strange, when I am true,
What He hates I will not do;
Sneers no more my heart can move;
Him upon the cross I love!

Know ye whence my strength is drawn,
Fearless thus the fight to wage?
Why my heart can laugh to scorn
Fleshly weakness, Satan's rage?
'Tis, I know the love of Christ,
Mighty is that love unpriced!
What can grieve me, what can move?
Him upon the cross I love!

Once the eyes that now are dim,
Shall discern the changeless love
That hath led us home to Him,

That hath crown'd us far above:
Would to God that all below
What that love is now might know,
And their hearts this word approve:
Him upon the cross I love!

V. At the Sepulchre
Viktor Strauss.

Thou sore-oppress'd,
The Sabbath rest
In yon still grave art keeping!
All Thy labour now is done,
Past is all Thy weeping!

The strife is o'er,
Nought hurts Thee more,
The heart at last hath slumber'd,
That in conflict sore for us
Bore our sins unnumber'd.

Thou awful tomb,
Once fill'd with gloom!
How blessed and how holy
Art thou now, since in the grave
Slept the Saviour lowly!

How calm and blest
The dead now rest
Who in the Lord departed!
All their works do follow them,
Yea, they sleep glad-hearted.

O lead us Thou,
To rest e'en now,
With all who sorely anguish'd
'Neath the burden of their sins,
Long in woe have languish'd.

O Blessed Rock!
Soon grant Thy flock
To see Thy Sabbath morning!
Strife and pain will all be past
When that day is dawning.

VI. Our Rest
George Werner. 1638.

Lord Jesus, who, our souls to save,
Didst rest and slumber in the grave,
Now grant us all in Thee to rest,
And here to live as seems Thee best.

Give us the strength, the dauntless faith,
That Thou hast purchased with Thy death,
And lead us to that glorious place,
Where we shall see the Father's face.

O Lamb of God! who once wast slain,
We thank Thee for that bitter pain!
Let us partake Thy death that we
May enter into life with Thee!

EASTER

    1. Christ the Lord is risen again!
    2. Ere yet the dawn hath fill'd the skies
    3. I say to all men, far and near
    4. O risen Lord! O conquering King!
    5. Sad with longing, sick with fears

I. The Song of Triumph

Bohemian Brethren.

Christ the Lord is risen again!
Christ hath broken every chain!
Hark, the angels shout for joy,
Singing evermore on high,
Hallelujah.

He who gave for us His life,
Who for us endured the strife,
Is our Paschal Lamb to-day!
We too sing for joy, and say:
Hallelujah.

He who bore all pain and loss
Comfortless upon the cross,
Lives in glory now on high,
Pleads for us and hears our cry:
Hallelujah.

He whose path no records tell,
Who descended into hell,
Who the strong man arm'd hath bound,
Now in highest heaven is crown'd:
Hallelujah.

He who slumber'd in the grave,
Is exalted now to save;
Now through Christendom it rings
That the Lamb is King of kings!
Hallelujah.

Now He bids us tell abroad,
How the lost may be restored,
How the penitent forgiven,
How we too may enter heaven.

Hallelujah.

Thou our Paschal Lamb indeed,
Christ, to-day Thy people feed;
Take our sins and guilt away,
That we all may sing for aye,
Hallelujah.

II. Christ our Champion
J. Heermann. 1630.

Ere yet the dawn hath fill'd the skies
Behold my Saviour Christ arise,
He chaseth from us sin and night,
And brings us joy and life and light.
Hallelujah.

O stronger Thou than Death and Hell,
Where is the foe Thou canst not quell?
What heavy stone Thou canst not roll
From off the prison'd anguish'd soul?
Hallelujah.

If Jesus lives, can I be sad?
I know He loves me, and am glad;
Though all the world were dead to me,
Enough, O Christ, if I have Thee!
Hallelujah.

He feeds me, comforts and defends,
And when I die His angel sends
To bear me whither He is gone,
For of His own He loseth none.
Hallelujah.

No more to fear or grief I bow,
God and the angels love me now;
The joys prepared for me to-day
Drive fear and mourning far away;
Hallelujah.

Strong Champion! For this comfort see
The whole world brings her thanks to Thee;
And once we too shall raise above
More sweet and loud the song we love;
Hallelujah.

III. The Whole World restored in Christ
Novalis. 1772-1801.

I say to all men, far and near,
That He is risen again;
That He is with us now and here,
And ever shall remain.

And what I say, let each this morn
Go tell it to his friend,
That soon in every place shall dawn
His kingdom without end.

Now first to souls who thus awake
Seems earth a fatherland,
A new and endless life they take
With rapture from His hand.

The fears of death and of the grave
Are whelm'd beneath the sea,
And every heart now light and brave
May face the things to be.

The way of darkness that He trod
To Heaven at last shall come,
And he who hearkens to His word
Shall reach His Father's home.

Now let the mourner grieve no more,
Though his beloved sleep,
A happier meeting shall restore
Their light to eyes that weep.

Now every heart each noble deed
With new resolve may dare,
A glorious harvest shall the seed
In brighter regions bear.

He lives, His presence hath not ceased,
Though foes and fears be rife;
And thus we hail in Easter's feast
A world renew'd to life!

IV. The Resurrection from the Death of Sin
J. H. Böhmer. 1706.

O risen Lord! O conquering King!
O Life of all that live!
To-day that peace of Easter bring
Which only Thou canst give!
Once death, our foe,
Had laid Thee low,
Now hast Thou rent his bonds in twain,
For Thou art risen who once wast slain!

The power of Thy great majesty
Bursts rocks and tombs away,
Thy victory raises us with Thee
Into the glorious day;
Now Satan's might
And Death's dark night
Have lost their power this blessed morn
And we to higher life are born.

Oh that our hearts might inly know
Thy victory over death,
And gazing on Thy conflict glow
With eager dauntless faith;
Thy quenchless light,
Thy glorious might
Still comfortless and lonely leave
The soul that cannot yet believe.

Then break through our hard hearts Thy way,
O Jesus, conquering King!
Kindle the lamp of faith to-day,
Teach our faint hearts to sing
For joy at length,
That in Thy strength
We too may rise whom sin had slain,
And Thy eternal rest attain.

And when our tears for sin o'erflow,
Do Thou in love draw near,
The precious gift of peace bestow,
Shine on us bright and clear;
That so may we,
O Christ, from Thee

Drink in the life that cannot die,
And keep true Easter feasts on high.

Yes, let us truly know within
Thy rising from the dead,
And quit the grave of death and sin,
And keep that gift, our Head,
That Thou didst leave
For all who cleave
To Thee through all this earthly strife--
So shall we enter into life.

V. The Walk to Emmaus
L. E. S. Müller.

Sad with longing, sick with fears,
Toward Emmaus slowly go
Two whose eyes are dim with tears,
And their hearts oppress'd with wo,
Of their ruin'd hopes they talk;
Yet while thus they sadly walk,
Jesus is not far away,
And their fears shall soon allay.

Ah! and still how many a heart
Onward toils in silent grief,
Mourning o'er its woes apart,
Hopeless now of all relief;
Oft it seeks to walk alone,
But to weep its fill unknown;
Yet my Jesus cometh now,
Asking, wherefore weepest thou?

Many a time I've felt indeed
That He leaves me ne'er alone,
In the hour of utmost need
Then Himself He maketh known;
When in sorrow I consume
As though He no more could come,
Lo! I find Him more than near,
Quickly with His help He's here.

Truest Friend, who canst not fail me,
Evermore abide with me;
When the world would most assail me,
Then Thy presence let me see;
When its heaviest thunders roll,
Shelter Thou my trembling soul,
Come and in my spirit rest,
I will do what seems Thee best.

When I dread some coming ill,
Lord, then bid me think of this,
That my Saviour loves me still,
And that I am surely His:
More of Thy word let me learn,
Till my heart within me burn,

Fill'd with love, and in Thy Light
Learn to know her Lord aright.

Comfort those who, fill'd with gloom,
Lonely on their journey go,
Or within their silent room
Cry to Thee from depths of wo;
When they leave the world apart,
There to weep out all their heart,
Let them hear Thy whisper mild;
Wherefore dost thou mourn, my child?

When life's day hath fleeted by,
When the night of death is near,
When in vain the darken'd eye
Seeks some stay, some helper here:
Then Thy followers' prayer fulfil,
Then abide Thou with us still,
Till Thou give us peace and rest
Stay, O stay, Thou noble guest!

ASCENSION
1. To-day our Lord went up on high
2. Since Christ is gone to heaven, His home
3. Conquering Prince and Lord of glory!
4. My Jesus, if the seraphim

I. The Way opened
J. Zwick. 1538.

To-day our Lord went up on high,
And so our songs we raise;
To Him with strong desire we cry
To keep us in His grace,
For we poor sinners here beneath
Are dwelling still 'mid woe and death,
All hope in Him we place.
Hallelujah.

Thank God that now the way is made!
The cherub-guarded door,
Through Him on whom our help was laid,
Stands open evermore;
Who knoweth this is glad at heart,
And swift prepares him to depart
Where Christ is gone before.
Hallelujah.

Our heavenward course begins when we
Have found our Father, God,
And join us to His sons, and flee
The paths that once we trod;
For He looks down, and they look up,
They feel His love, they live in hope,
Until they meet their Lord.
Hallelujah.

Then all the depths of joy that lie
In this day we shall know,
When we are made like Him on high,
Whom we confess below,
When bathed in life's eternal flood
We dwell with Him, the highest Good:
God grant us this to know!
Hallelujah.

II. Christ's Ascension the Ground of Ours
Josua Wegelin. 1636.

Since Christ is gone to heaven, His home
I too must one day share;
And in this hope I overcome
All anguish, all despair;
For where the Head is, well we know
The members He hath left below
In time He gathers there.

Since Christ hath reach'd His glorious throne
And mighty gifts are His,
My heart can rest in heaven alone,
On earth my Lord I miss,
I long to be with Him on high,
And heart and thoughts would hourly fly
Where now my treasure is.

From Thy ascension let such grace,
My Lord, be found in me,
That steadfast faith may guide my ways
Unfaltering up to Thee,
And at Thy voice I may depart
With joy to dwell where Thou, Lord, art;
Oh grant this prayer to me!

III. The Kingdom of Christ
Tersteegen. 1731.

Conquering Prince and Lord of glory!
Majesty enthroned in light!
All the heavens are bow'd before Thee,
Far beyond them spreads Thy might
Shall I fall not at Thy feet,
And my heart with rapture beat,
Now Thy glory is display'd,
Thine ere yet the worlds were made?

Far and wide, Thou heavenly Sun,
Now Thy brightness streams abroad,
And Heaven's host anew hath won
Light and gladness from its Lord;
Hark, how yon unnumber'd throng
Welcome Thee with joyous song:
See Thy children weak and few
Here would cry Hosanna too.

Of Thy cup shall I not drink,
Now Thy glories o'er me shine?
Shall my courage ever sink,
Now I know all power is Thine?
I will trust Thee, O my King,
And will fear no earthly thing,
Henceforth will I bow the knee
To no ruler, save to Thee.

Power and Spirit now o'erflow,
On me also be they pour'd,
Till Thy last and mightiest foe
Hath been made Thy footstool, Lord;
Yea, let earth's remotest end
To Thy righteous sceptre bend,
Make Thy way before Thee plain,
O'er all hearts and spirits reign.

Lo! Thy presence filleth now
All Thy Church in every place,
To my heart, oh enter Thou,
See it thirsteth for Thy grace;
Come, Thou King of glory, come,
Deign to make my heart Thy home,

There abide and rule alone,
As upon Thy heavenly throne!

Parting, dost Thou bring Thy life,
God and heaven, most inly near:
Let me rise o'er earthly strife,
As though still I saw Thee here,
And my heart transplanted hence,
Strange to earth and time and sense,
Dwell with Thee in heaven e'en now,
Where our only joy art Thou!

IV. The Throne of Grace
Wolfgang C. Dessler. 1692.

My Jesus, if the seraphim,
The burning host that near Thee stand,
Before Thy Majesty are dim,
And veil their face at Thy command;
How shall these mortal eyes of mine,
Now dark with evil's hateful night,
Endure to gaze upon the light
That aye surrounds that throne of Thine?

Yet grant the eye of faith, O Lord,
To pierce within the Holy Place,
For I am saved and Thou adored,
If I am quicken'd by Thy grace.
Behold, O King, before Thy throne
My soul in lowly love doth bend,
Oh show Thyself her gracious Friend,
And say, "I choose thee for mine own."

Have mercy, Lord of love, for long
My spirit for Thy mercy sighs,
My inmost soul hath found a tongue,
"Be merciful, O God," she cries!
I know Thou wilt not bid me go,
Thou canst not be ungracious, Lord,
To one for whom Thy blood was pour'd,
Whose guilt was cancell'd by Thy woe.

Here in Thy gracious hands I fall,
To Thee I cling with faith's embrace,
O righteous Sovereign, hear my call,
And turn, O turn, to me in grace!
For through Thy sorrows I am just,
And guilt no more in me is found,
Thus reconciled, my soul is bound
To Thee in endless love and trust.

And let Thy wisdom be my guide,
Nor take Thy light from me away,
Thy grace be ever at my side,
That from the path I may not stray
Which Thou dost love, but evermore
In steadfast faith my course fulfil,

And keep Thy word, and do Thy will,
Thy love within, Thy heaven before!

Reach down and arm me with Thy hand,
And strengthen me with inner might,
That I through faith may strive and stand
Though craft and force against me fight:
So shall the kingdom of Thy love
Be through me and within me spread,
That honours Thee, our glorious Head,
And crowneth us in realms above.

Yes, yes, to Thee my soul would cleave,
O choose it, Saviour, for Thy throne!
Couldst Thou in love to me once leave
The glory that was all Thine own,
So honour Thou my life and heart
That Thou mayst find a heaven in me,
And when this house decay'd shall be,
Then grant the heaven where now Thou art.

To Thee I rise in faith on high,
O bend Thou down in love to me!
Let nothing rob me of this joy,
That all my soul is fill'd with Thee;
As long as I have life and breath,
Thee will I honour, fear, and love,
And when this heart hath ceased to move,
Yet Love shall live and conquer death.

WHITSUNTIDE
1. Holy Spirit, once again
2. Sweetest joy the soul can know
3. The Church of Christ that He hath hallow'd here
4. Hark, the Church proclaims her honour
5. Spread, oh spread, thou mighty Word

I. The Work of the Holy Spirit
Anon.

Holy Spirit, once again
Come, Thou true Eternal God!
Nor Thy power descend in vain,
Make us ever Thine abode;
So shall Spirit, joy, and light
Dwell in us, where all was night.

Pour into our heart and mind
Wisdom, counsel, truth, and love;
That we be to nought inclined,
Save what Thou mayst well approve;
Let Thy knowledge spread and grow,
Working error's overthrow.

Guide us, Lord, from day to day,
Keep us in the paths of grace,
Clear all hindrances away
That might foil us in the race;
When we stumble hear our call,
Work repentance for our fall.

Witness in our hearts that God
Counts us children through His Son,
That our Father's gentle rod
Smites us for our good alone,
So when tried, perplex'd, distrest,
In His love we still may rest.

Quicken us to seek His face
Freely, with a trusting heart,
In our prayers O breathe Thy grace,
Go with us when we depart,
So shall our requests be heard,
And our faith to joy be stirr'd.

And whene'er a yearning strong
Presses out the bitter cry,
"Ah my God, how long, how long?"
Then O let me find Thee nigh,
And Thy words of healing balm
Bring me courage, patience, calm.

Spirit Thou of strength and power,
Thou new Spirit God hath given,
Aid us in temptation's hour,
Train and perfect us for heaven,
Arm us in the battle-field,
Leave us never there to yield.

Lord, preserve us in the faith,
Suffer nought to drive us thence,
Neither Satan, scorn, nor death,
Be our God and our defence,
Though the flesh resist Thy will,
Let Thy word be stronger still.

And at last when we must die,
Oh assure the sinking heart
Of the glorious realm on high
Where Thou healest every smart,
Of the joys unspeakable
Where our God would have us dwell.

II. The Spirit of Wisdom, Love, and Joy
Paul Gerhardt. 1653.

Sweetest joy the soul can know,
Fairest Light was ever shed,
Who alike in joy or woe,
Leavest none unvisited;
Spirit of the Highest God,
Lord from whom is life bestow'd,
Who upholdest everything,
Hear me, hear me, while I sing!

For the noblest gift Thou art
That a soul e'er sought or won,
Have I wish'd Thee to my heart,
Then my wishing all is done;
Ah then yield Thee, nor refuse
Here to dwell, for Thou didst choose
This my heart, from e'en its birth,
For Thy temple here on earth.

Thou art shed like gentlest showers
From the Father and the Son,
Bringest to this earth of ours
Purest blessing from their throne;
Suffer then, O noble Guest,
That rich gift by Thee possest,
Which Thou givest at Thy will
All my soul and flesh to fill.

Thou art wise, before Thee stand
Hidden things unveil'd to Thee,
Countest up the grains of sand,
Fathomest the deepest sea,
And Thou knowest well how blind,
Dark and crooked is my mind;
Give me wisdom, in Thy light
Let me please my God aright.

Thou art holy, enterest in
Where pure hearts Thy coming wait,
But Thou fleest shame and sin,
Craft and falsehood Thou dost hate;
Wash me then, O Well of grace,
Every stain and spot efface,

Let me flee what Thou dost flee,
Grant me what Thou lov'st to see.

Thou art loving, hatest strife,
As a lamb of patient mood,
Calm through all our restless life,
E'en to sinners kind and good;
Grant me too this noble mind,
To be calm and true and kind,
Loving every friend or foe,
Grieving none whom Thou dost know.

Well contented is my heart,
If but Thou reject me not;
If but Thou wilt ne'er depart,
I am blest whate'er my lot;
Thine for ever make me now,
And to Thee, my Lord, I vow
Here and yonder to employ
Every power for Thee with joy.

Be my help when danger's nigh,
When I sink hold Thou me up,
Be my life when I must die,
In the grave be Thou my hope;
Bring me when I rise again
To the land that knows no pain,
Where Thy followers from Thy stream
Drink for ever joys supreme.

Catherine Winkworth

III. The unity of the Spirit
A. G. Spangenberg. 1747.

The Church of Christ that He hath hallow'd here
To be His house, is scatter'd far and near,
In North and South and East and West abroad,
And yet in earth and heaven, through Christ her Lord,
The Church is one.

One member knoweth not another here,
And yet their fellowship is true and near,
One is their Saviour, and their Father one,
One Spirit rules them, and among them none
Lives to himself.

They live to Him who bought them with His blood,
Baptized them with His Spirit pure and good,
And in true faith and ever-burning love
Their hearts and hope ascend to seek above
The eternal Good.

O Spirit of the Lord, all life is Thine,
Now fill Thy Church with life and power divine,
That many children may be born to Thee
And spread Thy knowledge like the boundless sea,
To God's great praise.

IV. The Strength of the Church
S. Preiswerk.

Hark, the Church proclaims her honour
And her strength is only this:
God hath laid His choice upon her,
And the work she doth is His.

He His Church hath firmly founded,
He will guard what He began;
We, by sin and foes surrounded,
Build her bulwarks as we can.

Frail and fleeting are our powers,
Short our days, our foresight dim,
And we own the choice not ours,
We were chosen first by Him.

Onward then! for nought despairing,
Calm we follow at His word,
Thus through joy and sorrow bearing
Faithful witness to our Lord.

Though we here must strive with weakness,
Though in tears we often bend,
What His might began in meekness
Shall achieve a glorious end.

V. The Diffusion of the Gospel
Bahnmaier.

Spread, oh spread, thou mighty Word,
Spread the kingdom of the Lord,
Wheresoe'er His breath has given
Life to beings meant for heaven.

Tell them how the Father's will
Made the world, and keeps it still,
How He sent His Son to save
All who help and comfort crave.

Tell of our Redeemer's love,
Who for ever doth remove
By His holy sacrifice,
All the guilt that on us lies.

Tell them of the Spirit given
Now, to guide us up to heaven,
Strong and holy, just and true,
Working both to will and do.

Word of Life! most pure and strong,
Lo! for Thee the nations long;
Spread, till from its dreary night
All the world awakes to light.

Up, the ripening fields ye see,
Mighty shall the harvest be,
But the reapers still are few,
Great the work they have to do.

Lord of harvest, let there be
Joy and strength to work for Thee,
Till the nations far and near
See Thy Light, and learn Thy fear.

TRINITY
1. Thee Fount of blessing we adore!
2. O Father-eye, that hath so truly watch'd
3. True mirror of the Godhead! Perfect Light!

I. A Morning Hymn
Tersteegen. 1731.

Thee Fount of blessing we adore!
Lo! we unlock our lips before
Thy Godhead's deep of holiness,
Oh deign to hear us now and bless.

The Lord, the Maker, with us dwell,
In soul and body shield us well,
And guard us with His sleepless might
From every ill by day and night!

The Lord, the Saviour, Light Divine,
Now cause His face on us to shine,
That seeing Him, with perfect faith
We trust His love for life and death!

The Lord, the Comforter, be near,
Imprint His image deeply here,
From bonds of sin and dread release,
And give us His unchanging peace!

O Triune God! Thou vast abyss!
Thou ever-flowing Fount of bliss,
Flow through us, heart and soul and will
With endless praise and blessing fill!

II. Our Father, Redeemer, Guide
Spitta.

O Father-eye, that hath so truly watch'd,
O Father-hand, that hath so gently led,
O Father-heart, that by my prayer is touch'd,
That loved me first when I was cold and dead:
Still do Thou lead me on with faithful care
The narrow path to heaven where I would go,
And train me for the life that waits me there,
Alike through love and loss, through weal and wo.

O my Redeemer, who for me wast slain,
Who bringest me forgiveness and release,
Whose death has ransom'd me to God again,
That now my heart can rest in perfect peace;
Still more and more do Thou my soul redeem,
From every bondage set me wholly free,
Though Evil oft the mightiest power may seem,
Still make me more than conqueror, Lord, in Thee.

O Holy Spirit, who with gentlest breath
Dost teach to pray, dost comfort or reprove,
Who givest us all joy and hope and faith,
Through whom we live at peace with God in love;
Still do Thou shed Thine influence abroad,
Let me the Father's image ever wear,
Make me a holy temple of my God,
Where dwells for ever calm adoring prayer!

III. An Evening Hymn
J. Franck. 1653.

True mirror of the Godhead! Perfect Light!
Thou Three in One, whose never-slumbering might
Enfolds the world within its sheltering wings,
And holds in being all created things!

We praise Thee with the earliest morning ray,
We praise Thee with the parting beam of day;
All things that live and move, by sea and land,
For ever ready at Thy service stand.

Exhaustless Treasure! Being limitless!
What gaze hath ever pierced Thy deep abyss?
Deep Fount of Life! Light inaccessible!
How great Thy power, O God, what tongue can tell?

Thy Christendom is singing night and day,
"Glory to Him, the mighty God, for aye,
By Whom, through Whom, in Whom all beings are!"
Grant us to echo on this song afar!

Thy Name is great, Thy kingdom in us dwell,
Thy will constrain and feed and guide us well;
Spare us, redeem us in the evil hour,
For Thine the glory, Thine the rule, the power.

Services

    Morning Prayer
    Evening Prayer
    Baptism
    The Holy Communion
    For Travellers
    At the Burial of the Dead

MORNING PRAYER.

1. Light of light enlighten me
2. Blessed Jesus, at Thy word
3. Once more the day-light shines abroad
4. When anguish'd and perplexed, with many a sigh and tear
5. O Thou Most Highest! Guardian of mankind!
6. As a bird in meadows fair
7. The golden morn flames up the Eastern sky

See also from Lyra Germanica: The Christian Year, Morning Hymns.

I. For The Sabbath Morning

B. Schmolck. 1731.

Light of light enlighten me
Now anew the day is dawning;
Sun of grace, the shadows flee,
Brighten Thou my Sabbath morning,
With Thy joyous sunshine blest
Happy is my day of rest!

Fount of all our joy and peace,
To Thy living waters lead me,
Thou from earth my soul release
And with grace and mercy feed me;
Bless Thy word that it may prove
Rich in fruits that Thou dost love.

Kindle Thou the sacrifice
That upon my lips is lying;
Clear the shadows from mine eyes
That, from every error flying,
No strange fire may in me glow
That Thine altar doth not know.

Let me with my heart to-day,
Holy, Holy, Holy, singing,
Rapt awhile from earth away,
All my soul to Thee upspringing,
Have a foretaste inly given
How they worship Thee in Heaven.

Rest in me and I in Thee,
Build a Paradise within me;
Oh reveal Thyself to me,
Blessèd Love, who diedst to win me;
Fed from Thine exhaustless urn
Pure and bright my lamp shall burn.

Hence all care, all vanity,
For the day to God is holy;
Come Thou glorious Majesty
Deign to fill this temple lowly,
Nought to-day my soul shall move
Simply resting in Thy love.

Catherine Winkworth

II. Before Public Worship
T. Clausnitzer. 1671.

Blessed Jesus, at Thy word
We are gather'd all to hear Thee;
Let our hearts and souls be stirr'd
Now to seek and love and fear Thee;
By Thy teachings sweet and holy
Drawn from earth to love Thee solely.

All our knowledge, sense, and sight
Lie in deepest darkness shrouded,
Till Thy Spirit breaks our night
With the beams of truth unclouded;
Thou alone to God canst win us,
Thou must work all good within us.

Glorious Lord, Thyself impart!
Light of light from God proceeding,
Open Thou our ears and heart,
Help us by Thy Spirit's pleading,
Hear the cry Thy people raises,
Hear, and bless our prayers and praises!

III. In Time of War and Persecution
Bohemian Brethren.

Once more the day-light shines abroad,
O Brethren let us praise the Lord,
Whose grace and mercy thus have kept
The nightly watch while we have slept.

To Him let us together pray
With all our heart and soul to-day,
That He would keep us in His love,
And all our guilt and sin remove.

Eternal God! Almighty Friend,
Whose deep compassions have no end,
Whose never-failing strength and might
Have kept us safely through the night:

Now send us from Thy heavenly throne
Thy grace and help through Christ Thy Son,
That with Thy strength our hearts may glow,
And fear nor man nor ghostly foe.

Ah Lord God! hear us we implore!
Be Thou our Guardian evermore,
Our mighty Champion and our shield
That goeth with us to the field.

We offer up ourselves to Thee,
That heart and word and deed may be
In all things guided by Thy mind,
And in Thine eyes acceptance find.

Thus, Lord, we bring through Christ Thy Son
Our morning offering to Thy throne;
Now be Thy precious gift outpour'd,
And help us for Thine honour, Lord!

IV. In Time of Distress
WRITTEN DURING THE THIRTY YEARS' WAR.
M. A. von Löwenstern.

When anguish'd and perplexed, with many a sigh and tear
I lift mine eyes up to the hills, and pour out all my woe,
Thou bendest down Thine ear,
And never from Thy face, dear Lord, uncomforted I go.

My help and my defence come, faithful God, from Thee,
By Whom the heavens were fixed, and earth's foundations laid;
Man cannot succour me,
Before Thy throne alone I find my refuge and my aid.

Thou watchest that my foot should neither slip nor stray,
Thou guidest me Thyself through all my dark and troubled course,
Thou pointest me the way
Amid the snares of sin and death, and this world's craft and force.

Guardian of Israel! Thou dost slumber not, nor sleep,
Thine eye is open day and night, still watching over those
Who true allegiance keep
To Jesus' banner of the Cross, and bravely meet His foes.

And when Thou bidd'st me leave this world of strife and pain,
Grant me in Thee a steadfast hope, and gentle quick release,
Knowing we rise again
To dwell where death and war are not, in endless joy and peace.

V. The Christian's Morning Sacrifice
Joachim Neander. 1679.

O Thou Most Highest! Guardian of mankind!
Supreme exhaustless Good Thou art!
To Thee I offer soul and heart:
Praise Him all creatures with your strength and mind,
For He is kind!

Yes, Lord, 'tis of Thy power alone to-day
That still I draw my living breath,
Thy grace preserves me still from death,
O Father-heart, reject me not, but stay
With me to-day.

O Israel's God, I bring Thee now my will,
That would be Thine whate'er it cost,
Love Thy good gifts, yet love Thee most;
This is my prayer while yet the morn is still,
Take Thou my will.

O Fount of grace, in love be Thou my guide,
Thine eye look down on me in power,
Whate'er I do or am each hour
Prepare me for th' eternal life, abide
Still at my side.

The soul and body Thou dost hold in life,
Be ever ready in Thy fear
To fight for truth and justice here,
And trusting Thee to meet the final strife,
For Thou art Life.

Bless all my works and ways, my light increase,
Order my doings for the best,
In all my toil be Thou my rest,
Until at last I lay me down in peace
That ne'er shall cease.

VI. A Morning Song of Gladness
Anon. About 1580

As a bird in meadows fair
Or in lonely forest sings,
Till it fills the summer air
And the greenwood sweetly rings,
So my heart to Thee would raise,
O my God, its song of praise,
That the gloom of night is o'er
And I see the sun once more.

If Thou, Sun of Love, arise,
All my heart with joy is stirr'd,
And to greet Thee upward flies
Gladsome as yon little bird.
Shine Thou in me clear and bright
Till I learn to praise Thee right;
Guide me in the narrow way,
Let me ne'er in darkness stray.

Bless to-day whate'er I do,
Bless whate'er I have and love;
From the paths of virtue true
Let me never, never rove;
By Thy Spirit strengthen me
In the faith that leads to Thee,
Then an heir of life on high
Fearless I may live and die.

VII. A Morning Prayer
Spitta

The golden morn flames up the Eastern sky,
And what dark night had hid from every eye
All-piercing day-light summons clear to view:
And all the forests, vale or plain or hill,
That slept in mist enshrouded, dark and still,
In gladsome light are glittering now anew.

Shine in my heart, and bring me joy and light,
Sun of my darken'd soul, dispel its night,
And shed in it the truthful day abroad;
And all the many gloomy folds lay bare
Within this heart, that fain would learn to wear
The pure and glorious likeness of its Lord.

Glad with Thy light, and glowing with Thy love,
So let me ever speak and think and move
As fits a soul new-touch'd with life from Heaven,
That seeks but so to order all her course
As most to show the glory of that Source
By whom alone her strength, her life are given.

I ask not, take away this weight of care;
No, for that love I pray that all can bear,
And for the faith that whatsoe'er befall
Must needs be good, and for my profit prove,
Since from my Father's heart most rich in love,
And from His bounteous hands it cometh all.

I ask not that my course be calm and still;
No, here too, Lord, be done Thy holy will;
I ask but for a quiet childlike heart;
Though thronging cares and restless toil be mine,
Yet may my heart remain for ever Thine,
Draw it from earth, and fix it where Thou art.

I ask Thee not to finish soon the strife,
The toil, the trouble of this earthly life;
No, be my peace amid its grief and pain;
I pray not, grant me now Thy realm on high;
No, ere I die let me to evil die,
And through Thy cross my sins be wholly slain.

Catherine Winkworth

True Morning Sun of all my life, I pray
That not in vain Thou shine on me to-day,
Be Thou my light when all around is gloom;
Thy brightness, hope, and courage on me shed,
That I may joy to see when life is fled
The setting sun that brings the pilgrim home.

EVENING PRAYER
    1. The night is come, wherein at last we rest
    2. Sink not yet, my soul, to slumber
    3. Lord, a whole long day of pain
    4. Now darkness over all is spread
    5. Abide among us with Thy grace
See also Lyra Germanica: The Christian Year, Evening Hymns.

I. Trust in God
Bohemian Brethren.

The night is come, wherein at last we rest,
God order this and all things for the best!
Beneath His blessing fearless we may lie
Since He is nigh.

Drive evil thoughts and spirits far away,
Master, watch o'er us till the dawning day,
Body and soul alike from harm defend,
Thine angel send.

Let holy prayers and thoughts our latest be,
Let us awake with joy, still close to Thee,
In all serve Thee, in every deed and thought
Thy praise be sought.

Give to the sick as Thy beloved sleep,
And help the captive, comfort those who weep,
Care for the widows' and the orphans' woe,
Keep far our foe.

For we have none on whom for help to call,
Save Thee, O God in heaven, who car'st for all,
And wilt forsake them never, day or night,
Who love Thee right.

Father, Thy Name be praised, Thy Kingdom come,
Thy will be wrought as in our heavenly home,
Keep us in life, forgive our sins, deliver
Us now and ever! Amen.

II. An Evening Thanksgiving
J. Rist. 1642.

Sink not yet, my soul, to slumber,
Wake, my heart, go forth and tell
All the mercies without number
That this by-gone day befell;
Tell how God hath kept afar
All things that against me war,
Hath upheld me and defended,
And His grace my soul befriended.

Father merciful and holy,
Thee to-night I praise and bless,
Who to labour true and lowly
Grantest ever meet success;
Many a sin and many a woe,
Many a fierce and subtle foe
Hast Thou check'd that once alarm'd me,
So that nought to-day has harm'd me.

Yes, our wisdom vainly ponders,
Fathoms not Thy loving thought;
Never tongue can tell the wonders
That each day for us are wrought;
Thou hast guided me to-day
That no ill hath cross'd my way,
There is neither bound nor measure
In Thy love's o'erflowing treasure.

Now the light, that nature gladdens,
And the pomp of day is gone,
And my heart is tired and saddens
As the gloomy night comes on;
Ah then, with Thy changeless light
Warm and cheer my heart to-night,
As the shadows round me gather
Keep me close to Thee, my Father.

Of Thy grace I pray Thee pardon
All my sins, and heal their smart;
Sore and heavy is their burden,
Sharp their sting within my heart;
And my foe lays many a snare
But to tempt me to despair,

Only Thou, dear Lord, canst save me,
Let him not prevail to have me.

Have I e'er from Thee departed,
Now I seek Thy face again,
And Thy Son, the loving-hearted,
Made our peace through bitter pain.
Yes, far greater than our sin,
Though it still be strong within,
Is the Love that fails us never,
Mercy that endures for ever.

Brightness of the eternal city!
Light of every faithful soul!
Safe beneath Thy sheltering pity
Let the tempests past me roll;
Now it darkens far and near,
Still, my God, still be Thou here;
Thou canst comfort, and Thou only,
When the night is long and lonely.

When the twilight now hath vanish'd,
Send Thy blessing on my sleep,
Every sin and terror banish'd,
Let my rest be calm and deep.
Soul and body, mind and health,
Wife and children, house and wealth,
Friend and foe, the sick, the stranger,
Keep Thou safe from harm and danger.

Keep me safe till morn is breaking,
Nightly terrors drive Thou hence,
Let not sickness keep me waking;
Sudden death and pestilence,
Fire and water, noise of war,
Keep Thou from my house afar;
Let me die not unrepented,
That my soul be not tormented.

O Thou mighty God, now hearken
To the prayer Thy child hath made;
Jesus, while the night-hours darken
Be Thou still my hope, my aid;
Holy Ghost, on Thee I call,
Friend and Comforter of all,
Hear my earnest prayer, oh hear me!
Lord, Thou hearest, Thou art near me.

III. In Sickness
Heinrich Puchta.

Lord, a whole long day of pain
Now at last is o'er!
Ah how much we can sustain
I have felt once more;
Felt how frail are all our powers,
And how weak our trust;
If Thou help not, these dark hours
Crush us to the dust.

Could I face the coming night
If Thou wert not near?
Nay, without Thy love and might
I must sink with fear:
Round me falls the evening gloom,
Sights and sounds all cease,
But within this narrow room
Night will bring no peace.

Other weary eyes may close,
All things seek their sleep,
Hither comes no soft repose,
I must wake and weep.
Come then, Jesus, o'er me bend,
Give me strength to cope
With my pains, and gently send
Thoughts of peace and hope.

Draw my weary heart away
From this gloom and strife,
And these fever pains allay
With the dew of life;
Thou canst calm the troubled mind,
Thou its dread canst still,
Teach me to be all resign'd
To my Father's will.

Then if I must wake and weep
All the long night through,
Thou the watch with me wilt keep,
Friend and Guardian true;
In the darkness Thou wilt speak
Lovingly with me,

Though my heart may vainly seek
Words to breathe to Thee.

Wheresoe'er my couch is made
In Thy hands I lie,
And to Thee alone for aid
Turns my restless eye;
Let my prayer grow weary never,
Strengthen Thou th' oppress'd,
In Thy shadow, Lord, for ever
Let me gently rest.

IV. For a Wakeful Night
Pastor Josephsen.

Now darkness over all is spread,
No sounds the stillness break,
Ah when shall these sad hours be fled,
Am I alone awake?

Ah no, I do not wake alone,
Alone I do not sleep,
Around me ever watcheth One
Who wakes with those that weep.

On earth it is so dark and drear,
With Him so calm and bright,
The stars in solemn radiance clear
Shine there through all our night.

'Tis when the lights of earth are gone
The heavenly glories shine;
When other comfort I have none,
Thy comfort, Lord, is mine.

Be still, my throbbing heart, be still,
Cast off thy weary load,
And make His holy will thy will,
And rest upon thy God.

How many a time the night hath come,
Yet still return'd the day;
How many a time thy cross, thy gloom,
Ere now hath pass'd away.

And these dark hours of anxious pain
That now oppress thee sore,
I know will vanish soon again,
Then I shall fear no more:

For when the night hath lasted long,
We know the morn is near,
And when the trial's sharp and strong
Our Help shall soon appear.

V. At the Close of the Sabbath
Stegmann. 1630.

Abide among us with Thy grace,
Lord Jesus, evermore,
Nor let us e'er to sin give place,
Nor grieve Him we adore.

Abide among us with Thy word,
Redeemer whom we love,
Thy help and mercy here afford,
And life with Thee above.

Abide among us with Thy ray,
O Light that lighten'st all,
And let Thy truth preserve our way,
Nor suffer us to fall.

Abide with us to bless us still,
O bounteous Lord of peace;
With grace and power our spirits fill,
Our faith and love increase.

Abide among us as our shield,
O Captain of Thy host;
That to the world we may not yield,
Nor e'er forsake our post.

Abide with us in faithful love,
Our God and Saviour be,
Thy help at need, oh let us prove,
And keep us true to Thee.

Catherine Winkworth

BAPTISM
1. Blessed Jesus, here we stand
2. O Father-heart, who hast created all
3. Thy parents' arms now yield thee
4. Seeing I am Jesus' lamb
5. I am baptized into Thy name

I. The Command
Schmolck. 1672-1737.

Blessed Jesus, here we stand,
Met to do as Thou hast spoken,
And this child at Thy command
Now we bring to Thee, in token
That to Christ it here is given,
For of such shall be His Heaven.

Yes, Thy warning voice is plain,
And we fain would keep it duly,
"He who is not born again,
Heart and life renewing truly,
Born of water and the Spirit,
Will My kingdom ne'er inherit."

Therefore hasten we to Thee,
Take the pledge we bring, oh take it!
Let us here Thy glory see,
And in tender pity make it
Now Thy child, and leave it never,
Thine on earth, and Thine for ever.

Turn the darkness into light,
To Thy grace receive and save it;
Heal the serpent's venom'd bite,
In the font where now we lave it;
Let Thy Spirit pure and lowly
Banish thought or taint unholy.

Make it, Head, Thy member now,
Sheperd, take Thy lamb, and feed it,
Prince of Peace, its peace be Thou,
Way of life, to Heaven oh lead it,
Vine, this branch may nothing sever,
Grafted firm in Thee for ever.

Now upon Thy heart it lies,
What our hearts so dearly treasure,
Heavenward lead our burden'd sighs,
Pour Thy blessing without measure,
Write the name we now have given,
Write it in the book of Heaven.

II. The Name
A. Knapp.

O Father-heart, who hast created all
In wisest love, we pray
Look on this babe, who at Thy gracious call
Is entering on life's way,
Bend o'er it now with blessing fraught,
And make Thou something out of nought,
O Father-heart!

O Son of God, who diedst for us, behold
We bring our child to Thee,
Thou tender Shepherd take it to Thy fold,
Thine own for aye to be;
Defend it through this earthly strife,
And lead it on the path of life,
O Son of God!

O Holy Ghost, who broodest o'er the wave,
Descend upon this child;
Give it undying life, its spirit lave
With waters undefiled;
Grant it while yet a babe to be
A child of God, a home for Thee,
O Holy Ghost!

O Triune God, what Thou command'st is done,
We speak, but Thine the might:
This child hath scarce yet seen our earthly sun,
Yet pour on it Thy light,
In faith and hope, in joy and love,
Thou Sun of all below, above,
O Triune God!

III. The Blessing
Albert Knapp.

Thy parents' arms now yield thee,
With love all glowing warm,
To Him who best can shield thee,
To that Eternal Arm
That all the heavens upholdeth,
And bids the dead arise,
That tender babes enfoldeth
And leads them toward the skies.

Wash'd in the blood that gushes
From out His wounded heart,
Wrapp'd in the peace that hushes
All earthly grief and smart,
Go forth upon thy journey,
Grow up in strength and age,
And seek with joy and wisdom
Thy holy heritage.

Oh sweet will sound the voices
That hail thee from above,
Where heaven's bright host rejoices
Before the Eternal Love;
"Now canst thou wander never,
Now past is all thy strife,
Oh bless the hour for ever
That call'd thee into life."

IV. For a Christian Child
Luise H. von Hayn. 1724-1782.

Seeing I am Jesus' lamb,
Ever glad at heart I am
O'er my Shepherd kind and good,
Who provides me daily food,
And His lamb by name doth call,
For He knows and loves us all.

Guided by His gentle staff
Where the sunny pastures laugh,
I go in and out and feed,
Lacking nothing that I need;
When I thirst my feet He brings
To the fresh and living springs.

Must I not rejoice for this?
He is mine, and I am His,
And when these bright days are past,
Safely in His arms at last
He will bear me home to heaven;
Ah what joy hath Jesus given!

V. Renewal of the Vow
Rambach. 1720.

I am baptized into Thy name,
O Father, Son, and Holy Ghost!
Among Thy seed a place I claim,
Among Thy consecrated host;
Buried with Christ, and dead to sin,
Thy Spirit now shall live within.

My loving Father, here dost Thou
Proclaim me as Thy child and heir;
Thou faithful Saviour bidd'st me now
The fruit of all Thy sorrows share;
Thou Holy Ghost wilt comfort me
When darkest clouds around I see.

And I have promised fear and love,
And to obey Thee, Lord, alone;
I felt Thy Spirit in me move,
And dared to pledge myself Thine own,
Renouncing sin to keep the faith,
And war with evil to the death.

My faithful God, upon Thy side
This covenant standeth fast for aye,
If I tranfgress through fear or pride,
O cast me therefore not away,
If I have sore my soul defiled,
Yet still forgive, restore Thy child.

I bring Thee here, my God, anew
Of all I am or have the whole,
Quicken my life, and make me true,
Take full possession of my soul,
Let nought within me, nought I own,
Serve any will but Thine alone.

Hence Prince of darkness, hence my foe!
Another Lord hath purchased me!
My conscience tells of sin, yet know,
Baptized in Christ I fear not thee!
Away vain World, Sin, leave me now,
I turn from you; God hears my vow.

Catherine Winkworth

And never let me waver more,
O Father, Son, and Holy Ghost,
Till at Thy will this life is o'er
Still keep me in Thy faithful host,
So unto Thee I live and die
And praise Thee evermore on high.

THE HOLY COMMUNION
1. Lord Jesus Christ, my faithful Shepherd, hear!
2. Deck thyself, my soul, with gladness
3. O Love, who formedst me to wear
4. Now take my heart and all that is in me
5. Jesus whom Thy Church doth own
6. Oh how could I forget Him
7. O Living Bread from Heaven

I. The Preparation
Johann Heermann. 1630.

Lord Jesus Christ, my faithful Shepherd, hear!
Feed me with Thy grace, draw inly near.
By Thee redeem'd, in Thee alone I live,
All I need 'tis Thou canst give:
Kyrie Eleison!
Ah Lord, Thy timid sheep now feed
With joy upon Thy heavenly mead,
Lead us to the crystal river
Whence our life is flowing ever:
Kyrie Eleison!

For Thou art calling all the toil-oppress'd,
All the weary to Thy rest;
The pardon of their sins is here bestow'd,
Thou dost free them from their load:
Kyrie Eleison!
Ah come, Thyself put forth Thine hand,
Unbind this heavy iron band,
Set me from my sorrows free,
Give me strength to follow Thee:
Kyrie Eleison!

Thou fain wouldst heart and soul to Thee incline,
Take me from myself and make me Thine;
Thou art the Vine and I the branch, oh grant
I may grow in Thee a living plant:
Kyrie Eleison!
For nought but sins I find in me,
Yet are they done away in Thee;
Mine are anguish, fear, unrest,
But in Thee, Lord, I am blest:
Kyrie Eleison!

II. The Thanksgiving
J. Frank. 1653.

Deck thyself, my soul, with gladness,
Leave the gloomy haunts of sadness,
Come into the daylight's splendour,
There with joy thy praises render
Unto Him, whose boundless grace
Grants thee at His feast a place;
He whom all the heavens obey
Deigns to dwell in thee to-day.

Hasten as a bride to meet Him,
And with loving reverence greet Him,
Who with words of life immortal
Now is knocking at thy portal;
Haste to make for Him a way,
Cast thee at His feet, and say:
Since, O Lord, Thou com'st to me,
Never will I turn from Thee.

Ah how hungers all my spirit,
For the love I do not merit!
Ah how oft with sighs fast thronging
For this food have I been longing!
How have thirsted in the strife
For this draught, O Prince of Life,
Wish'd, O Friend of man, to be
Ever one with God through Thee!

Here I sink before Thee lowly,
Fill'd with joy most deep and holy,
As with trembling awe and wonder
On Thy mighty works I ponder;
On this banquet's mystery,
On the depths we cannot see;
Far beyond all mortal sight
Lie the secrets of Thy might.

Sun, who all my life dost brighten,
Light, who dost my soul enlighten,
Joy, the sweetest man e'er knoweth,
Fount, whence all my being floweth,
Here I fall before Thy feet,
Grant me worthily to eat

Of this blessed heavenly food,
To Thy praise, and to my good.

Jesus, Bread of Life from Heaven,
Never be Thou vainly given,
Nor I to my hurt invited;
Be Thy love with love requited;
Let me learn its depths indeed,
While on Thee my soul doth feed;
Let me here so richly blest,
Be hereafter too Thy guest.

Catherine Winkworth

III. The exceeding great Love of our Master and only Saviour Jesus Christ
Angelus. 1657.

O Love, who formedst me to wear
The image of Thy Godhead here;
Who soughtest me with tender care
Through all my wanderings wild and drear;
O Love, I give myself to Thee,
Thine ever, only Thine to be.

O Love, who ere life's earliest dawn
On me Thy choice hast gently laid;
O Love, who here as man wast born
And like to us in all things made;
O Love, I give myself to Thee,
Thine ever, only Thine to be.

O Love, who once in Time wast slain,
Pierced through and through with bitter woe;
O Love, who wrestling thus didst gain
That we eternal joy might know;
O Love, I give myself to Thee,
Thine ever, only Thine to be.

O Love, of whom is truth and light,
The Word and Spirit, life and power,
Whose heart was bared to them that smite,
To shield us in our trial hour;
O Love, I give myself to Thee,
Thine ever, only Thine to be.

O Love, who thus hast bound me fast,
Beneath that gentle yoke of Thine;
Love, who hast conquer'd me at last
And rapt away this heart of mine;
O Love, I give myself to Thee,
Thine ever, only Thine to be.

Love, who lovest me for aye,
Who for my soul dost ever plead;
O Love, who didst my ransom pay,
Whose power sufficeth in my stead,
O Love, I give myself to Thee,

Thine ever, only Thine to be.

O Love, who once shalt bid me rise
From out this dying life of ours;
O Love, who once above yon skies
Shalt set me in the fadeless bowers:
O Love, I give myself to Thee,
Thine ever, only Thine to be.

IV. The Christian Sacrifice
Angelus. 1657.

Now take my heart and all that is in me,
My Lord beloved, take it from me to Thee;
I would have Thine
This soul and flesh of mine
Would order thought and word and deed
As Thy most holy will shall lead.

Thou feedest me with heavenly bread and wine,
Thou pourest through me streams of life divine;
Oh noble Face,
So sweet, so full of grace,
I ponder as Thy cross I see,
How best to give myself to Thee.

Behold, through all the eternal ages, still
My heart shall choose and love Thy holy will;
Wouldst Thou my death,
I die to Thee in faith;
Wouldst Thou that I should longer live,
To Thee the choice I wholly give.

But Thou must also deign to be my own,
To dwell in me, to make my heart Thy throne,
My God indeed,
My Help in time of need,
My Head from whom no power can sever,
The Bridegroom of my soul for ever!

V. The Christian Fellowship
Tersteegen. 1731.

Jesus whom Thy Church doth own
As her Head and King alone,
Bless me Thy poor member too;
And Thy Spirit's influence give
That to Thee henceforth I live,
Daily Thou my strength renew.

Let Thy living Spirit flow
Through Thy members all below,
With its warmth and power divine;
Scatter'd far apart they dwell,
Yet in every land, full well,
Lord, Thou knowest who is Thine.

Those who serve Thee I would serve,
Never from their union swerve,
Here I cry before Thy face:
"Zion, God give thee good speed,
Christ thy footsteps ever lead,
Make thee steadfast in His ways!"

Save her from the world her foe,
Satan quickly overthrow,
Cast him down beneath her feet;
Through the Spirit slay within
Love of ease, the world, and sin,
Let her find Thee only sweet.

Those o'er whom Thy billows roll
Strengthen Thou to leave their soul
In Thy hands, for Thou art Love;
Make them through their bitter pain
Pure from pride and sinful stain,
Fix their hopes and hearts above.

Unto all Thyself impart,
Fashion'd after Thine own heart
Make Thy children like to Thee;
Humble, pure, and calm, and still,
Loving, single as Thy will,
And as Thou wouldst have them be.

Catherine Winkworth

And from those I love, I pray,
Turn not, Lord, Thy face away,
Hear me while for them I plead;
Be Thou their Eternal Friend,
Unto each due blessing send,
For Thou knowest all they need.

Ah Lord, at this gracious hour
Visit all their souls with power;
Let Thy gladness in them shine;
Draw them with Thy love away
From vain pleasures of a day,
Make them wholly ever Thine.

Dearly were we purchased, Lord,
When Thy blood for us was pour'd;
Think, O Christ, we are Thine own!
Hold me, guide me, as a child,
Through the battle, through the wild,
Leave me nevermore alone.

Till at last I meet on high
With the faithful host who cry
Hallelujah night and day;
Pure from stain we there shall see
Thee in us, and us in Thee,
And be one in Thee for aye.

VI. The Remembrance
Kern. Died 1835.

Oh how could I forget Him
Who ne'er forgetteth me?
Or tell the love that let Him
Come down to set me free?
I lay in darkest sadness,
Till He made all things new,
And still fresh love and gladness
Flow from that heart so true.

How could I ever leave Him
Who is so kind a Friend?
How could I ever grieve Him
Who thus to me doth bend?
Have I not seen Him dying
For us on yonder tree?
Do I not hear Him crying,
Arise and follow Me!

For ever will I love Him
Who saw my hopeless plight,
Who felt my sorrows move Him,
And brought me life and light;
Whose arm shall be around me
When my last hour is come,
And suffer none to wound me,
Though dark the passage home.

He gives me pledges holy,
His body and His blood,
He lifts the scorn'd, the lowly,
He makes my courage good,
For He will reign within me,
And shed His graces there;
The heaven He died to win me
Can I then fail to share?

In joy and sorrow ever
Shine through me, Blessed Heart,
Who bleeding for us never

Didst shrink, from sorest smart!
Whate'er I've loved or striven
Or borne, I bring to Thee;
Now let Thy heart and heaven
Stand open, Lord, to me!

Catherine Winkworth

VII. After Participation
Rist. 1651.

O Living Bread from Heaven,
How richly hast Thou fed Thy guest!
The gifts Thou now hast given
Have fill'd my heart with joy and rest.
O wondrous food of blessing,
O cup that heals our woes,
My heart this gift possessing
In thankful song o'erflows;
For while the life and strength in me
Were quicken'd by this food,
My soul hath gazed awhile on Thee,
O highest, only Good!

My Lord, Thou here hast led me
Within Thy temple's holiest place,
And there Thyself hast fed me
With all the treasures of Thy grace;
And Thou hast freely given
What earth could never buy,
The bread of life from heaven,
That now I shall not die;
And Thou hast suffer'd me in faith
To drink the blessed wine
That heals the soul from inner death,
And makes her wholly Thine.

Thou givest all I wanted,
The food whose power can death destroy,
And Thou hast freely granted
The cup of full eternal joy;
Ah Lord, I do not merit
The favour Thou hast shown,
And all my soul and spirit
Bow down before Thy throne;
Since Thou hast suffer'd me to eat
The food of angels here,
Nor Sin, nor foes that I can meet,
Nor Death I now may fear.

O Love incomprehended!
That wrought in Thee, my Saviour, thus
That Thou shouldst have descended

Catherine Winkworth

From highest heaven to dwell with us!
Creator, that hath brought Thee
To succour such as I,
Who else had vainly sought Thee!
Then grant me now to die
To sin, and live alone to Thee,
That when this time is o'er,
Thy face, O Saviour, I may see
In heaven for evermore.

For as a shadow passes
I pass, but Thou dost still endure;
I wither like the grasses,
But Thou art rich, though I am poor;
Oh boundless is Thy kindness,
And righteous is Thy power;
And I in sinful blindness
Am erring hour by hour,
And yet Thou comest, dost not spurn
A sinner, Lord, like me!
Ah how can I Thy love return,
What gift have I for Thee?

A heart that hath repented,
And mourns for sin with bitter sighs,--
Thou, Lord, art well-contented
With this my only sacrifice.
I know that in my weakness
Thou wilt despise me not,
But grant me in Thy meekness
The favour I have sought;
Yes, Thou wilt deign in grace to heed
The song that now I raise,
For meet and right is it indeed
That I should sing Thy praise.

Grant what I have partaken
May through Thy grace so work in me,
That sin be all forsaken,
And I may cleave alone to Thee,
And all my soul be heedful
How she Thy love may know,
For this alone is needful,
Thy love should in me glow;
And let no beauty please mine eyes,
No joy allure my heart,
But what in Thee, my Saviour, lies,
What Thou dost here impart.

O well for me that strengthen'd
With heavenly bread and wine, if here
My course on earth be lengthen'd,
I now may serve Thee free from fear;
Away then earthly pleasure,
All earthly gifts are vain,
I seek a heavenly treasure,
My home I long to gain,
Where I shall live and praise my God,
And none my peace destroy,
Where all the soul is overflow'd
With pure eternal joy.

FOR TRAVELLERS
    1. In God's name let us on our way!
    2. Wherever I go, whate'er my task
    3. O Lord, be this our vessel now
    4. Thou, solemn Ocean, rollest to the strand
    5. Now we must leave our father-land
    6. On our sails all soft and sweetly

I. At the Outset of any Journey
Anon.

In God's name let us on our way!
The Father's help and grace we pray,
His love shall guard us round about
From foes within and arms without.
Hallelujah.

And Christ, be Thou our Friend and Guide,
Through all our wanderings at our side,
Help us all evil to withstand
That wars against Thy least command.
Hallelujah.

The Holy Spirit o'er us brood
With all His gifts of richest good,
With hope and strength when dark our road
And bring us home again in God!
Hallelujah.

II. On a Long and Perilous Journey
Written on a Journey to Russia and Persia, undertaken by the Author as Physician to the Embassy from Holstein.
Paul Flemming. 1631.

Wherever I go, whate'er my task,
The counsel of my God I ask,
Who all things hath and can;
Unless He give both thought and deed
The utmost pains can ne'er succeed,
And vain the wisest plan.

For what can all my toil avail?
My care, my watching all must fail,
Unless my God is there;
Then let Him order all for me
As He in wisdom shall decree;
On Him I cast my care.

For nought can come, as nought hath been,
But what my Father hath foreseen,
And what shall work my good;
Whate'er He gives me I will take,
Whate'er He chooses I will make
My choice with thankful mood.

I lean upon His mighty arm,
It shields me well from every harm,
All evil shall avert;
If by His precepts still I live
Whate'er is useful He will give,
And nought shall do me hurt.

But only may He of His grace
The record of my guilt efface,
And wipe out all my debt;
Though I have sinn'd He will not straight
Pronounce His judgment, He will wait,
Have patience with me yet.

I travel to a distant land
To serve the post wherein I stand,
Which He hath bade me fill;
And He will bless me with His light,
That I may serve His world aright,

Catherine Winkworth

And make me know His will.

And though through desert wilds I fare,
Yet Christian friends are with me there,
And Christ Himself is near;
In all our dangers He will come,
And He who kept me safe at home,
Can keep me safely here.

Yes, He will speed us on our way,
And point us where to go and stay,
And help us still and lead;
Let us in health and safety live,
And time and wind and weather give,
And whatsoe'er we need.

When late at night my rest I take,
When early in the morn I wake,
Halting or on my way,
In hours of weakness or in bonds,
When vex'd with fears my heart desponds,
His promise is my stay.

Since then my course is traced by Him
I will not fear that future dim,
But go to meet my doom,
Well knowing nought can wait me there
Too hard for me through Him to bear;
I yet shall overcome.

To Him myself I wholly give,
At His command I die or live,
I trust His love and power:
Whether to-morrow or to-day
His summons come, I will obey,
He knows the proper hour.

But if it please that love most kind,
And if this voice within my mind
Be whispering not in vain,
I yet shall praise my God ere long
In many a sweet and joyful song,
In peace at home again.

To those I love will He be near,
With His consoling light appear,
Who is my shield and theirs;
And He will grant beyond our thought
What they and I alike have sought
With many tearful prayers.

Then, O my soul, be ne'er afraid,
On Him who thee and all things made
With calm reliance rest;
Whate'er may come, where'er we go,
Our Father in the heavens must know
In all things what is best.

III. Prayers at Sea
F. Winkelmann.

O Lord, be this our vessel now
A worthy temple unto Thee,
Though none may hear its bells but Thou
And this our little company;
Our church's roof, yon mighty dome,
Shall ring with hymns we learnt at home,
Our floor the boundless tossing wave,
Our field, our path, perchance our grave.

Where shall we aid and comfort find
With toils and perils all around?
Command, O mighty God, the wind
To bear us whither we are bound,
Oh bring us to our home once more
From weary wanderings safe to shore;
And those who follow us with prayer
Keep Thou in Thy most tender care.

And as the needle while we rove,
To one point still is true and just,
So let our hope and faith and love
Be fix'd on One in whom we trust;
His word is mighty still to save,
He still can walk the stormiest wave,
And hold His followers with His hand,
For His are heaven and sea and land.

IV. On the Sea-Shore
de la Motte Fouqué.

Thou, solemn Ocean, rollest to the strand
Laden with prayers from many a far-off land,
To us thy thousand murmurs at our feet
One cry repeat.

Through all thy myriad tones that never cease
We hear of death and love, the cross and peace,
New churches bright with hope and glad with psalms,
And martyrs' palms.

Then on! and come whate'er our God sees fit!
To yon frail wave-toss'd planks we now commit
Our lives, our all, and leave our native land
At His command.

We take thee for our chariot, stormy Sea!
Borne safely on to serve our God by thee,
For thou and we alike obey His word
And own Him Lord.

And whether thy chill deeps become our grave,
Or far away our blood shall stain thy wave,
Or we shall cross with joyous songs thy foam
Back to our home:

Be it as He ordains whose name is Love!
Whether our lot or life or death shall prove,
To Life Eternal surely guides His will,
And we are still.

V. The Parting
Albert Knapp.

Now we must leave our father-land,
And wander far o'er ocean's foam;
Broken is kinship's dearest band,
Forsaken stands our ancient home;
But One will ever with us go
Through busiest day and stillest night;
And heaven above, the deeps below
Shrink back abash'd before His sight.

Then be the issue life or death,
Let Him do as it seems Him best,
The messenger of Christian faith
Looks not in this world for his rest.
If but His hand still hold us fast,
His presence hourly fold us round,
The anchor of our souls is cast
Firm in the One eternal ground.

The voice of Everlasting Love,
That rang with living power through us,
Is worthy thus our souls to move,
Worthy to fill a lifetime thus;
Here none was e'er deceived or lost,
Howe'er his earthly hopes might fade;
Then well for him who weighs the cost
Ere yet his final choice is made.

Yes, scatter'd are our brothers now
O'er land and ocean far apart,
Yet to one Master still they bow,
In Him they still are one in heart;
For as one sin, one poison ran
Through all our race since Adam's fall;
There is one hope, one life for man
In Him who bore the sins of all.

Sweet for each other oft to plead,
And feel our oneness in the Son,
Ah then we daily meet indeed
In spirit at our Father's throne!
Our bodies are but parted here,
And fade in this dark land away

The earthly shadows disappear,
The harvest ripens for that Day.

Soon Time for us shall cease to reign,
The Saviour calls us home in peace;
At last we all shall meet again,
And dwell together all in bliss,
Where faith to clearest vision yields;--
Triumphant light for sorrowing gloom,
For desert wastes fair Eden's fields,
For tearful paths a blessed home!

VI. On the Voyage
de la Motte Fouqué.

On our sails all soft and sweetly,
Yet with bold resistless force,
Breathe the winds of heaven, and fleetly
Wing us on our watery course;
Swift, and swifter, furrowing deep
Through the mighty waves, that keep
Not a trace where we have been,
On we speed to lands unseen!

Sink thou deeply in our mind,
Type of life, most apt and true!
Though we leave no track behind,
Yet we plough our furrows too,
Where, from out a world of bliss,
Falls the seed unseen of this,
And an unseen distant home
Beckons o'er the desert foam.

Be our voyage, brethren, such
That if direst peril came,
Wreck and ruin could not touch
Ought but this our weary frame;
That may gladly sleep, the while
Still and blest the soul shall smile,
In the eternal peace of Heaven,
That our God hath surely given.

Oh that in that blessed peace
Many and many a soul may rest!
Oh through us may God increase
Soon the number of the blest!
Free through us the souls that now
'Neath a bitter bondage bow;
Whom yet darkest error binds!
Speed, oh speed us on, ye winds!

AT THE BURIAL OF THE DEAD
    1. Now lay we calmly in the grave
    2. Now weeping at the grave we stand
    3. Christ will gather in His own
    4. Though Love may weep with breaking heart
    5. Gentle Shepherd, Thou hast still'd
    6. Thou'rt mine, yes, still thou art mine own!
    See also from Lyra Germanica, The Christian Year, Hymns for the Burial of the Dead

I. The Sure and Certain Hope
Michael Weiss. 1531.

Now lay we calmly in the grave
This form, whereof no doubt we have
That it shall rise again that Day
In glorious triumph o'er decay.

And so to earth again we trust
What came from dust, and turns to dust,
And from the dust shall surely rise
When the last trumpet fills the skies.

His soul is living now in God
Whole grace his pardon hath bestow'd,
Who through His Son redeem'd him here
From bondage unto sin and fear.

His trials and his griefs are past,
A blessed end is his at last,
He bore Christ's yoke, and did His will,
And though he died, he liveth still.

He lives where none can mourn and weep,
And calmly shall this body sleep
Till God shall Death himself destroy,
And raise it into glorious joy.

He suffer'd pain and grief below,
Christ heals him now from all his woe,
For him hath endless joy begun,
He shines in glory like the sun.

Catherine Winkworth

Then let us leave him to his rest,
And homeward turn, for he is blest,
And we must well our souls prepare,
When death shall come, to meet him there.

Then help us, Christ, our Hope in loss!
Thou hast redeem'd us by Thy cross
From endless death and misery;
We praise, we bless, we worship Thee!

II. The Departure of a Christian
Spitta.

Now weeping at the grave we stand
And sow the seed in tears,
The form of him who in our band
On earth no more appears.
Ah no, for he hath safely come
Where we too would attain;
He dwells within our Father's home,
And death to him was gain.

Now he beholds what we believe,
He has what here we want,
The sins no more his soul can grieve
That here the pilgrim haunt;
The Lord hath claim'd him for His own,
And sent him calm release;
We weep, but it is we alone,
He dwells in perfect peace.

He wears the crown of life on high,
He bears the shining palm,
Where angels "Holy, holy," cry,
He joins their glorious psalm.
But we poor pilgrims journey on
Through this dark land of woe,
Until we go where he is gone,
And all his joy shall know.

III. The Lord doth all Things Well
Moravian Hymn-Book.

Christ will gather in His own
To the place where He is gone,
Where their heart and treasure lie,
Where our life is hid on high.

Day by day the voice saith, "Come,
Enter thine eternal home;"
Asking not if we can spare
This dear soul it summons there.

Had He ask'd us, well we know
We should cry, oh spare this blow!
Yes, with streaming tears should pray,
"Lord, we love him, let him stay!"

But the Lord doth nought amiss,
And since He hath order'd this,
We have nought to do but still
Rest in silence on His will.

Many a heart no longer here,
Ah! was all too inly dear;
Yet, O Love, 'tis Thou dost call,
Thou wilt be our All in all.

IV. The Light in Darkness
F. A. Krummacher.

Though Love may weep with breaking heart,
There comes, O Christ, a Day of Thine,
There is a Morning Star must shine,
And all these shadows shall depart.

Though Faith may droop and tremble here,
That Day of light shall surely come;
His path has led him safely home;
When twilight breaks the dawn is near.

Though Hope seem now to have hoped in vain,
And Death seem king of all below,
There yet shall come the Morning-glow,
And wake our slumberers once again.

V. The Death of a little Child
Meinhold.

Gentle Shepherd, Thou hast still'd
Now Thy little lamb's long weeping;
Ah how peaceful, pale, and mild,
In its narrow bed 'tis sleeping,
And no sigh of anguish sore
Heaves that little bosom more.

In this world of care and pain,
Lord, Thou wouldst no longer leave it,
To the sunny heavenly plain
Dost Thou now with joy receive it,
Clothed in robes of spotless white,
Now it dwells with Thee in light.

Ah Lord Jesus, grant that we
Where it lives may soon be living,
And the lovely pastures see
That its heavenly food are giving,
Then the gain of death we prove
Though Thou take what most we love.

VI. On the Death of His Son
Paul Gerhardt. 1650.

Thou'rt mine, yes, still thou art mine own!
Who tells me thou art lost?
But yet thou art not mine alone,
I own that He who cross'd
My hopes, hath greatest right in thee;
Yea, though He ask and take from me
Thee, O my son, my heart's delight,
My wish, my thought, by day and night.

Ah might I wish, ah might I choose,
Then thou, my Star, shouldst live,
And gladly for thy sake I'd lose
All else that life can give.
Oh fain I'd say: Abide with me,
The sunshine of my house to be,
No other joy but this I crave,
To love thee, darling, to my grave!

Thus saith my heart, and means it well,
God meaneth better still;
My love is more than words can tell,
His love is greater still;
I am a father, He the Head
And Crown of fathers, whence is shed
The life and love from which have sprung
All blessed ties in old and young.

I long for thee, my son, my own,
And He who once hath given,
Will have thee now beside His throne,
To live with Him in heaven.
I cry, Alas! my light, my child!
But God hath welcome on him smiled,
And said: "My child, I keep thee near,
For there is nought but gladness here."

Oh blessed word, oh deep decree,
More holy than we think!
With God no grief or woe can be,
No bitter cup to drink,
No sickening hopes, no want or care,
No hurt can ever reach him there;

Catherine Winkworth

Yes, in that Father's shelter'd home
I know that sorrow cannot come.

We pass our nights in wakeful thought
For our dear children's sake;
All day our anxious toil hath sought
How best for them to make
A future safe from care or need,
Yet seldom do our schemes succeed;
How rarely does their future prove
What we had plann'd for those we love!

How many a child of promise bright
Ere now hath gone astray,
By ill example taught to slight
And quit Christ's holy way.
Oh fearful the reward is then,
The wrath of God, the scorn of men!
The bitterest tears by mortal shed
Are his, who mourns a child misled.

But now I need not fear for thee,
Where thou art, all is well;
For thou thy Father's Face dost see,
With Jesus thou dost dwell!
Yes, cloudless joys around him shine,
His heart shall never ache like mine,
He sees the radiant armies glow
That keep and guide us here below:

He hears their singing evermore,
His little voice too sings,
He drinks of wisdom deepest lore,
He speaks of secret things,
That we can never see or know
Howe'er we seek or strive below,
While yet amid the mists we stand
That veil this dark and tearful land.

Oh that I could but watch afar,
And hearken but awhile,
To that sweet song that hath no jar,
And see his heavenly smile,
As he doth praise the holy God,
Who made him pure for that abode!
In tears of joy full well I know
This burden'd heart would overflow.

And I should say: Stay there, my son,
My wild laments are o'er,
O well for thee that thou hast won,
I call thee back no more;
But come, thou fiery chariot, come,
And bear me swiftly to that home,
Where he with many a loved one dwells,
And evermore of gladness tells!

Then be it as my Father wills,
I will not weep for thee;
Thou livest, joy thy spirit fills,
Pure sunshine thou dost see,
The sunshine of eternal rest:
Abide, my child, where thou art blest;
I with our friends will onward fare,
And, when God wills, shall find thee there.

PART II. THE INNER LIFE

  Penitence
  Praise and Thanksgiving
  The Life of Faith
  Songs of the Cross
  The Final Conflict and Heaven

PENITENCE

  1. Lord Jesus Christ, in Thee alone
  2. Alas! my Lord and God
  3. Jesus, pitying Saviour, hear me
  4. O Jesus, Lord of majesty!
  5. O God, Thou faithful God
  6. Thou Who breakest every chain
  7. Courage, my sorely-tempted heart!

I. The Only Helper

J. Schneesing. 1522.

Lord Jesus Christ, in Thee alone
My hope on earth I place;
For other comforter is none,
Nor help save in Thy grace.
There is no man nor creature here,
No angel in the heavenly sphere,
Who at my need can succour me;
I cry to Thee,
For Thou canst end my misery.

My sin is very sore and great,
I mourn beneath its load;
Oh free me from this heavy weight
Through Thy most precious blood;
And with Thy Father for me plead
That Thou hast suffer'd in my stead,
The burden then from me is roll'd;
Lord, I lay hold
On Thy dear promises of old.

And of Thy grace on me bestow
True Christian faith, O Lord,
That all the sweetness I may know

That in Thy cross is stored,
Love Thee o'er earthly pride or pelf,
And love my neighbour as myself;
And when at last is come my end,
Be Thou my Friend,
From all assaults my soul defend.

Glory to God in highest heaven,
The Father of all love;
To His dear Son, for sinners given
Whose grace we daily prove;
To God the Holy Ghost we cry,
That we may find His comfort nigh,
And learn how, free from sin and fear,
To please Him here,
And serve Him in the sinless sphere.

II. Submission
Rutilius. 1604; and Gross. 1627.

Alas! my Lord and God,
How heavy is my load,
My sins are great and weigh me to the ground;
The yoke doth sorely press,
And yet in my distress
Through all the world no helper can be found.

And fled I in my fear
Far far away from here,
To earth's remotest end--Thou still wert there.
My anguish and my pain
Would yet with me remain;
I could not flee away from my despair.

'Tis Thou canst help alone,
I cast me at Thy throne,
Reject me not, though I deserve it, Lord;
Ah think of all Thy Son
For me, for me, hath done,
Nor let me feel Thy sharp avenging sword.

And if it must be so,
That punishment and woe
Must follow sin, then let me bear it here;
Low at Thy feet I bow,
Oh let me suffer now,
But spare me yonder, then in love appear.

Oh Lord, forget my sin,
And deign to put within
A calm obedient heart, a patient mind,
That I may murmur not,
Though bitter seem my lot,
For hearts unthankful can no blessing find.

Do Thou, O Lord, with me
As seemeth best to Thee,
For Thou wilt strengthen me to bear the rod,
For this alone I pray,
Oh cast me not away,
For ever from Thy grace, Thou pitying God.

Nay, that Thou wilt not do,
I know Thy word is true,
My faith can rest in quiet hope on Thee,
The death of Christ, I know,
Hath freed me from my woe,
And open'd heaven to sinners and to me.

Lord Jesus, where Thou art
All doubt and dread depart,
My refuge is the cross where Thou wast slain,
Where Thou, Lord, for our sake
Didst all our griefs partake,
And die our comfort and our grace to gain.

Here at my Saviour's side,
Here let me still abide,
Then death may come, but little he destroys;
Though soul and body part,
I live where Thou, Lord, art,
My sins wiped out amid eternal joys.

All praise to God alone,
Who claims me for His own,
Through Christ my Lord; O let me trust Him then,
And lean in fullest faith
On what my Saviour saith,
He who believeth shall be saved; Amen.

III. In great inward Distress
Tersteegen. 1731.

Jesus, pitying Saviour, hear me,
Draw Thou near me,
Turn Thee, Lord, in grace to me;
For Thou knowest all my sorrow,
Night and morrow
Doth my cry go up to Thee.

Lost in darkness, girt with dangers,
Round me strangers,
Through an alien land I roam,
Outward trials, bitter losses,
Inward crosses,
Lord, Thou know'st have sought me home.

See the fetters that have bound me,
Snares surround me,
Free the captive, hear my call;
Ah from sin my soul I never
Can deliver,
I am weak and helpless all.

Though the tempter's wiles and cunning
I am shunning,
Yet they vex and wound me sore;
Oft I waver, oft I languish,
Fill'd with anguish,
Strength and rest are mine no more.

Peace I cannot find, oh take me,
Lord, and make me
From the yoke of evil free;
Calm this longing never-sleeping,
Still my weeping,
Grant me hope once more in Thee.

Sin of courage hath bereft me,
And hath left me
Scarce a spark of faith or hope;
Bitter tears my heart oft sheddeth
As it dreadeth
I am past Thy mercy's scope.

Lord, wilt Thou be wroth for ever?
Oh deliver
Me from all I most deserved;
'Tis Thyself, dear Lord, hast sought me,
Thou hast taught me
Thee to seek from whom I swerved.

Thou, my God and King, hast known me,
Yet hast shown me
True and loving is Thy will;
Though my heart from Thee oft ranges,
Through its changes,
Lord, Thy love is faithful still.

Satan watches to betray me,
He would slay me,
Quicken Thou my faith and powers,
Let me, though Thy face Thou'rt hiding,
Still confiding,
Look to Thee in darkest hours.

Bless my trials thus to sever
Me for ever
From the love of self and sin;
Let me through them see Thee clearer,
Find Thee nearer,
Grow more like to Thee within.

In the patience that Thou lendest
All Thou sendest
I embrace, I will be still;
Bend this stubborn heart I pray Thee
To obey Thee,
Calmly waiting on Thy will.

Here I bring my will, oh take it,
Thine, Lord, make it,
Calm this troubled heart of mine;
In Thy strength I too may conquer,
Wait no longer,
Show in me Thy grace Divine.

IV. The Weakness and Restlessness of Sin
Tersteegen. 1731.

O Jesus, Lord of majesty!
O glorious King, eternal Son!
In mercy bend Thou down to me,
As now I cast me at Thy throne.

Enslaved to vanity, and weak,
An alien power in me hath sway,
My strength is gone, howe'er I seek
I cannot break my bonds away.

How oft my heart against my will
Is torn and tossing to and fro,
I cannot, as I would, fulfill
The good that yet I love and know.

How many ties oppress and bind
The soul that yearneth to be free;
Distracted, vanquish'd, oft the mind
That fain would rest at peace in Thee.

I practice me in self-controul,
Yet rest and calm in vain pursue
Self-will is rooted in my soul,
And thwarts me still, whate'er I do.

I hate it, but its life is strong,
I fear, yet cannot it forsake;
Ah Lord, how long it seems, how long,
Until Thy grace my yoke shall break!

Ah Jesus, when, when, wilt Thou lead
The prisoner from this drear abode?
When shall I feel that I am freed,
And Thou art with me, Son of God?

Oh take this heart, that I would give
For ever to be all Thine own;
I to myself no more would live;
Come, Lord, be Thou my King alone.

Yes, take my heart, and in it rule,
Direct it as it pleases Thee;
I will be silent in Thy school,
And learn whate'er Thou teachest me.

What lives by life that is not Thine,
I yield it to Thy righteous doom;
What yet resists Thy power Divine,
Oh let Thy fire of love consume.

And then within the heart abide
That Thou halt cleansed to be Thy throne;
A look from Thee shall be my guide,
I watch but till Thy will is known.

Yes, make me Thine,--though I am weak,
Thy service makes us strong and free;
My Lord and King, Thy face I seek,
For ever keep me true to Thee.

Catherine Winkworth

V. A Christian's Daily Prayer
Johann Heermann. 1630.

O God, Thou faithful God,
Thou Fountain ever flowing,
Without Whom nothing is
All perfect gifts bestowing;
O pure and healthy frame
O give me, and within
A conscience free from blame,
A soul unhurt by sin.

And grant me, Lord, to do,
With ready heart and willing,
Whate'er Thou shalt command,
My calling here fulfilling,
And do it when I ought,
With all my strength, and bless
The work I thus have wrought,
For Thou must give success.

And let me promise nought
But I can keep it truly,
Abstain from idle words,
And guard my lips still duly;
And grant, when in my place
I must and ought to speak,
My words due power and grace,
Nor let me wound the weak.

If dangers gather round,
Still keep me calm and fearless;
Help me to bear the cross
When life is dark and cheerless;
To overcome my foe
With words and actions kind;
When counsel I would know,
Good counsel let me find.

And let me be with all
In peace and friendship living,
As far as Christians may;
And if Thou aught art giving
Of wealth and honours fair,
Oh this refuse me not,

That nought be mingled there
Of goods unjustly got.

And if a longer life
Be here on earth decreed me,
And Thou through many a strife
To age at last wilt lead me,
Thy patience in me shed,
Avert all sin and shame,
And crown my hoary head
With pure untarnish'd fame.

Let nothing that may chance,
Me from my Saviour sever;
And dying with Him, take
My soul to Thee for ever;
And let my body have
A little space to sleep
Beside my fathers' grave,
And friends that o'er it weep.

And when the Day is come,
And all the dead are waking,
Oh reach me down Thy hand,
Thyself my slumbers breaking;
Then let me hear Thy voice,
And change this earthly frame,
And bid me aye rejoice
With those who love Thy name.

VI. The Deliverer from Bondage
Gottfried Arnold. 1697.

Thou Who breakest every chain,
Thou Who still art ever near,
Thou with Whom disgrace and pain
Turn to joy and heaven e'en here;
Let Thy further judgments fall
On the Adam strong within,
Till Thy grace hath freed us all
From the prison-house of sin.

'Tis Thy Father's will toward us,
Thou shouldst end Thy work at length;
Hence in Thee are centred thus
Perfect wisdom, love, and strength,
That Thou none shouldst lose of those
Whom He gave Thee, though they roam
'Wilder'd here amid their foes,
Thou shouldst bring them safely home.

Ah Thou wilt, Thou canst not cease,
Till Thy perfect work be done;
In Thy hands we lie at peace,
Knowing all Thy love hath won,
Though the world may blindly dream
We are captives poor and base,
And the cross's yoke may deem
Sign of meanness and disgrace.

Look upon our bonds, and see
How doth all creation groan
'Neath the yoke of vanity,
Make Thy full redemption known;
Still we wrestle, cry, and pray,
Held in bitter bondage fast,
Though the soul would break away
Into higher things at last.

Lord, we do not ask for rest
For the flesh, we only pray
Thou wouldst do as seems Thee best,
Ere yet comes our parting day;
But our spirit clings to Thee,
Will not, dare not, let Thee go,

Until Thou have set her free
From the bonds that cause her woe.

Conqueror conquer, Ruler reign,
King assert Thy sovereign right,
Till no slavery more remain
Spread the kingdom of Thy might!
Lead the captives freely out,
Through the covenant of Thy blood,
From our dark remorse and doubt,
For Thou willest but our good.

Ours the fault it is, we own,
We are slaves to self and sloth,
Yet oh leave us not alone
In the living death we loathe;
Crush'd beneath our burden's weight,
Crying at Thy feet we fall,
Point the path, though steep and strait,
Thou didst open once for all.

Ah how dearly were we bought
Not to serve the world or sin;
By the work that Thou hall wrought
Must Thou make us pure within,--
Wholly pure and free, in us
Be Thine image now restored:
Fill'd from out Thy fulness thus
Grace for grace is on us pour'd.

Draw us to Thy cross, O Love,
Crucify with Thee whate'er
Cannot dwell with Thee above,
Lead us to those regions fair!
Courage! long the time may seem,
Yet His day is coming fast;
We shall be like them that dream
When our freedom dawns at last.

VII. The Safe Refuge
J. H. Böhmer. 1704.

Courage, my sorely-tempted heart!
Break through thy woes, forget their smart;
Come forth and on Thy Bridegroom gaze,
The Lamb of God, the Fount of grace;
Here is thy place!

His arms are open, thither flee!
There rest and peace are waiting thee,
The deathless crown of righteousness,
The entrance to eternal bliss;
He gives thee this!

Then combat well, of nought afraid,
For thus His follower thou art made,
Each battle teaches thee to fight,
Each foe to be a braver knight,
Arm'd with His might.

If storms of fierce temptation rise,
Unmoved I'll face the frowning skies;
If but the heart is true indeed,
Christ will be with me in my need,--
His own could bleed.

I flee away to Thy dear cross,
For hope is there for every loss,
Healing for every wound and woe,
There all the strength of love I know
And feel its glow.

Before the Holy One I fall,
The Eternal Sacrifice for all;
His death has freed us from our load,
Peace on the anguish'd soul bestow'd,
Brought us to God.

How then should I go mourning on?
I look to Thee,--my fears are gone,
With Thee is rest that cannot cease,
For Thou hast wrought us full release,
And made our peace.

Thy word hath still its glorious powers,
The noblest chivalry is ours;
O Thou, for whom to die is gain,
I bring Thee here my all, oh deign
To accept and reign!

PRAISE AND THANKSGIVING
1. Now thank we all our God
2. All praise and thanks to God most High
3. O, heaven and earth, and sea and air
4. I who so oft in deep distress
5. O mighty Spirit! Source whence all things sprung!
6. In Thee is gladness
7. Thank God it hath resounded

I. The Chorus of God's Thankful Children
Martin Rinckart. 1636.

Now thank we all our God,
With heart and hands and voices,
Who wondrous things hath done,
In Whom His world rejoices;
Who from our mother's arms
Hath bless'd us on our way
With countless gifts of love,
And still is ours to-day.

Oh may this bounteous God
Through all our life be near us,
With ever joyful hearts
And blessed peace to cheer us;
And keep us in His grace,
And guide us when perplex'd,
And free us from all ills
In this world and the next.

All praise and thanks to God
The Father, now be given,
The Son, and Him who reigns
With them in highest heaven,
The One eternal God,
Whom earth and heaven adore,
For thus it was, is now,
And shall be evermore!

II. The Goodness of God
J. J. Schütz. 1673.

All praise and thanks to God most High,
The Father of all Love!
The God who doeth wondrously,
The God who from above
My soul with richest solace fills,
The God who every sorrow stills;
Give to our God the glory!

The hosts of heaven Thy praises tell,
All thrones bow down to Thee,
And all who in Thy shadow dwell,
In earth and air and sea,
Declare and laud their Maker's might,
Whose wisdom orders all things right;
Give to our God the glory!

And for the creatures He hath made
Our God shall well provide;
His grace shall be their constant aid,
Their guard on every side;
His kingdom ye may surely trust,
There all is equal, all is just;
Give to our God the glory!

I sought Him in my hour of need;
Lord God, now hear my prayer!
For death He gave me life indeed,
And comfort for despair;
For this my thanks shall endless be,
Oh thank Him, thank Him too with me
Give to our God the glory!

The Lord is never far away,
Nor sunder'd from His flock;
He is their refuge and their stay,
Their peace, their trust, their rock,
And with a mother's watchful love
He guides them wheresoe'er they rove:
Give to our God the glory!

Catherine Winkworth

And when earth cannot comfort more,
Nor earthly help avail,
The Maker comes Himself, whose store
Of blessing cannot fail,
And bends on them a Father's eyes
Whom earth all rest and hope denies:
Give to our God the glory!

Ah then till life hath reach'd its bound,
My God, I'll worship Thee,
The chorus of Thy praise shall sound
Far over land and sea;
Oh soul and body now rejoice,
My heart send forth a gladsome voice:
Give to our God the glory!

All ye who name Christ's holy Name,
Give to our God the glory!
Ye who the Father's power proclaim,
Give to our God the glory!
All idols under foot be trod,
The Lord is God! The Lord is God!
Give to our God the glory!

III. The Glory of God in Creation
Joachim Neander. 1679

O, heaven and earth, and sea and air,
Their Maker's glory all declare;
And thou, my soul, awake and sing,
To Him Thy praises also bring.

Through Him the glorious Source of Day
Drives all the clouds of night away;
The pomp of stars, the moon's soft light,
Praise Him through all the silent night.

Behold, how He hath everywhere
Made earth so wondrous rich and fair;
The forest dark, the fruitful land,
All living things do show His hand.

Behold, how through the boundless sky
The happy birds all swiftly fly;
And fire and wind and storm are still
The ready servants of His will.

Behold the waters' ceaseless flow
For ever circling to and fro;
The mighty sea, the bubbling well,
Alike their Maker's glory tell.

My God, how wondrously dost Thou
Unfold Thyself to us e'en now!
O grave it deeply on my heart
What I am, Lord, and what Thou art!

IV. The Faithfulness of God
Paul Gerhardt. 1606-1676.

I who so oft in deep distress
And bitter grief must dwell,
Will now my God with gladness bless,
And all His mercies tell;
Oh hear me then, my God and King,
While of Thy Holy Name I sing,
Who doest all things well.

Our fathers who are now no more
Have praised Thee in their day,
They taught their children oft of yore
The wonders of Thy way;
Our children shall not rest, and still
They shall not all the measure fill,
Nor all exhaust the lay.

To Thee how many thankful songs
Have gone up ere my days,
And yet to me a part belongs
In that great hymn of praise;
I too must tell Thy wondrous might,
And praise Thy covenant just and right,
And Thine all-conquering grace.

And many a pious heart shall learn
The songs I make to Thee,
Far o'er the stars that yonder burn
Shall rise our harmony,
Thy Majesty, Thy mighty Hand
Shall be reveal'd to every land,
And all Thy goodness see!

For who is gracious, Lord, as Thou?
Who hath so much forgiven?
Who still to us would pitying bow
Who thus with grace have striven?
For lost in sins the whole world lies,
Her ceaseless crimes would scale the skies,
And cry aloud to heaven.

Yes, it must be a faithful heart
That thus can love us still,
Who oft reject the better part,
And thankless choose the ill;
But God can be nought else but good,
And therefore doth His mercies' flood
All things with blessing fill.

For this the works that Thou hast made
Do thank Thee and rejoice,
Thy saints shall bless Thee for Thine aid,
And make Thy ways their choice,
And tell abroad from hour to hour
Thy glorious rule, Thy kingdom's power,
With far-resounding voice.

Yes, they shall praise it, till its fame
Through all the world shall ring,
And all men learn to know Thy name
And gifts and service bring;
Eternal is Thy glorious throne,
Thy rule is like Thyself alone,
O just, Eternal King!

And yet in death or pain or loss,
The Lord is with us all,
Lightens the pressure of the cross,
Upholds us when we fall;
He stems the swelling tide of woes,
And when we sink beneath its blows
He comes, ere yet we call.

All eyes do wait on Thee, O Lord,
Who keepest us from dearth,
Who scatterest rich supplies abroad
For all the wants of earth;
Thou openest oft Thy bounteous hand,
And all in sea and air and land
Are fill'd with food and mirth.

Thy thoughts are good, and Thou art kind
E'en when we think it not;
How many an anxious faithless mind
Sits grieving o'er its lot,
And frets and pines by day and night,
As God had lost it out of sight,
And all its wants forgot!

Catherine Winkworth

Ah no! God ne'er forgets His own,
His heart is far too true,
He ever seeks their good alone,
His love is daily new;
And though thou deem that things go ill,
Yet He in all He doeth, still
Is holy, just and true.

The Lord to them is ever nigh
Who truly keep His word,
Whene'er in faith to Him they cry
Their prayer is surely heard;
He knoweth well who love Him well,
His love shall yet their clouds dispel,
And grant the hope deferr'd.

To those who love Him He denies
No good thing that they seek;
He sees their sorrow, counts their sighs,
And hearkens when they speak,
And surely frees them from their woes;
But those who hate them He o'erthrows,
And makes their boasting weak.

Yet this is but a little part
Of what I fain would sing;
But daily shall my voice and heart
New thanks and praises bring;
Oh help me all that live and move,
Help me to speak His faithful love,
And praise our glorious King.

V. The Holiness of God brought near to Man in Christ
J. J. Rambach. 1720.

O mighty Spirit! Source whence all things sprung!
O glorious Majesty of perfect Light!
Hath ever worthy praise to Thee been sung,
Or mortal heart endured to meet Thy sight?
If they who sin have never known
Must veil their faces at Thy throne,
Oh how shall I, who am but sin and dust,
Approach untrembling to the Pure and Just?

The voice of conscience in the soul hath shown
Some far-off glimpses of Thy holiness,
And yet more clearly hast Thou made it known
In Thy dear word that tells us of Thy grace;
But with all-glorious light divine
In His face we behold it shine,
The sinless One, who this dark earth has trod
To win through sorrow sinners back to God.

The brightness of Thy glory was the Son;
Thy law engraven on His heart He wore,
And on His forehead that all clearly shone
That Aaron's forehead but in shadow bore;[3]
And even to death did He obey
To take the guilt of sin away,
And made a curse for man, and dying thus,
He won the power of holiness for us.

Now may Thine image in us shine anew
In holy righteousness and innocence;
Now, strengthen'd by Thy Son, a service true
Thy people render, pure from all offence;
But all their light is only dim,
A shadow'd broken light from Him,
Who that we might be holy bore our load,
In Whom we dare to meet the Holy God.

VI. To the Saviour
I. Lindemann. 1580-1630.

In Thee is gladness
Amid all sadness,
Jesus, Sunshine of my heart!
By Thee are given
The gifts of heaven,
Thou the true Redeemer art!
Our souls Thou wakest,
Our bonds Thou breakest,
Who trusts Thee surely
Hath built securely,
He stands for ever:
Hallelujah.
Our hearts are pining
To see Thy shining,
Dying or living
To Thee are cleaving,
Nought can us sever;
Hallelujah.

If He is ours,
We fear no powers
Of earth or Satan, sin or death!
He sees and blesses
In worst distresses,
He can change them with a breath!
Wherefore the story
Tell of His glory
With heart and voices;
All heaven rejoices
In Him for ever;
Hallelujah.
We triumph o'er sadness,
We sing in our gladness,
We love Thee, we praise Thee,
And yonder shall raise Thee,
Glad hymns for ever;
Hallelujah.

VII. For Public Peace
Written at the close of the Thirty Years' War.
Paul Gerhardt. 1648.

Thank God it hath resounded,
The blessed voice of joy and Peace!
And murder's reign is bounded,
And spear and sword at last may cease.
Arise, take down thy lyre,
My country, and once more
Uplift in full-toned choir
Thy happy songs of yore;
Oh raise thy heart to God and say:
Thy covenants, Lord, endure,
Thy mercies do not pass away,
Thy promises are sure.

For nothing do we merit,
But fiery wrath and sharpest rod,
A race of froward spirit,
Whose shameless sins still mock our God;
And He indeed hath sent us
Full many a bitter stroke,
And yet, do we repent us,
Or learn to bear His yoke?
Nay, as we were so still we are,
But God abideth true,
His help shall still the noise of war,
The captives' bonds undo.

O welcome day, that brought us
This precious noble gift of Peace!
For war hath deeply taught us
What sorrows come where she doth cease;
In her our God now layeth
All hope, all happiness;
Who woundeth her, or slayeth,
Doth, like a madman, press
The arrow to his own heart's core,
And quench with impious hand
The golden torch of Peace once more,
That glads at last our land.

Catherine Winkworth

This ye could teach us only,
So dull and hard these hearts of ours,
Ye homes, now stripp'd and lonely,
Ye wasted cities, ruin'd towers;
Ye fields once fairly blooming,
With golden harvests graced,
Where forests now are glooming,
Or spreads a dreary waste;
Ye graves, with corpses piled, where lies
Full many a hero brave,
Whose like no more shall meet our eyes,
Who died, yet could not save.

O man, with bitter mourning
Remember now the bygone years,
When thou hast met God's warning
With careless scoff, not contrite tears;
Yet like a loving Father,
He lays aside His wrath,
And seeks with kindness rather
To lure thee to His path;
He tries if love may yet constrain
The heart that hath withstood
His rod,--oh let Him not in vain
Now strive with thee for good!

Thou careless world awaken!
Awake, awake, all ye that sleep,
Ere yet ye be o'ertaken
With ruin sudden, swift, and deep!
But he who knows Christ liveth,
May hope and fear no ill,
The Peace that now He giveth
Hath deeper meaning still,
For He will surely teach us this:
"The end is nigh at hand,
When ye in perfect rest and peace
Before your God shall stand."

THE LIFE OF FAITH

1. Faith is a living power from heaven
2. Who keepeth not God's word, yet saith
3. I know in Whom I put my trust
4. Lord, all my heart is fix'd on Thee
5. Now at last I end the strife
6. Who would make the prize his own
7. Oh dearest Lord! to feel that Thou art near
8. Here behold me, as I cast me
9. Up! yes, upward to thy gladness
10. A pilgrim here I wander
11. Now the pearly gates unfold

I. Faith

Bohemian Brethren.

Faith is a living power from heaven,
That grasps the promise God hath given,
A trust that cannot be o'erthrown,
Fix'd heartily on Christ alone.

Faith finds in Christ whate'er we need
To save or strengthen us indeed,
Receives the grace He sends us down,
And makes us share His cross and crown.

Faith in the conscience worketh peace,
And bids the mourner's weeping cease;
By Faith the children's place we claim,
And give all honour to One Name.

Faith feels the Spirit's kindling breath
In love and hope that conquer death;
Faith worketh hourly joy in God,
And trusts and blesses e'en the rod.

We thank Thee then, O God of heaven,
That Thou to us this faith hast given
In Jesus Christ Thy Son, Who is
Our only Fount and Source of bliss;

Catherine Winkworth

And from His fulness grant each soul
The rightful faith's true end and goal,
The blessedness no foes destroy,
Eternal love and light and joy.

II. Faith that worketh by Love
C. F. Gellert. 1757.

Who keepeth not God's word, yet saith,
I know the Lord, is wrong;
In him is not that blessed faith
Through which the truth is strong;
But he who hears and keeps the word,
Is not of this world, but of God.

The faith His word hath caused to shine
Will kindle love in thee;
More wouldst thou know of things divine,
Deeper thy love must be;
True faith not only gives thee light,
But strength to love and do the right.

Jesus hath wash'd away our sin,
And we are children now;
Who feels such hope as this within,
To evil cannot bow;
Rather with Christ all scorn endure,
So we be like our Maker pure!

For he doth please the Father well
Who simply can obey;
In him the love of God doth dwell
Who steadfast keeps His way;
A daily active life of love,
Such fruits a living faith must prove.

He is in God, and God in him,
Who still abides in love;
'Tis love that makes the Cherubim
Obey and praise above;
For God is love, the loveless heart
Hath in His life and joy no part.

III. The Christian's Trust
E. M. Arndt.

I know in Whom I put my trust,
I know what standeth fast,
When all things here dissolve like dust
Or smoke before the blast:
I know what still endures, howe'er
All else may quake and fall,
When lies the prudent men ensnare,
And dreams the wise enthral.

It is the Dayspring from on high,
The adamantine Rock,
Whence never storm can make me fly,
That fears no earthquake's shock;
My Jesus Christ, my sure Defence,
My Saviour, and my Light,
That shines within, and scatters thence
Dark phantoms of the night:

Who once was borne, betray'd and slain,
At evening to the grave;
Whom God awoke, Who rose again,
A Conqueror strong to save;
Who pardons all my sin, who sends
His Spirit pure and mild;
Whose grace my every step befriends,
Who ne'er forgets His child!

Therefore I know in Whom I trust,
I know what standeth fast,
When all things form'd of earthly dust
Are whirling in the blast;
The terrors of the final foe
Can rob me not of this,
And this shall crown me once, I know,
With never-fading bliss.

IV. The Anchor of the Soul
Schalling. 1594.

Lord, all my heart is fix'd on Thee,
I pray Thee, be not far from me,
With grace and love divine.
The whole wide world delights me not,
Of heaven or earth, Lord, ask I not,
If only Thou art mine;
And though my heart be like to break,
Thou art my trust that nought can shake,
My portion, and my hidden joy,
Whose cross could all my bonds destroy;
Lord Jesus Christ!
My God and Lord! My God and Lord!
Forsake me not who trust Thy word!

Rich are Thy gifts! 'Twas God that gave
Body and soul, and all I have
In this poor life I live;
That I may use them to Thy praise,
And man's true welfare all my days,
Thy grace I pray Thee give;
From all false doctrine keep me, Lord;
All lies and malice from me ward;
In every cross uphold Thou me,
That I may bear it patiently;
Lord Jesus Christ!
My God and Lord! My God and Lord!
In death Thy comfort still afford.

Ah Lord, let Thy dear angels come
At my last end to bear me home
To Paradise for aye;
And in its narrow chamber keep
My body safe in painless sleep
Until Thy judgment Day;
And then from death awaken me,
That these mine eyes with joy may see,
O Son of God, Thy glorious face,
My Saviour, and my Fount of Grace!
Lord Jesus Christ!
Receive my prayer, receive my prayer,
Thy love for ever I'll declare.

V. The Resolve
Tersteegen. 1731.

Now at last I end the strife,
To my God I give my life
Wholly, with a steadfast mind;
Sin, I will not hearken more,
World, I turn from thee, 'tis o'er,
Not a look I'll cast behind.

Hath my heart been wavering long,
Have I dallied oft with wrong,
Now at last I firmly say:
All my will to this I give,
Only to my God to live,
And to serve Him night and day.

Lord, I offer at Thy feet
All I have most dear and sweet,
Lo! I keep no secret hoard:
Try my heart, and lurks there aught
False within its inmost thought,
Take it hence this moment, Lord!

I will shun no toil or wo,
Where Thou leadest I will go,
Be my pathway plain or rough;
If but every hour may be
Spent in work that pleases Thee,
Ah, dear Lord, it is enough!

One thing will I seek alone,
Nothing outward shall be known,
Sought, or toil'd for, more by me;
Strange to earth and all her care,
Well content with pilgrim's fare,
Shall my life be hid in Thee.

Thee I make my choice alone,
Make for ever, Lord, Thine own
All my powers of soul and mind;
Here I give myself away,
Let the covenant stand for aye
That my hand to-day hath sign'd.

VI. The Christian Race
J. Mentzer. 1704.

Who would make the prize his own,
Runs as swiftly as he can;
Who would gain an earthly crown,
Strives in earnest as a man;
Trains himself betimes with care
For the conflict he would share,
Casts aside whate'er could be
Hindrance to His victory.

Lord, Thou biddest me aspire
To a prize so high, so grand,
That it sets my soul on fire
To be found amidst Thy band:
Oh how brightly shineth down
From Thy heights the starry crown
And the throne to victors given,
Who for Thee have bravely striven!

Yet it seems I strive in vain,
Lord, in pity look on me,
Thou my weakness must sustain,
Set me now from all things free
That would keep me from my goal;
Come, Thyself prepare my soul,
Give me joy and strength and life,
Help me in the race, the strife.

Well our utmost efforts worth
Is the crown I see afar,
Though the blinded sons of earth
Care not for our holy war;
An exceeding great reward
Is that crown of grace, my Lord;
Be Thyself my Strength divine,
And the prize shall soon be mine.

VII. The Christian's Joy
Christian Gregor. 1778.

Oh dearest Lord! to feel that Thou art near
Brings deepest peace, and hushes every fear;
To see Thy smile, to hear Thy gracious voice,
Makes soul and body inwardly rejoice
With praise and thanks.

We cannot see as yet Thy glorious face,
Not yet our eyes behold its love and grace,
But Thee our inmost soul can surely feel,
Oh clearly, Lord, canst Thou Thyself reveal,
Though all unseen!

Oh well for him who ever day and night
Still only seeks to feed on Thee aright!
In him a well of joy for ever springs,
And, all day long his heart is glad and sings:
Who is like Thee?

For Thou dost love to meet us as a Friend,
Our comfort, healing, hope, and joy to send;
Patient to pity and to calm our woe,
And daily to forgive us all we owe,
Of Thy rich grace.

Or though we weep soon bid our tears to cease,
And make us feel how strong Thy love and peace;
And let the soul see Thee within, and learn
From need and love alike to Thee to turn
With ceaseless gaze.

A warm and loving heart, a childlike mind,
Through every change mayst Thou within us find;
The comfort of Thy holy sorrows keep
Our hearts at rest, in peace most calm and deep,
In joy or woe!

So shall we all, until Thy heaven we see,
Like children evermore be glad in Thee,
Though many a time the sudden tear may start,--
If only Thou wilt touch the throbbing heart
And still its pain!

Thou reachest down to us Thy wounded hand,
And at Thy cross, dear Lord, ashamed we stand,
Remembering all Thy truth through weal and woe,
Until our eyes with tears must overflow
Of thanks and praise.

VIII. Under Clouds
Joachim Neander. 1679.

Here behold me, as I cast me
At Thy throne, O glorious King!
Tears fast thronging, childlike longing,
Son of Man, to Thee I bring.
Let me find Thee--let me find Thee!
Me a poor and worthless thing.

Look upon me, Lord, I pray Thee,
Let Thy Spirit dwell in mine;
Thou hast sought me, Thou hast bought me,
Only Thee to know I pine;
Let me find Thee--let me find Thee!
Take my heart and grant me Thine.

Nought I ask for, nought I strive for,
But Thy grace so rich and free,
That Thou givest whom Thou lovest,
And who truly cleave to Thee;
Let me find Thee--let me find Thee!
He hath all things who hath Thee.

Earthly treasure, mirth and pleasure,
Glorious name, or richest hoard,
Are but weary, void and dreary,
To the heart that longs for God;
Let me find Thee--let me find Thee!
I am ready, mighty Lord.

IX. Aspiration
J. C. Schade. 1699.

Up! yes, upward to thy gladness
Rise, my heart, and soul, and mind!
Cast, oh cast away thy sadness,
Rise where thou thy Lord canst find.
He is thy home,
And thy life alone is He;
Hath the world no place for thee,
With Him is room.

On, still onward, mounting nigher
On the wings of faith to Him!
On, still onward, ever higher,
Till the mournful earth grows dim!
God is thy Rock;
Christ thy Champion cannot fail thee,
Howsoe'er thy foes assail thee,
Fear not their shock.

Firm, yes firmly, ever cleaving
Unto Christ the strong and true,
All, yes all, to God still leaving,
For His love is daily new,
Be steadfast here;
Soon thy foes shall be o'erthrown,
Since He wills thy good alone,
Be of good cheer.

Hide thee, in His chamber hide thee,
Christ hath open'd now the door;
Tell Him all that doth betide thee,
All thy sorrows there outpour;
He hears thy cry;
Men may hate thee and deceive thee,
But He cannot, will not leave thee,
He still is nigh.

High, oh high, o'er all things earthy,
Raise thy thoughts, my soul, to heaven;
One alone of thee is worthy,
All thou hast to Him be given;
Thy Lord He is
Who so truly pleads to have thee,

Catherine Winkworth

Who in love hath died to save thee
Then thou art His.

Up then, upwards! seek thou only
For the things that are above;
Sin thou hatest, earth is lonely,
Rise to Him whom thou dost love,--
There art thou blest;
All things here must change and die,
Only with our Lord on high
Is perfect rest.

X. Song of the Christian Pilgrim
Paul Gerhardt. 1606-1676.

A pilgrim here I wander,
On earth have no abode,
My fatherland is yonder,
My home is with my God.
For here I journey to and fro,
There in eternal rest
Will God His gracious gift bestow
On all the toil-oppress'd.

For what hath life been giving,
From youth up till this day,
But constant toil and striving?
Far back as thought can stray,
How many a day of toil and care,
How many a night of tears,
Hath pass'd in grief that none could share,
In lonely anxious fears!

How many a storm hath lighten'd
And thunder'd round my path!
And winds and rains have frighten'd
My heart with fiercest wrath:
And cruel envy, hatred, scorn,
Have darken'd oft my lot,
And patiently reproach I've borne,
Though I deserved it not.

Then through this life of dangers
I onward take my way;
But in this land of strangers
I do not think to stay,
Still forward on the road I fare
That leads me to my home,
My Father's comfort waits me there,
When I have overcome.

Ah yes, my home is yonder,
Where all the angelic bands
Praise Him with awe and wonder,
In whose Almighty hands
All things that are and shall be, lie,
By Him upholden still,

Catherine Winkworth

Who casteth down and lifts on high
At His most holy will.

That home have I desired,
'Tis there I would be gone
Till I am well-nigh tired,
O'er earth I've journey'd on;
The longer here I roam, I find
The less of real joy
That e'er could please or fill my mind,
For all hath some alloy.

The lodging is too cheerless,
The sorrow is too much;
Ah come, my heart is fearless,
Release it with Thy touch,
When Thy heart wills, and make an end
Of all this pilgrimage,
And with Thine arm and strength defend,
When foes against me rage.

Where now my spirit stayeth
Is not her true abode,
This earthly house decayeth,
And she will drop its load,
When comes the hour to leave beneath
What now I use and have;
And when I've yielded up my breath
Earth gives me but a grave.

But Thou, my joy and gladness,
O Thou, my Life and Light,
Wilt raise me from this sadness,
This long tempestuous night,
Into the perfect gladsome day,
Where bathed in joy divine,
Among Thy saints, and bright as they,
I too shall ever shine.

There shall I dwell for ever,
Not as a guest alone,
With those who cease there never
To worship at Thy throne;
There in my heritage I rest,
From baser things set free,
And join the chorus of the blest
For ever, Lord, to Thee!

XI. Longing for Home
Wolfgang C. Deszler. 1692.

Now the pearly gates unfold,
O Thou Joy of highest heaven,
Who ere earth was made, of old
Light of light for light wast given!
Hasten, Lord, and quickly come,
Bring the bride Thou hast betroth'd,
In Thine own pure radiance clothed,
Safe to Thine eternal home,
Where no more the night of sin
Spreads its fear and gloom within.

All my spirit thirsts to see,
Lord, Thy face unveil'd and bright;
And to stand from sin set free,
Spotless Lamb, amid Thy light.
But I leave it,--Thou dost well,
And my heaven is here and now,
Daystar of my soul, if Thou
Wilt but deign in me to dwell;
For without Thee could there be
Joy in heaven itself for me?

Bliss from Thee my soul hath won,
Spite of darkly threat'ning ill;
And my heart calls Thee its Sun,
And the sea of care grows still
In the shining of Thy smile;
For Thy love's all-quickening ray
Chases night and pain away,
That my heart grows light the while;
Heavenly joys in Thee are mine,
Far from Thee I mourn and pine.

Graft me into Thee for ever,
Tree of Life, that I may grow
Stronger heavenward, drooping never
For the sharpest storms that blow,
Bearing fruits of faith and truth;
Then transplant me out of time
Into that eternal clime
Where I shall renew my youth,
When earth's wither'd leaves shall bloom

Catherine Winkworth

Fresh in beauty from the tomb.

Life, to whom as to my Head
I unite me, through my soul
Now Thy quickening life-stream shed,
And Thy love's warm current roll,
Freshening all with strength and grace;
Be Thou mine, I am Thine own,
Here and ever Thine alone,
All my hope in Thee I place;
Heaven and earth are nought to me,
Save, O Life of life, with Thee!

SONGS OF THE CROSS
1. Can I my fate no more withstand
2. O Christ, Thou bright and Morning Star
3. When in the hour of utmost need
4. O Faithful God! O, pitying Heart
5. Ah God, my days are dark indeed
6. Why art thou thus cast down, my heart?
7. All things hang on our possessing
8. My God, in Thee all fulness lies
9. Who puts his trust in God most just
10. What pleases God, O pious soul
11. Whate'er my God ordains is right
12. Wherefore should I grieve and pine?
13. Seems it in my anguish lone

I. Queen Maria of Hungary's Song

Composed most probably in 1526, when she was compelled to flee from Buda on account of her adherence to the Reformed Doctrine, after the Battle of Mohacz; in which her husband and the flower of the Hungarian nobility fell in defending their country against the Turks.

Can I my fate no more withstand,
Nor 'scape the hand
That for my faith would grieve me;
This is my strength, that well I know
In weal or woe
God's love the world must leave me
God is not far, though hidden now,
He soon shall rise and make them bow
Who of His word bereave me.

Judge as ye will my cause this hour,
Yours is the power,
God bids me strive no longer;
I know what mightiest seems to-day
Shall pass away,
Time than your rule is stronger.
The Eternal Good I rather choose,
And fearless all for this I lose;
God help me thus to conquer!

All has its day, the proverb saith:
This is my faith,
Thou, Christ, wilt be beside me,

Catherine Winkworth

And look on all this pain of mine
As were it Thine,
When sharpest woes betide me;
Must I then tread this path--I yield;
World, as thou wilt, God is my shield,
And He will rightly guide me!

II. In Outward and Inward Distress
From the Dark Times of the Thirty Years' War.
Anon.

O Christ, Thou bright and Morning Star,
Now shed Thy light abroad;
Shine on us from Thy throne afar
In this dark place, dear Lord,
With Thy pure glorious word.

O Jesus, Comfort of the poor,
I lift my heart to Thee,
I know Thy mercies still endure
And Thou wilt pity me;
I trust alone to Thee.

I cannot rest, I may not sleep,
No joy or peace I know,
My soul is torn with anguish deep
And fears a deeper woe;
O Christ, Thy pity show!

For Thou didst suffer for my soul,
Her burdens to remove;
Oh make me through Thy sorrows whole,
Refresh me with Thy love;
Lord, help me from above.

Then Jesus, glory, honour, praise,
I'll ever sing to Thee;
Increase my faith that Thou wilt raise
Me once where I shall see
Eternal joys with Thee!

III. The only Refuge in Time of Trouble
Paul Eber. 1511-1569.

When in the hour of utmost need
We know not where to look for aid,
When days and nights of anxious thought
Nor help nor counsel yet have brought:

Then this our comfort is alone,
That we may meet before Thy throne,
And cry, O faithful God, to Thee
For rescue from our misery:

To Thee may raise our hearts and eyes,
Repenting sore with bitter sighs,
And seek Thy pardon for our sin,
And respite from our griefs within:

For Thou hast promised graciously
To hear all those who cry to Thee,
Through Him whose Name alone is great,
Our Saviour and our Advocate.

And thus we come, O God, to-day,
And all our woes before Thee lay,
For tried, forsaken, lo! we stand,
Perils and foes on every hand.

Ah hide not for our sins Thy face,
Absolve us through Thy boundless grace,
Be with us in our anguish still,
Free us at last from every ill.

That so with all our hearts we may
Once more our glad thanksgivings pay,
And walk obedient to Thy word,
And now and ever praise the Lord.

IV. Under a Heavy Private Cross or Bereavement
Paul Gerhardt. 1606-1676.

O Faithful God! O, pitying Heart,
Whose goodness hath no end;
I know this cross with all its smart
Thy hand alone doth send!
Yes, Lord, I know it is Thy love,
Not wrath or hatred bids me prove
The load 'neath which I bend.

'Twas ever wont with Thee, my God,
To chasten oft a son;
He whom Thou lovest feels Thy rod,
Tears flow ere joy is won;
Thou leadest us through darkest pain
Back to the joyous light again
Thus ever hast Thou done.

For e'en the Son Thou most dost love
Here trod the path of woe;
Ere He might reach His throne above
He bore the cross below;
Through anguish, scorn, and poverty,
Through bitterest death He pass'd, that we
The bliss of heaven might know.

And if the pure and sinless One
Could thus to sorrow bow,
Shall I who so much ill have done
Resist the cross? O Thou
In whom doth perfect patience shine,
Whoe'er would fain be counted Thine
Must wear Thy likeness now.

Yet, Father, each fresh aching heart
Will question in its woe,
If Thou canst send such bitter smart
And yet no anger know?
How long the hours beneath the cross!
How hard to learn that love and loss
From one sole Fountain flow!

Catherine Winkworth

But what I cannot, Thou true Good,
Oh work Thyself in me;
Nor ever let my trials' flood
O'erwhelm my faith in Thee;
Keep me from every murmur, Lord,
And make me steadfast in Thy word,
My tower of refuge be!

If I am weak, Thy tender care
Shall bid me fear no ill;
With ceaseless cries and tears and prayer
The long sad hours I'll fill;
The heart that yet can hope and trust,
And cry to Thee, though from the dust,
Is all unconquer'd still!

O Thou who diedst to give us life,
Full well to Thee is known
The cross, and all the inner strife
Of those who weep alone,
And 'neath their burden well-nigh faint;
The aching heart's unspoken plaint
Finds echo in Thine own.

Ah Christ, do Thou within me speak,
For Thou canst comfort best;
The tower and stronghold of the weak,
The weary wanderer's rest,
Our shadow in the noon-day hours,
And when the tempest round us lowers,
Our shelter safe and blest!

O Holy Spirit, sent of God,
In whom all gladness lies,
Refresh my soul, lift off her load,
From Thee all sadness flies;
Thou know'st the glories yet to come,
The joy, the solace, of that home,
Where we shall one day rise.

There in Thy presence we shall see
Glories beyond our ken;
The cross known here to none but Thee
Shall turn to gladness then;
There smiles for all our tears are given,
And for our woes the joys of heaven
Lord, I believe! Amen!

V. The one True Friend
Conrad Hojer. 1584.

Ah God, my days are dark indeed,
How oft this aching heart must bleed,
The narrow way, how fill'd with pain
That I must pass ere heaven I gain!
How hard to teach this flesh and blood
To seek alone the Eternal Good!

Ah whither now for comfort turn?
For Thee, my Jesus, do I yearn,
In Thee have I, howe'er distrest,
Found ever counsel, aid, and rest;
I cannot all forsaken be
While still my heart can trust in Thee.

Jesus, my only God and Lord,
What sweetness in Thy name is stored!
So dark and hopeless is no grief
But Thy sweet Name can bring relief,
So keen no sorrows' rankling dart
But Thy sweet Name can heal my heart.

The world can show no truth like Thine,
And therefore will I not repine;
I know Thou wilt forsake me not,
Thy truth is fix'd, though dark my lot;
Thou art my Shepherd, and Thy sheep
From every real harm Thou'lt keep.

Jesus, my boast, my light, my joy,
The treasure nought can e'er destroy,
No words, no song that I can frame
Speak half the sweetness of Thy name;
They only all its power shall prove
Whose hearts have learnt Thy faith and love.

How many a time I've sadly said,
Far better were it I were dead,
Far better ne'er the light to see,
If I had not this joy in Thee;
For he who hath not Thee in faith,
His very life is merely death.

Catherine Winkworth

Jesus, my Bridegroom, and my crown,
If Thou but smile, the world may frown,
In Thee lie depths of joy untold,
Far richer than her richest gold;
Whene'er I do but think of Thee,
Thy dews drop down and solace me;

Whene'er I hope in Thee, my Friend,
Thy comfort and Thy peace descend;
Whene'er in grief I pray and sing
I feel new courage in me spring;
Thy Spirit witnesses that this
Is foretaste of the eternal bliss.

Then while I live this life of care
The cross for Thee I'll gladly bear;
Grant me a patient willing mood,
I know that it shall work my good;
Help me to do my talk aright,
That it may stand before Thy sight.

Let me this flesh and blood controul,
From sin and shame preserve my soul,
And keep me steadfast in the faith,
Then I am Thine in life and death;
Jesus, Consoler, bend to me,
Ah would I were e'en now with Thee!

VI. Under the Pressure of Care or Poverty
Written most probably either during the great Famine in Nuremburg in 1551, or the time of the Siege in 1561.
Hans Sachs.

Why art thou thus cast down, my heart?
Why troubled, why dost mourn apart,
O'er nought but earthly wealth?
Trust in thy God, be not afraid,
He is thy Friend who all things made.

Dost think thy prayers He doth not heed?
He knows full well what thou dost need,
And heaven and earth are His;
My Father and my God, who still
Is with my soul in every ill.

Since Thou my God and Father art,
I know Thy faithful loving heart
Will ne'er forget Thy child;
See I am poor, I am but dust,
On earth is none whom I can trust.

The rich man in his wealth confides,
But in my God my trust abides;
Laugh as ye will, I hold
This one thing fast that He hath taught,--
Who trusts in God shall want for nought.

Yes, Lord, Thou art as rich to-day
As Thou hast been and shalt be aye,
I rest on Thee alone;
Thy riches to my soul be given,
And 'tis enough for earth and heaven.

What here may shine I all resign,
If the eternal crown be mine,
That through Thy bitter death
Thou gainedst, O Lord Christ, for me
For this, for this, I cry to Thee!

All wealth, all glories, here below,
The best that this world can bestow,
Silver or gold or lands,
But for a little time is given,

Catherine Winkworth

And helps us not to enter heaven.

I thank Thee, Christ, Eternal Lord,
That Thou hast taught me by Thy word
To know this truth and Thee;
O grant me also steadfastness
Thy heavenly kingdom not to miss.

Praise, honour, thanks, to Thee be brought,
For all things in and for me wrought
By Thy great mercy, Christ.
This one thing only still I pray,
Oh cast me ne'er from Thee away.

VII. The Resting-Place amid Changes
Anon. in a Nuremburg Hymnbook of 1676.

All things hang on our possessing
God's free love and grace and blessing,
Though all earthly wealth depart;
He who God for his hath taken,
'Mid the changing world unshaken
Keeps a free heroic heart.

He who hitherto hath fed me,
And to many a joy hath led me,
Is and shall be ever mine;
He who did so gently school me,
He who still doth guide and rule me,
Will not leave me now to pine.

Shall I weary me with fretting
O'er vain trifles, and regretting
Things that never can remain?
I will strive but that to win me
That can shed true rest within me,
Rest the world must seek in vain.

When my heart with longing sickens,
Hope again my courage quickens,
For my wish shall be fulfill'd,
If it please His love most tender;
Life and soul I all surrender
Unto Him on whom I build.

Well He knows how best to grant me
All the longing hopes that haunt me,
All things have their proper day;
I would dictate to Him never,
As God wills so be it ever,
When He wills, I will obey.

If on earth He bids me linger,
He will guide me with His finger
Through the years that now look dim;
All that earth has fleets and changes
As a river onward ranges,
But I rest in peace on Him.

VIII. Rest in the Lord
Anon.

My God, in Thee all fulness lies,
All want in me, from Thee apart;
In Thee my soul hath endless joys,
In me is but an aching heart;
Poor as the poorest here I pine,
In Thee a heavenly kingdom's mine.

Thou seest whatsoe'er I need,
Thou seest it, and pitiest me;
Thy swift compassions hither speed,
Ere yet my woes are told to Thee;
Thou hearest, Father, ere we cry,
Shall I not still before Thee lie?

I leave to Thee whate'er is mine,
And in Thy will I calmly rest;
I know that richest gifts are Thine,
Thou canst and Thou wilt make me blest,
For Thou hast promised, and our Lord
Will never break His promised word.

Thou lov'st me, Father, with the love
Wherewith Thou lovedst Christ Thy Son,
And so a brightness from above
Still glads me though my tears may run,
For in Thy love I find and know
What all the world could ne'er bestow.

Then I can let the world go by,
And yet be still and rest in Thee,
I sit, I walk, I stand, I lie,
Thou ever watchest over me,
And when the yoke is pressing sore
I think, my God lives evermore!

IX. The Christian's Confidence

Probably by Joachim Magdeburg, a Pastor who died in 1560--long a favourite Hymn at death-beds; said to be found in a stained glass window in Nordhausen with the date 1592, printed at latest 1598.

Who puts his trust in God most just
Hath built his house securely;
He who relies on Jesus Christ,
Shall reach His heaven most surely:
Then fix'd on Thee my trust shall be,
For Thy truth cannot alter;
While mine Thou art, not death's worst smart
Shall make my courage falter.

Though fiercest foes my course oppose,
A dauntless front I'll show them;
My champion Thou, Lord Christ, art now,
Who soon shalt overthrow them!
And if but Thee I have in me
With Thy good gifts and Spirit,
Nor death nor hell, I know full well,
Shall hurt me, through Thy merit.

I rest me here without a fear,
By Thee shall all be given
That I can need, O Friend indeed,
For this life or for heaven.
O make me true, my heart renew,
My soul and flesh deliver!
Lord, hear my prayer, and in Thy care
Keep me in peace for ever.

X. Childlike Submission
Paul Gerhardt. 1653.

What pleases God, O pious soul,
Accept with joy, though thunders roll
And tempests lower on every side,
Thou knowest nought can thee betide
But pleases God.

The best will is our Father's will,
And we may rest there calm and still,
Oh make it hour by hour thine own,
And wish for nought but that alone
Which pleases God.

His thought is aye the wisest thought,
How oft man's wisdom comes to nought,
Mistake or weakness in it lurks,
It brings forth ill, and seldom works
What pleases God.

His mind is aye the gentlest mind,
His will and deeds are ever kind,
He blesses when against us speaks
The evil world, that rarely seeks
What pleases God.

His heart is aye the truest heart,
He bids all grief and harm depart,
Defending, shielding day and night
The man who knows and loves aright
What pleases God.

He governs all things here below,
In Him lie all our weal and woe,
He bears the world within His hand,
And so to us bear sea and land
What pleases God.

And o'er His little flock He yearns,
And when to evil ways it turns,
The Father's rod oft smiteth sore,
Until it learns to do once more
What pleases God.

What most would profit us He knows,
And ne'er denies aught good to those
Who with their utmost strength pursue
The right, and only care to do
What pleases God.

If this be so, then World, from me
Keep if thou wilt, what pleases thee;
But thou, my soul, be well content
With God and all things He hath sent;
As pleases God.

And must thou suffer here and there,
Cling but the firmer to His care,
For all things are beneath His sway,
And must in very truth obey
What pleases God.

True faith will grasp His mercy fast,
And hope bring patience at the last,
Then both within thy heart enshrine,
So shall the heritage be thine
That pleases God.

To thee for ever shall be given
A kingdom and a crown in heaven,
And there shall be fulfill'd in thee,
And thou shalt taste and hear and see
What pleases God.

Catherine Winkworth

XI. *The quiet hoping Heart*

Written for the comfort of a Sick Friend, who set it to Music, and on his recovery frequently caused it to be sung before his house by the School-Choir. S. Rodigast. 1675.

Whate'er my God ordains is right,
His will is ever just;
Howe'er He order now my cause
I will be still and trust.
He is my God,
Though dark my road,
He holds me that I shall not fall,
Wherefore to Him I leave it all.

Whate'er my God ordains is right,
He never will deceive;
He leads me by the proper path,
And so to Him I cleave,
And take content
What He hath sent;
His hand can turn my griefs away,
And patiently I wait His day.

Whate'er my God ordains is right,
He taketh thought for me,
The cup that my Physician gives
No poison'd draught can be,
But medicine due;
For God is true,
And on that changeless truth I build,
And all my heart with hope is fill'd.

Whate'er my God ordains is right,
Though I the cup must drink
That bitter seems to my faint heart,
I will not fear nor shrink;
Tears pass away
With dawn of day,
Sweet comfort yet shall fill my heart,
And pain and sorrow all depart.

Whate'er my God ordains is right,
My Light, my Life is He,
Who cannot will me aught but good,
I trust Him utterly;

For well I know,
In joy or woe,
We once shall see as sunlight clear
How faithful was our Guardian here.

Whate'er my God ordains is right,
Here will I take my stand;
Though sorrow, need, or death make earth
For me a desert land,
My Father's care
Is round me there,
He holds me that I shall not fall,
And so to Him I leave it all.

XII. The Courage of perfect Trust
Paul Gerhardt. 1653.

Wherefore should I grieve and pine?
Is not Christ the Lord still mine?
Who can sever me from Him?
Who can rob me of the heaven
Which the Son of God hath given
Unto faith though weak and dim?

Naked, helpless, was I born
When my earliest breath was drawn,
Naked must I wander forth,
As a shadow flits away
At the coming of the day,
Bearing nought with me from earth.

Soul and body, life and goods,
Are not mine, are only God's,
Given me by His loving will;
Would He take back aught of His,
Let Him take it, not for this
Shall my song of praise be still.

Sendeth He some cross to bear,
Cometh sorrow, need, or care,
Shall it all my peace destroy?
He who sends can end it too,
Well He knows in season due,
How to turn my griefs to joy.

Many a day of happiness
Hath He sent who loves to bless,
Shall I not bear aught for God?
He is kind, we know that He
Ne'er forsakes us utterly,
Love lies hidden in His rod.

What is there my foes can do,
Though they be nor weak nor few,
Save to scorn and mock my woe?
Let them laugh, and let them mock,
God my Saviour and my Rock
Soon shall all their schemes o'erthrow.

With a glad and fearless mien
Should a Christian man be seen,
Wheresoe'er be cast his lot;
Yea, though death seem close at hand,
Calm and quiet let him stand,
And his spirit tremble not.

Him no death has power to kill,
But from many a dreaded ill
Bears his spirit safe away:
Shuts the door of bitter woes,
Opens yon bright path that glows
With the light of perfect day.

There in deepest joy my heart
Shall be heal'd from all the smart
Of the wounds that pierced it here;
Here can no true good be found,
Seeming goods that here abound
In a moment disappear.

Wealth that this world can command,
Is it aught but barren sand,
Bringing cares and troubles sore?
There, there are the gifts unpriced
Where my Shepherd Jesus Christ
Shall refresh me evermore.

Fount of joy, my Lord Divine,
Thine I am, and Thou art mine,
Nought can part my soul from Thee;
I am Thine, for Thou didst give
Once Thy life that I might live,
Dearly didst Thou purchase me.

Thou art mine, because my heart
Ne'er will let Thee more depart,
Clings to Thee her joy, her light;
Bring me, bring me to that place
Where, enclasped in Thine embrace,
Love at last is blest with sight.

XIII. The Sufficiency of God
C. Titius. 1641-1703.

Seems it in my anguish lone,
As though God forsook His own,
Yet I hold this knowledge fast,
God will surely help at last.

Though awhile it be delay'd
He denieth not His aid;
Though it come not oft with speed,
It will surely come at need.

As a father not too soon
Grants his child the long'd-for boon,
So our God gives when He will;
Wait His leisure and be still.

I can rest in thoughts of Him,
When all courage else grows dim,
For I know my soul shall prove
His is more than father's love.

Would the powers of ill affright,
I can smile at all their might;
Or the cross be pressing sore,
God, my God, lives evermore!

Man may hate me causelessly,
Man may plot to ruin me,
Foes my heart may pierce and rend;
God in heaven is still my Friend.

Earth may all her gifts deny,
Safe my treasure still on high,
And if heaven at last be mine,
All things else I can resign.

I renounce thee willingly,
World, I hate what pleases thee,
Baneful every gift of thine,
Only be my God still mine.

Lyra Germanica: Hymns for the Sundays & Chief Festivals of The Christian Year - Book I & II

Ah Lord, if but Thee I have
Nought of other good I crave,
Bright is even death's dark road,
If but Thou art there, my God.

THE FINAL CONFLICT AND HEAVEN
1. I know my end must surely come
2. Who knows how near my end may be?
3. World, farewell! Of thee I'm tired
4. My cause is God's, and I am still
5. O Lord my God, I cry to Thee
6. Lord Jesus Christ, my Life, my Light
7. Lord God, now open wide Thy heaven
8. Lord, now let Thy servant
9. When now at last the hour is come
10. Jerusalem, thou city fair and high
11. Now fain my joyous heart would sing
12. Wake, awake, for night is flying
13. When the Lord recalls the banish'd

I. The Uncertainty of Life
Salomo Franck. 1711.

I know my end must surely come,
But know not when or where or how,
It may be I shall hear my doom
To-night, to-morrow, nay or now
Ere yet the present hour is fled,
This living body may be dead.

Lord Jesus, let me daily die,
And at the last Thy presence give,
Then Death his utmost power may try,
He can but make me truly live,
Then welcome my last hour shall be,
When, where, and how it pleases Thee.

II. Preparation for Death
Said to be written on occasion of the sudden death of Duke George of Saxe-Eisenach, while hunting.
Emilia Juliana, Countess of Schwarzburg Rudolstadt. 1686.

Who knows how near my end may be?
Time speeds away, and Death comes on;
How swiftly, ah! how suddenly,
May Death be here, and Life be gone!
My God, for Jesu's sake I pray
Thy peace may bless my dying day.

The world that smiled when morn was come
May change for me ere close of eve;
So long as earth is still my home
In peril of my death I live;
My God, for Jesu's sake I pray
Thy peace may bless my dying day.

Teach me to ponder oft my end,
And ere the hour of death appears,
To cast my soul on Christ her Friend,
Nor spare repentant cries and tears;
My God, for Jesu's sake I pray
Thy peace may bless my dying day.

And let me now so order all,
That ever ready I may be
To say with joy, whate'er befall,
Lord, do Thou as Thou wilt with me
My God, for Jesu's sake I pray
Thy peace may bless my dying day.

Let heaven to me be ever sweet,
And this world bitter let me find,
That I, 'mid all its toil and heat,
May keep eternity in mind;
My God, for Jesu's sake I pray
Thy peace may bless my dying day.

O Father, cover all my sins
With Jesu's merits, who alone
The pardon that I covet wins,
And makes His long-sought rest my own;
My God, for Jesu's sake I pray

Catherine Winkworth

Thy peace may bless my dying day.

His sorrows and His cross I know
Make death-beds soft, and light the grave,
They comfort in the hour of woe,
They give me all I fain would have;
My God, for Jesu's sake I pray
Thy peace may bless my dying day.

From Him can nought my soul divide,
Nor life nor death can part us now;
I lay my hand upon His side,
And say, My Lord and God art Thou;
My God, for Jesu's sake I pray
Thy peace may bless my dying day.

In holy baptism long ago,
I join'd me to the living Vine,
Thou lovest me in Him, I know,
In Him Thou dost accept me Thine;
My God, for Jesu's sake I pray
Thy peace may bless my dying day.

And I have eaten of His flesh
And drunk His blood,--nor can I be
Forsaken now, nor doubt afresh,
I am in Him and He in me;
My God, for Jesu's sake I pray
Thy peace may bless my dying day.

Then death may come or tarry yet,
I know in Christ I perish not,
He never will His own forget,
He gives me robes without a spot;
My God, for Jesu's sake I pray
Thy peace may bless my dying day.

And thus I live in God at peace,
And die without a thought of fear,
Content to take what God decrees,
For through His Son my faith is clear,
His grace shall be in death my stay,
And peace shall bless my dying day.

III. A Weary Pilgrim's Song
J. G. Albinus. 1652.

World, farewell! Of thee I'm tired,
Now toward heaven my way I take;
There is peace the long-desired,
Lofty calm that nought can break;
World, with thee is war and strife,
Thou with cheating hopes art rife,
But in heaven is no alloy,
Only peace and love and joy.

When I reach that home of gladness,
I shall feel no more this load,
Feel no sickness, want, or sadness,
Resting in the arms of God.
In the world woes follow fast,
And a bitter death comes last,
But in heaven shall nought destroy
Endless peace and love and joy.

What are earthly joys? a weary
Chase of mist, or wind-borne foam!
In this desert black and dreary
Sins and vices have their home;
Thine, O World, are war and strife,
Mocking pleasures, dying life;
But in heaven is no annoy,
Only peace and love and joy.

Oh the music and the singing
Of the host redeem'd by love!
Oh the hallelujahs ringing
Through the halls of light above!
Thine, O World, the scornful sneer,
Misery thy reward, and fear;
But in heaven is no annoy,
Only peace and love and joy.

Here is nought but care and mourning,
Comes a joy, it will not stay;
Fairly shines the sun at dawning,
Night will soon o'ercloud the day;
World, with thee we weep and pine,
Gnawing care and grief are thine;

Catherine Winkworth

But in heaven is no alloy,
Only peace and love and joy.

Onwards then! not long I wander,
Ere my Saviour comes for me,
And with Him abiding yonder
All His glory I shall see;
For there's nought but sorrow here,
Toil and pain and many a fear,
But in heaven is no annoy,
Only peace and love and joy.

Well for him whom death has landed
Safely on yon blessed shore,
Where in joyful worship banded,
Sing the faithful evermore;
For the world hath strife and war,
All her works and hopes they mar,
But in heaven is no annoy,
Only peace and love and joy.

Time, thou speedest on but slowly,
Hours, how tardy is your pace,
Ere with Him the High and Holy
I hold converse face to face;
World, with partings thou art rife,
Fill'd with tears and storms and strife;
But in heaven can nought destroy
Endless peace and love and joy.

Therefore will I now prepare me,
That my work may stand His doom,
And when all is sinking round me,
I may hear not "Go"--but "Come!"
World, the voice of grief is here,
Outward seeming, care, and fear,
But in heaven is no alloy,
Only peace and love and joy!

IV. In Time of dangerous Duty
J. Pappus. 1598.

My cause is God's, and I am still,
Let Him do with me as He will;
Whether for me the fight is won,
Or scarce begun,
I ask no more--His will be done!

My sins are more than I can bear,
Yet not for this will I despair,
I know to death and to the grave
The Father gave
His dearest Son, that He might save.

In Him my Saviour I abide,
I know for all my sins He died,
And risen again to work my good,
The burning flood
Hath quench'd with His most precious blood.

To Him I live and die alone,
Death cannot part Him from His own;
Living or dying I am His
Who only is
Our comfort, and our gate of bliss.

This is my solace, day by day,
When snares and death beset my way,
I know that at the morn of doom
From out the tomb
With joy to meet Him I shall come.

Then I shall see God face to face,
I doubt it not, through Jesu's grace,
Amid the joys prepared for me!
Thanks be to Thee
Who givest us the victory!

O Jesus Christ, Thou Son of God,
Who once for me didst bear the rod,
Ah hide me in Thy wounded heart
When I depart;
My help, my hope, Thou only art!

Amen, dear God! now send us faith,
And at the last a happy death;
And grant us all ere long to be
In heaven with Thee,
To praise Thee there eternally.

Catherine Winkworth

V. In the near prospect of Death
Nicholas Selnecker. 1587.

O Lord my God, I cry to Thee,
In my distress Thou helpest me;
To Thee myself I all commend,
Oh swiftly now Thine angel send
To guide me home, and cheer my heart,
Since Thou dost call me to depart!

O Jesu Christ, Thou Lamb of God,
Once slain to take away our load,
Now let Thy cross, Thine agony,
Avail to save and solace me;
Thy death to open heaven, and there
Bid me the joy of angels share.

O Holy Spirit, at the end,
Sweet Comforter, be Thou my Friend!
When death and hell assail me sore,
Leave me, oh leave me, nevermore,
But bear me safely through that strife,
As Thou hast promised, into life!

VI. In Weakness and Distress of Mind
M. Behemb. 1606.

Lord Jesus Christ, my Life, my Light,
My strength by day, my trust by night,
On earth I'm but a passing guest,
And sorely with my sins oppress'd.

Far off I see my fatherland,
Where through Thy grace I hope to stand,
But ere I reach that Paradise
A weary way before me lies.

My heart sinks at the journey's length,
My wasted flesh has little strength,
Only my soul still cries in me,
Lord, fetch me home, take me to Thee!

Oh let Thy sufferings give me power
To meet the last and darkest hour;
Thy prayer refresh and comfort me,
Thy bonds and fetters set me free!

That thirst and bitter draught of Thine
Help me to bear with patience mine,
Thy piercing cry avail my soul,
When floods of anguish o'er me roll!

And when my lips grow white and chill,
Thy Spirit cry within me still,
And help my soul Thy heaven to find,
When these poor eyes grow dark and blind!

And when the spirit flies away,
Thy parting words shall be my stay,
Thy cross the staff whereon I lean,
My couch the grave where Thou hast been.

Since Thou hast died, the Pure, the Just,
I take my homeward way in trust,
The gates of heaven, Lord, open wide,
When here I may no more abide.

And when the last great Day is come,
And Thou our Judge shalt speak the doom,
Let me with joy behold the light,
And set me then upon Thy right.

Renew this wasted flesh of mine,
That like the sun it there may shine,
Among the angels pure and bright,
Yea, like Thyself in glorious light.

Ah then I have my heart's desire,
When singing with the angels' choir,
Among the ransom'd of Thy grace,
For ever I behold Thy face!

VII. Resignation
T. Kiel. 1620.

Lord God, now open wide Thy heaven,
My parting hour is near;
My course is run, enough I've striven
Enough I've suffer'd here;
Weary and sad
My soul is glad
That she may lay her down to rest;
Now all on earth I can resign,
But only let Thy heaven be mine.

As Thou, Lord, hast commanded me,
Have I with perfect faith
Embraced my Saviour, and to Thee
I calmly look in death;
With willing heart
I hence depart,
I hope to stand before Thy face:
Yes, all on earth I can resign,
If but Thy heaven at last be mine.

Then let me go like Simeon
In peace with Thee to dwell,
For I commend me to Thy Son,
And He will guard me well,
And guide me straight
To the golden gate;
And in this hope I calmly die;
Yes, all on earth I can resign,
If but Thy heaven may now be mine.

VIII. The Faithful Servant Longing for Peace
David Böhme. 1605-1657.

Lord, now let Thy servant
Pass in peace away;
I have had enough of life,
Here I would not stay:
Let me go, if such Thy will,
With a heart at rest and still.

Here, Lord, have I wrestled,
Suffer'd many a woe,
Fought as fearless warriors fight,
Conquer'd many a foe,
Kept the faith with them of old,
Help'd to guard and warn Thy fold.

Many an hour of sorrow,
Many an anguish'd tear,
Many a thorny path was mine
With Thy people here;
O'er my sins I've had to mourn,
Many a cross and trial borne.

All at last is ended,
Fight and race are o'er,
God will free me from all ills
Now for evermore;
To a better life I go,
Than this tearful earth can show.

Peace shall I find yonder,
And be free from sin,
No more strife and wars without,
No more foes within,
All around me shall be peace,
And the joy that cannot cease.

Where they bear the sceptre,
There a crown for me
Is laid up through Jesu's grace,
Bright that crown shall be:
Deepest calm my soul shall fill,
And this longing shall be still.

Catherine Winkworth

My Redeemer liveth,
He shall bid me rise
From the gloomy realm of death,
There all sorrow lies,
And I need not fear to wake,
Since His voice my sleep shall break.

He will change this body,
Make it like His own,
When the dead arise from earth,
When the trump is blown,
I shall see Him face to face,
Here my steadfast hope I place.

Therefore of His mercy
Ever will I sing,
All my heart and soul to Him
Praise and thanks shall bring;
Praise Him now, and praise Him then,
When the heavens shall cry, Amen!

IX. The Christian Soldier rejoicing that he has overcome
Spener. 1676.

When now at last the hour is come,
That I have long'd for many a time,
When God with joy should call me home
From this strange land, this wintry clime;
Thy victim, Death, escapes no more,
The hour draws on when I shall be
From all the bonds of earth set free,
And life's long battle shall be o'er.

To combat for His glory here
The Father sent me forth;--and lo!
The hour of victory draws near,
And conquer'd now is every foe;
And I have borne me in the strife
As true and fearless warriors ought,
And bravely to the last have fought
Through all the wars and woes of life.

My cry, when rough the march and dark,
Was, watch and strive till thou hast won,
Press forward fearless to the mark!
As now, thank God, at last I've done.
Now it is o'er, I cannot miss;
Through every danger to the death
True to my Lord I've kept the faith,
And freely risk'd all else for this.

It lacketh now a few short hours,
And I am in eternity;
The wreath of fadeless heavenly flowers
Is twined already there for me,
The crown is waiting for me there,
Until the fight is wholly fought,
And all my soul is thither caught,
Where shining palms the conquerors bear.

But when that morning shall appear,
When our great judge, the Son of God,
Shall give to those who loved Him here
Their gracious undeserved reward,

Catherine Winkworth

Then in the glorious halls above,
I too among that host shall stand,
And take from His all-faithful hand
The crown of righteousness and love.

Nor shall I yonder stand alone,
I see the crownèd host appear,
The mighty host before His throne,
Who shine for ever pure and clear,
The souls of those, who on their way
Still hour by hour were longing here,
With burning love, and many a tear,
To see the glories of His Day.

X. Jerusalem
J. M. Meyfart. 1634.

Jerusalem, thou city fair and high,
Would God I were in thee!
My longing heart fain fain to thee would fly,
It will not stay with me;
Far over vale and mountain,
Far over field and plain,
It hastes to seek its Fountain
And quit this world of pain.

Oh happy day, and yet far happier hour,
When wilt thou come at last?
When fearless to my Father's love and power,
Whose promise standeth fast,
My soul I gladly render,
For surely will His hand
Lead her with guidance tender
To heaven her fatherland.

A moment's space, and gently, wondrously,
Released from earthly ties,
The fiery chariot bears her up to thee
Through all these lower skies,
To yonder shining regions,
While down to meet her come
The blessed angel legions,
And bid her welcome home.

Oh hail thou glorious city! now unfold
The gates of grace to me!
How many a time I long'd for thee of old,
Ere yet I was set free
From yon dark life of sadness,
Yon world of shadowy nought,
And God had given the gladness,
The heritage I sought.

Oh what the nation, what the glorious host,
Comes sweeping swiftly down?
The chosen ones on earth who wrought the most,
The Church's brightest crown,
Our Lord hath sent to meet me,
As in the far-off years

Catherine Winkworth

Their words oft came to greet me
In yonder land of tears.

The Patriarchs' and Prophets' noble train,
With all Christ's followers true,
Who bore the cross, and could the worst disdain
That tyrants dared to do,
I see them shine for ever,
All-glorious as the sun,
'Mid light that fadeth never,
Their perfect freedom won.

And when within that lovely Paradise
At last I safely dwell,
From out my blissful soul what songs shall rise,
What joy my lips shall tell,
While holy saints are singing
Hosannas o'er and o'er,
Pure Hallelujahs ringing
Around me evermore.

Innumerous choirs before the shining throne
Their joyful anthems raise,
Till Heaven's glad halls are echoing with the tone
Of that great hymn of praise,
And all its host rejoices,
And all its blessed throng
Unite their myriad voices
In one eternal song!

XI. The new Heavens and new Earth
J. Walther. 1557.

Now fain my joyous heart would sing
That lovely summer-time,
When God reneweth everything
In His celestial prime;
When He shall make new heavens and earth,
And all the creatures there
Shall spring from out that second birth
All-glorious, pure, and fair.

The perfect beauty of that sphere
No mortal tongue may speak,
We have no likeness for it here,
Our words are far too weak;
And we must wait till we behold
The hour of judgment true,
That to the soul shall all unfold
What God is, and can do.

For God ere long will summon all
Who once on earth were born,
This flesh shall hear the trumpet's call
And live again that morn,
And when in Christ His Son we wake,
These skies asunder roll,
And all the bliss of heaven shall break
Upon the raptured soul.

And He will lead the white-robed throng
To His fair Paradise,
Where from the marriage-feast the song
Of endless praise shall rise,
And from His fathomless abyss
Of perfect love and truth,
Shall flow perpetual joy and bliss,
In never-ending youth.

Ah God, now lead me of Thy love
Through this dark world aright;
Lord Christ defend me lest I rove,
Or lies delude my sight;
And keep me steadfast in the faith
Till these dark days have ceased,

Catherine Winkworth

And ready still in life or death
For Thy great marriage-feast.

And herewith will I end the song
Of that fair summer-time;
The blossoms shall burst out ere long
Of heaven's eternal prime,
The year begin, for ever new;
God grant us then on high
To see our vision here made true,
And eat the fruits of joy!

XII. The Final
Philip Nicolai. 1598.

Wake, awake, for night is flying,
The watchmen on the heights are crying;
Awake, Jerusalem, at last!
Midnight hears the welcome voices,
And at the thrilling cry rejoices:
Come forth, ye virgins, night is past.
The Bridegroom comes, awake,
Your lamps with gladness take
Hallelujah!
And for His marriage-feast prepare,
For ye must go to meet Him there.

Zion hears the watchmen singing,
And all her heart with joy is springing,
She wakes, she rises from her gloom;
For her Lord comes down all-glorious,
The strong in grace, in truth victorious,
Her Star is risen, her Light is come!
Ah come, Thou blessed One,
God's own Beloved Son,
Hallelujah!
We follow till the halls we see
Where Thou hast bid us sup with Thee!

Now let all the heavens adore Thee,
And men and angels sing before Thee
With harp and cymbal's clearest tone;
Of one pearl each shining portal,
Where we are with the choir immortal
Of angels round Thy dazzling throne;
Nor eye hath seen, nor ear
Hath yet attain'd to hear
What there is ours,
But we rejoice, and sing to Thee
Our hymn of joy eternally.

XIII. The End
S. G. Bürde. 1794.

When the Lord recalls the banish'd,
Frees the captives all at last,
Every sorrow will have vanish'd
Like a dream when night is past;
Then shall all our hearts rejoice,
And with glad resounding voice
We shall praise the Lord who sought us,
For the freedom He hath wrought us.

Lift Thy hand to aid us, Father,
Look an us who widely roam,
And Thy scatter'd children gather
In their long'd-for promised home;
Steep and weary is the way,
Shorten Thou the sultry day,
Faithful warriors hast Thou found us,
Let Thy peace for aye surround us.

In that peace we reap in gladness
What was sown in tearful showers:
There the fruit of all our sadness
Ripens,--there the palm is ours;
There our God upon His throne
Is our full reward alone;
They who all for God surrender
Bring their sheaves in heavenly splendour.

Footnotes:

1. See Bunsen's larger Gesangbuch, and Sketch of the History of the Church of the United Brethren by James Montgomery.

2. Spiritual Songs of Luther, translated by R. Massie, Esq. Hatchard and Co.

3. Exodus 28:36-38

www.ingramcontent.com/pod-product-compliance
Lightning Source LLC
Chambersburg PA
CBHW021828220426
43663CB00005B/168